Becoming a Social Worker

Becoming a Social Worker
A Guide for Students

Caroline Humphrey

Los Angeles | London | New Delhi
Singapore | Washington DC

First published 2011

Apart from any fair dealing for the purposes of research or private
study, or criticism or review, as permitted under the Copyright,
Designs and Patents Act, 1988, this publication may be reproduced,
stored or transmitted in any form, or by any means, only with the
prior permission in writing of the publishers, or in the case of
reprographic reproduction, in accordance with the terms of licences
issued by the Copyright Licensing Agency. Enquiries concerning
reproduction outside those terms should be sent to the publishers.

SAGE Publications Ltd
1 Oliver's Yard
55 City Road
London EC1Y 1SP

SAGE Publications Inc.
2455 Teller Road
Thousand Oaks, California 91320

SAGE Publications India Pvt Ltd
B 1/I 1 Mohan Cooperative Industrial Area
Mathura Road
New Delhi 110 044

SAGE Publications Asia-Pacific Pte Ltd
33 Pekin Street #02-01
Far East Square
Singapore 048763

Library of Congress Control Number: 2010924169

British Library Cataloguing in Publication data

A catalogue record for this book is available from the British Library.

ISBN 978-1-84920-057-8
ISBN 978-1-84920-058-5 (pbk)

Typeset by C&M Digitals (P) Ltd, Chennai, India
Printed and bound in Great Britain by TJ International Ltd, Padstow, Cornwall
Printed on paper from sustainable resources

Mixed Sources
Product group from well-managed
forests and other controlled sources
www.fsc.org Cert no. SGS-COC-2482
© 1996 Forest Stewardship Council
FSC

Contents

Acknowledgements

A heartfelt thanks to everyone who made this book possible by sharing with me their stories of social work education. First and foremost are the students who completed surveys, signed up for interviews and volunteered their portfolios from placements. They invested time and energy in this endeavour, often disclosing sensitive material about their personal and professional journeys for the sake of enhancing the education of future generations of students. Second are the social work educators whose stories about teaching, supervision and assessment provided a richer background context to understanding student learning. Finally, I am grateful for institutional support in the form of a HEFCE grant and a period of research leave for the writing of this textbook.

List of Illustrations

List of Abbreviations

Research Data

CH	Interviewer (author)
P	Portfolio report (from placement)
S	Student's voice (from interview)
T	Teacher's voice (from interview)

Professional Terms

AYE	Assessed year in employment
CPD	Continuing professional development
ICT	Information and communication technology
NQSW	Newly qualified social worker
PCS	Personal-cultural-structural (a model of anti-oppressive practice)
PLA	Practice learning assessor (i.e. a qualified practice teacher)
PLO	Practice learning opportunity (i.e. an agency placement)
PLO1	Initial placement (usually in the independent sector)
PLO2	Final placement (usually in the statutory sector)
PQ	Post-qualification
SWIT	Social worker in training

Institutional Acronyms

BASW	British Association of Social Workers
CCW	Care Council for Wales
CWDC	Children's Workforce Development Council
DCSF	Department of Children, Schools and Families (now Department of Education)
DfES	Department for Education and Skills (now Department of Education)

DH	Department of Health
ESWDET	Evaluation of Social Work Degree in England Team
GSCC	General Social Care Council
NISCC	Northern Ireland Social Care Council
NSPCC	National Society for the Prevention of Cruelty to Children
QAA	Quality Assurance Agency for Higher Education
SSSC	Scottish Social Services Council
SWTF	Social Work Task Force (England)
TOPSS	Training Organisation for the Personal Social Services (now Skills for Care)
UK	United Kingdom
USA	United States of America

Preface

Although this introductory textbook covers the traditional subject matter of social work education, it is distinctive insofar as it is grounded upon real-life stories supplied during a research project.

The research was conducted during 2004–08 in England. The main focus was upon students undertaking a BA in Social Work programme and the main methods of data collection were:

- surveys at the beginning and end of the programme with a cohort of 80 students
- interviews with 30 students at different stages of the programme
- six focus groups convened during initial placements
- reading of 40 portfolios, 15 from initial placements and 25 from final placements.

This was supplemented by interviews with 30 social work educators. The majority were qualified practice teachers in the community, some of whom occupied management roles, but a few academic tutors and unqualified agency supervisors were also involved in these interviews. The result is that this book is able to go 'behind the scenes' in social work education in various ways.

Part 1 offers an introduction to social work in the UK, along with an invitation to students to engage with their programmes and the profession as adult learners. It provides a map of personal and political journeys into the social work profession based upon surveys and interviews. It examines styles of teaching and learning in university and community settings, and includes reference to the 'hidden' curriculum and practicum where aspects of students' biographies are brought to the foreground simply by virtue of studying social problems and practising social work. Reflecting upon our own biographies can be just as vital to the social work journey as any official requirements.

Part 2 covers the substantive knowledge base and skill repertoire of the social work profession, along with the ethical and political values underpinning it. It illuminates the struggles which students and educators continue to experience in relation to theory and research, as well as concrete applications of theoretical frameworks and research projects in practice settings. It unpackages the meaning of 'practice wisdom' and shows how students develop into critically reflective practitioners. Case examples from interviews and portfolios are provided in relation to each of the Key Roles against which students are assessed, and in relation to the value dilemmas encountered by students during placements. Making mistakes and achieving breakthroughs are equally vital on any learning journey, and the case studies pay attention to both aspects of students' journeys.

Part 3 attends to the practicalities of becoming a qualified practitioner and embarking upon a social work career. It offers guidance to students on how to maximise their chances for success in academic assignments and practice placements, and how to maximise their chances for surviving and thriving in the real world of social work.

Part 1

Becoming a Social Worker in Training

1

Social Work in the UK

Introduction

This chapter provides an introduction to social work in the UK. We start by considering the history of the profession, which emerged from diverse origins in the nineteenth century, and then became part of a centralised welfare state apparatus in the twentieth century. We will then survey the contemporary landscape to show that social work in the twenty-first century is embedded in diverse organisations, and core terminology around sectors, staff and service users will be clarified. In section 1.3 the official knowledge, skills and values requirements for social work will be summarised in the text and in tables. The final section explains some of the debates which have been reshaping professional education – this will help to prepare you for your role as adult learners.

1.1 A Short History of Social Work

The history of social work in the UK is characterised by its commitment to the most vulnerable people in society and by the competing agendas for social care, social control and social change which come into play when we ask: why do people fall by the wayside and how can we help them?

1.1.1 The Origins of Social Work

Social work emerged as one of the by-products of the modern capitalist economy. The Industrial Revolution resulted in a mass migration to cities for work and ruptured many family and community bonds, so that when people became unemployed as a result of economic crises or disability they could become isolated, impoverished and homeless. Three types of responses to these predicaments can be identified, each with its own distinctive ideological bias.

First, the Poor Law refers to the institutions established by local government officials to contain those who were unable to fend for themselves in the capitalist economy. These included workhouses for able-bodied people who were homeless and jobless; alms houses for elderly and disabled people who were unable to work; houses of correction for delinquent youths; and orphanages for children (Payne, 2005a). The Poor Law was initiated in 1601 but as the numbers of vulnerable citizens grew century by century, it developed a more punitive ethos to deter people from entering the system. It reflected a conservative ideology insofar as local politicians sought to conserve the status quo whilst providing a safety net to care for and contain the socially excluded. The capitalist ideal was that of self-sufficiency whereby everyone should provide for themselves and their family, but the capitalist system required social order, and hence the containment of people who might otherwise be at liberty to disrupt this social order by vagrancy, criminality or insurrection. So the agenda for social care was allied to the agenda for social control (Mooney, 1998).

Second, a plethora of charities were established by Christian philanthropists in the late nineteenth century. They specialised in one-to-one casework with people who had fallen by the wayside on account of problems ranging from alcohol dependence to prostitution, although this was often supplemented by practical handouts in the form of food, blankets and other necessities of life. Most philanthropists assumed that such problems were rooted in defects in the character of individuals rather than defects in the constitution of society. Consequently, casework was governed by a conservative morality, with people being exhorted to change their lifestyles in the direction of continence and chastity (Woodroofe, 1961). But some philanthropists became critical of the wider society, leading them towards a more radical conception of social problems. For example, the NSPCC was known for its criticism of gender ideologies which vaunted male superiority. NSPCC officers uncovered domestic violence against women, physical abuse of children within families and sexual abuse of teenagers on the streets, most of which was perpetrated by men (Corby, 2005).

Third, a settlement movement developed in the late nineteenth and early twentieth centuries. Some wealthy individuals purchased land and property in inner-city areas where they could house homeless families, and where they offered crèches for children and day centres for elderly and disabled people. This marked the beginning of community work as they recognised the value of building supportive communities around people rather than confining them to harsh institutions or offering moral tutelage alongside charitable handouts (Popple, 1995). Several of the benefactors and student volunteers were active in the socialist and feminist movements where they campaigned for social justice and gender equality (Auchmuty, 1989). Here, the agenda for social care is allied to the agenda for social change. In other words, it is not enough to provide a safety net if society continues to spawn the same problems, so radical social workers campaign for changes in social structures and cultures (Langan and Lee, 1989; Stepney and Popple, 2008).

1.1.2 The Welfare State

In the early twentieth century, social work became a recognisable profession with its own training programmes, and several specialist branches flourished within the profession (Payne, 2005a). In the mid-twentieth century, social services became one arm of the welfare state which was set up within the wider project of reconstructing the nation after the Second World War (Lewis, 1998). Initially, it was assumed that the need for social work would be minimal as a result of new institutions and policies designed to provide education, health care, employment and social security for all. In fact, the need for social services continued to grow so that by the 1970s there was a large bureaucratic apparatus to deal with social problems – Social Services Departments in England and Wales; Social Work Departments in Scotland; and Health and Social Services Boards in Northern Ireland.

Nevertheless, demand for services continued to be greater than supply. Why was this?

At least three answers can be offered. First, the capitalist economy itself generates massive inequalities of income, wealth and life chances along with spiralling forms of social exclusion, so that at any one time a significant proportion of the population may need additional support (Pierson, 2002). Second, modernity is characterised by perpetual change which brings as many difficulties as it resolves. For example, improvements in health and medicine have brought about increased longevity, but many elderly people living with chronic disease or disability now require long-term specialist care (Bernard and Scharf, 2007). Third, evolution in human psychology tends to lag behind evolution in technology, so that age-old problems such as child abuse can be reproduced across all classes even when material conditions improve (Miller, 1987).

In the late twentieth century, social work was challenged on all fronts. Some were welcome challenges, notably the movement to deinstitutionalise mentally ill and mentally handicapped people and to rehabilitate them within supervised community settings (cf. Goffman, 1961; Jay Committee, 1979). Some challenges were greeted with ambivalence. In child care, the pendulum swung between prevention and protection as child abuse tragedies unfolded (Parton, 1991) and in adult care, social workers became care managers charged with securing the best value-for-money services within new welfare markets (Payne, 1995). But resource cutbacks compromised the chances of effectively implementing any reforms; instead a new managerialism developed to pressurise staff into delivering 'more for less' (Audit Commission, 1995). Economic cutbacks can reflect a lack of political commitment to social work and social problems; New Right governments objected to the 'nanny state' and preached the virtues of self-sufficiency (Clarke et al., 1987). It is not surprising that during this period social work underwent a further radicalisation in its fight for truth, justice and even its own survival as a social profession. This is encapsulated in its adherence to anti-oppressive practice (Dominelli, 1997, 2002) and its engagement with critical social movements (Humphrey, 2002). Social workers spend most of their working lives with citizens who are structurally and culturally excluded from mainstream society which makes them critical of the political economy as well as ideologies rooted in individualism. The profession also attracts people from subordinated groups, including disabled people, black and minority ethnic people, lesbians and gay men, who have suffered discrimination. So for many social workers anti-oppressive practice reflects their personal experiences and political convictions as well as their professional values.

1.1.3 Into the New Millennium

The New Labour governments which took us into the new millennium were supportive of social work in principle but sought to modernise it in practice; politicians invested money into the profession and into a range of organisations charged with developing and monitoring 'best practice' (cf. DH, 1998; Humphrey, 2003). Social work has been the subject of a wide-ranging review as key stakeholders try to work out the balance between prevention and intervention and to ensure that adequate staff and services are in place to meet the needs of future generations (Scottish Executive, 2006; Blewett et al., 2007; Welsh Assembly Government, 2007). One of the most important ideological shifts pertains to the recognition of service users and their user-led organisations as key stakeholders in the future development of social work – as Peter Beresford points out, without this, anti-oppressive practice is more of a rhetorical word than a living reality (Beresford, 2000, 2007).

Beyond this, the effects of globalisation have filtered through to social work in the UK. Students from overseas may come to UK universities to study social work and there are international exchanges so that some students may undertake placements in other countries (Dominelli and Bernard, 2003). Qualified social workers may migrate to other countries for work, although they usually need additional training to learn the language and the law (Healy, 2001). It is clear from research into international social work that although there is a family resemblance between the forms taken by social work, there is also variation in the ways it has been constructed (cf. Payne, 2005a; Lawrence et al., 2009). For example, in the Middle East, Africa, Asia and Latin America, social work is still closely linked to indigenous religious and spiritual traditions, but in the UK it has become part of a secular and scientific modernity. Students and practitioners need to be mindful of such matters, given that the UK is home to many minority ethnic communities as well as asylum seekers and refugees from across the globe.

1.2 Surveying the Contemporary Landscape

Familiarity with the organisation of social work is essential for students on placement, and familiarity with core terminology will equip students to think, talk and write about social work more clearly.

1.2.1 The Organisation of Social Work

In the UK, social workers and social care workers are employed in two broad types of settings known as 'the statutory sector' and 'the independent sector'. The statutory sector refers to organisations which have been established by statute (i.e. by Act of Parliament) to deliver services to citizens, and it includes central government, local government, the legal system, health care and education. Devolution in the UK during the 1990s – whereby each of the four countries of England, Wales, Scotland and Northern Ireland acquired its own distinct government – means that there is increasing scope for intercountry variation in the organisation of social services. In Northern Ireland, there is an integration of health and social work in Health and Social Care Trusts which cater for adults and children and operate independently of the local government apparatus. Elsewhere, statutory social work is largely based in local government, although some social workers in the statutory sector are employed in multi-professional teams outside of local government – for example, in courts or hospitals. Local government in Scotland is the home to Social Work Departments which deal with children, adults and offenders; Welsh local authorities also combine adult and child care services. There is an institutional segregation between statutory services for children and adults in England. Child care social work is based in Children's Services Authorities which combine education and social work, whilst multi-professional practice more generally has been consolidated by the establishment of Children's Trusts and Local Safeguarding Children Boards (DfES, 2004; HM Government, 2007a, 2010). Adult care social work is based in another branch of local government and is undergoing reforms with a view to creating a new National Care Service and a more robust adult protection apparatus (HM Government, 2007b, 2009a; DH, 2009).

The independent sector consists of voluntary agencies and private businesses. Voluntary agencies are registered charities ranging from nationwide institutions such as Mind and Age UK to local projects devoted to meeting the specialist needs of people who may fall through the gaps of statutory services, such as women suffering domestic violence and minority ethnic families. Private businesses are run on a for-profit basis, and most are large-scale operations supplying domiciliary care services and residential care homes to elderly and disabled people (Harris and Rochester, 2001). It should be noted that the statutory and independent sectors are increasingly interdependent since the statutory sector contracts out significant amounts of work to the independent sector, which then becomes more dependent upon this funding stream for its own financial viability.

1.2.2 Social Workers and Educators

The terms 'social work' and 'social care work' are sometimes used interchangeably, but it is important that students understand the difference between them. Social care is a general term which covers all the personal and social services provided to people in need, whilst social work is the specialist professional element of social care which has distinct statutory functions attached to it, including functions of social control in relation to people who may pose risks to themselves or others. Social care workers may have a variety of vocational qualifications secured through on-the-job training, but they are not qualified as social workers; they tend to work in residential, day care and domiciliary settings where they provide hands-on personal care, but they will not be charged with decision-making responsibilities around care planning. The term 'social worker' is a protected title under the law and it is a criminal offence for anyone who does not possess a social work degree and who is not registered as a qualified social worker to appropriate this title. Social workers are licensed to practise social work in terms of carrying out statutory roles, and they can expect to take on supervisory responsibilities vis-à-vis social care workers.

It is strange but true that qualified social workers who are employed to undertake social work tasks do not necessarily have the term 'social worker' in their actual job title. In England social workers in community care teams typically occupy the position of care managers, whilst those in Youth Offending Teams have the official title of youth justice workers. This reflects the multi-professional world of welfare insofar as an increasing number of posts are open to any professional who can offer the requisite skills and knowledge, so that occupational therapists are eligible to apply for care management posts and probation officers can occupy youth justice posts. Nevertheless, there are many posts which are reserved for qualified social workers, particularly in statutory child care teams, on account of the specialist legal functions attached to social work. Official job titles can also vary across the UK – in Scotland most social workers do have the official job title of 'social worker'.

Social work education is a general term which covers both the university-based curriculum and the community-based practicum. University educators may be called lecturers, academic tutors or supervisors – every student is allocated their own personal supervisor as soon as they register on a programme – and when you embark upon placements you will encounter another array of terms. Practice education encompasses within it both practice teaching and practice learning, and your practice teacher may also be called a supervisor, a practice learning assessor or a practice educator. Students become familiar with this linguistic kaleidoscope quite quickly, but it is helpful if you are aware of subtle and significant differences in the meanings of these terms. 'Practice teacher' has been the most prevalent term to date in social work education and this is reflected in this textbook. The term 'supervisor' is the most prevalent term in social care and social work organisations insofar as all social workers, social care workers, other staff and students will have regular supervision from their line manager. In the case of students, they have supervision from their practice teacher, and they may also have supervision from a line manager in the agency if the practice teacher is not based in the agency.

The terminology associated with practice education underwent a significant shift when the new degree programmes were established across the UK from 2003 onwards. In the new official language students became 'social workers in training', practice teachers became 'practice learning assessors' and placements became 'practice learning opportunities'. Essentially, the government was keen to emphasise students' responsibilities as adult learners, practice teachers' responsibilities for assessing competence and managers' responsibilities to provide a learning environment for professionals-in-the-making rather than to treat students as a ready source of cheap labour for over-stretched organisations (Humphrey, 2006). Whatever the merits of these principles, the new terminology was quite cumbersome. On the one hand, a set of acronyms arose to enable people to say and write one word rather than three or four, i.e. SWIT, PLA and PLO. On the other hand, the traditional language of students, practice teachers and placements continued to be used alongside the new language. The reforms to social work education in England from 2010 onwards will entrain another linguistic shift, albeit a much simpler one which entails reverting to the terms 'student' and 'placement' whilst ushering in the new term of 'practice educator' (SWTF, 2009). But for the foreseeable future there is likely to be a coexistence of diverse terms.

1.2.3 Service Users and Carers

Other terms which can also cause confusion for students are the terms applied to the people we work with, who may be called 'citizens', 'clients', 'consumers', 'customers', 'service users' or 'carers'. The welfare state was designed to cater to the needs of all citizens, but social workers only work with a fraction of citizens, usually the marginalised citizens who require specialist care or control, and who may include non-citizens such as asylum seekers. For most of the twentieth century, social workers referred to the people on their caseloads as 'clients', but this term came under criticism since it suggested that there could be a certain dependency or inferiority attached to being a client of social work (cf. Howe, 1993; Clarke, 1997). It is noteworthy that this criticism was specific to social work (i.e. it was not applied to clients in the private sector) and that it was specific to the UK (i.e. 'client' is the most prevalent term in international social work). In the 1980s, the

New Right government championed the terms 'consumers' and 'customers' as part of their quest to increase choice in the marketplace of health and social care, but this term was also controversial insofar as many of the people seen by social workers have few resources and therefore few choices in their lives, and some will be involuntary clients detained under mental health or criminal justice law (Clarke, 1997). By the 1990s, 'service users' became the most prevalent term in policy documents, although it does not command universal consensus. It is not only that there has been an unfortunate tendency to abbreviate this to 'user' which has more negative connotations, but also that there are some people who believe that they need services only to be refused them, and there are other people who regard themselves as 'survivors' of the system rather than users of the service. This is indeed why service users created their own self-organised groups linked to critical social movements to campaign for welfare reforms (cf. Rogers and Pilgrim, 1991; Beresford and Campbell, 1994). A distinct carers' movement also emerged, claiming that carers needed services and recognition in their own right, giving birth to the popular phrase 'service users and carers' (Blytheway and Johnson, 1998). By the twenty-first century, service user groups along with government regulators were referring to service users as 'experts by experience' who should contribute to social work education, research and policy making (Levin, 2004). This linguistic shift has not resolved all the conundrums since experience in itself is not always converted into expertise, and since the expertise of some people who come to the attention of social workers (notably child sex offenders) is of dubious value (McLaughlin, 2009).

There are two main lessons here for students. The first is that we need to be careful in our use of language since terms can harbour more or less accuracy and adequacy, and terms have their own history which can entrain a set of positive or negative associations for different audiences. You are free to draw upon the range of linguistic terms in speech and writing, but you should select the most appropriate term for each context. The second lesson is that this reconstruction of language reflects both the embeddedness of the profession in a political arena and its ongoing reconstruction. Many stakeholders want to have their say on social work – politicians, practitioners, service users and carers, journalists and researchers – and the perspectives of these stakeholders can shift over time, as can the balance of power between them. Policy and practice is then reconstructed in line with the prevailing conception of what social work is all about, where social workers have gone wrong in the past, and what priorities they should have in the future. In practical terms, this means that the ways in which we do social work at the start of our careers may be quite different to the ways in which we do social work at the end of our careers, so you need to be prepared for lifelong learning. In academic terms, it means that social constructionism is the most appropriate theoretical approach to make sense of social work in society (cf. Symonds and Kelly, 1998; Burr, 2003; Garrett, 2003).

1.3 Official Requirements for Education and Practice

Social work in the UK underwent a major transformation at the start of the twenty-first century so that there is now a prescribed curriculum for students, an official set of roles to be discharged by trainees and practitioners and a mandatory code of practice, along with regulatory bodies which inspect the standards of social work education and practice on a regular basis (Humphrey, 2006). In 2003–04, a variety of new degree programmes were rolled out across the UK, i.e. undergraduate students may embark upon a BA (Bachelor of Arts) or BSc (Bachelor of Science) in Social Work whilst postgraduate students can study the equivalent programmes at Master's level. The Department of Health (2002a) specified at the outset that academic and practical learning should be of equal weight in these programmes, and the importance of practical skills training has been reinforced in the aftermath of child protection inquiries in England (Laming, 2009).

Table 1A illustrates the knowledge base of social work covered in the curriculum at universities. At first sight, it will appear daunting, since student social workers have to draw upon several disciplines when other students may only be studying one discipline for the entirety of their degree. But social work is necessarily multi-disciplinary, as are other caring professions such as nursing and medicine. The main academic disciplines underpinning social work are law, policy, sociology and psychology, but remember that you do not need to know any of these disciplines inside-out; your task is to select relevant aspects and apply them to social work, and there are textbooks specifically designed for this (e.g. Nicolson et al., 2006; Llewellyn et al., 2008; Brammer, 2010). There are also professional knowledges around interventions, ethics, organisations and research; some of these are specific to social work, whilst others borrow from other caring professions.

The official job description for social workers is contained in the six Key Roles which make up the National Occupational Standards for Social Work. A summary of these Key Roles is provided in Table 1B, although students in Scotland will find that these Key Roles appear in a different numerical order (SSSC, 2003). The Key Roles revolve around assessments, interventions, partnership working, risk management, agency accountability and professional competence. Each Key Role is subdivided into Units of Practice, and during placements in the community students have to

TABLE 1A   *The Knowledge Base of Social Work*

Social workers need to draw from the following sets of knowledges:

1   Law – civil laws governing service provision, statutory interventions, human rights and data protection; criminal laws around harm and harassment.

2   Policy – social care, health, education, criminal justice, housing and welfare benefits are all relevant areas of social policy.

3   Sociology – social structures generating inequality and poverty; plus cultures in communities which may contribute to empowerment or oppression.

4   Psychology – human development across the lifespan including disabilities; plus identities and relationships formed in families and communities.

5   Interventions – models of the social work process and methods of working with individuals and groups in order to carry out the Key Roles.

6   Ethics – Codes of Practice as prescribed by regulatory bodies, supplemented by the core concepts of moral philosophy such as 'rights' and 'duties'.

7   Organisations – internal processes within organisations around management; plus interagency working and the costing and commissioning of services.

8   Research – basic understanding of the diverse methods used by researchers, as well as key research findings, as the foundation for evidence-based practice.

Sources: TOPSS (2002); CCW (2003a); NISCC (2003a); SSSC (2003)

TABLE 1B   *National Occupational Standards for Social Work*

Key Role 1 – Assessments. Work with individuals, families, carers, groups and communities ('I-F-C-G-C') to assess their needs and circumstances.

Unit 1: Prepare for social work contact.
Unit 2: Work with I-F-C-G-C to help them make informed decisions.
Unit 3: Assess needs and options in order to recommend a course of action.

Key Role 2 – Interventions. Plan, carry out, review and evaluate social work practice with individuals, families, carers, groups and communities and other professionals.

Unit 4: Respond to crisis situations.
Unit 5: Interact with I-F-C-G-C to achieve change and improve life chances.
Unit 6: Implement and evaluate plans with service users, carers and other professionals.
Unit 7: Support the development of networks to meet assessed needs.
Unit 8: Work with groups to promote individual growth and independence.
Unit 9: Address behaviour which presents risks.

Key Role 3 – Partnership Working. Support people to represent their needs, views and circumstances.

Unit 10: Advocate with and on behalf of individuals, families, carers and groups.
Unit 11: Participate in decision-making forums with other professionals.

Key Role 4 – Risk Management. Assess and manage risks to individuals, families, carers, groups and communities as well as self and colleagues.

Unit 12: Assess, minimise and manage risks to I-F-C-G-C.
Unit 13: Assess, minimise and manage risks to self and colleagues.

(Continued)

TABLE 1B   *(Continued)*

Key Role 5 – Agency Accountability. Manage and be accountable for your own social work practice within the organisation, with supervision and support.

Unit 14: Manage and be accountable for your own work.
Unit 15: Contribute to the management of resources and services.
Unit 16: Manage, present and share records and reports.
Unit 17: Work within multi-professional and multi-agency systems.

Key Role 6 – Professional Competence. Demonstrate professional competence in social work practice.

Unit 18: Research, evaluate and utilise current knowledge of best practice.
Unit 19: Work within agreed standards of social work practice.
Unit 20: Manage complex ethical issues, dilemmas and conflicts.
Unit 21: Contribute to the promotion of best social work practice.

Sources: TOPSS (2002); CCW (2003a); NISCC (2003a); SSSC (2003)

demonstrate competence in each of the 21 Units in order to pass the Key Roles. This may sound a tall order, especially when we realise that these Key Roles apply to qualified practitioners and managers as much as students, but students are only required to master these Key Roles in the sense of achieving the basic competence of a newly qualified social worker, and you have the rest of your careers to consolidate this mastery.

Students are obliged to register with the relevant regulatory body, i.e. General Social Care Council in England (GSCC), Care Council for Wales (CCW), Northern Ireland Social Care Council (NISCC) or Scottish Social Services Council (SSSC). Registration in turn requires compliance with the Code of Practice for Social Care Workers which has six positive standards as outlined in Table 1C. The Code makes it clear that we should promote independence where possible, whilst being prepared to intervene to protect people from harm where necessary. It is worth reading the small print which makes reference to a number of prohibited behaviours such as embarking upon personal relationships with service users – this can result in deregistration (GSCC, 2002a). It is a generic code of conduct which applies to all social care workers as well as student social workers, qualified social workers and social work managers. It is supplemented by a Code of Practice for Employers who have to ensure that their policies and procedures nurture the kind of environment in which staff can operate effectively (GSCC, 2002b).

Readers should expect further changes to social work education, particularly in England where a National Reform Programme has been established as a result of recommendations from the Social Work Task Force. This ten-year programme is charged with delivering improvements in

TABLE 1C   *Code of Practice for Social Care Workers*

Social workers, students and social care workers must adhere to these standards:

1   Protect the rights and promote the interests of service users and carers.

2   Establish and maintain the trust and confidence of service users and carers.

3   Promote the independence of service users whilst protecting them as far as possible from danger or harm.

4   Respect the rights of service users whilst seeking to ensure that their behaviour does not harm themselves or other people.

5   Uphold public trust and confidence in social care services.

6   Be accountable for the quality of their work and take responsibility for maintaining and improving their knowledge and skills.

Sources: GSCC (2002a); NISCC (2002); CCW (2003b); SSSC (2005)

academic and practice education, and overseeing changes in several areas ranging from the selection of students to the support and assessment of new graduates (SWTF, 2009).

1.4 The Nature of Professional Education

During the past quarter-century, there has been a revolution in our under-standing of professional education which has reshaped teaching and learn-ing, and familiarity with the three core debates will help students to engage more effectively with their professional programmes. The first debate is an educational one which can be dubbed 'pedagogy versus andragogy'. Traditionally, education was deemed to be 'pedagogy', a term applied to the guidance of children, with the implication that pupils arrived in classrooms as 'empty vessels' to be filled up with knowledge transmitted by their teachers. Malcolm Knowles (1990) argued that this was inappropriate in relation to adult learners who chose to enter higher education in order to fulfil their own life goals and who bring vast amounts of prior life experience with them, and he coined the term 'andragogy' for adult teaching and learning. Although the most common term for social work education is 'professional pedagogy', this refers to 'the education of adults for professional life' and it is rooted in the principles of modern andragogy rather than those of traditional pedagogy. It is now widely accepted that educators must engage with the experiences and concep-tions which adult learners bring from previous socialisation and education, since otherwise they can disengage from the curriculum whenever it appears to be irrelevant to them or in conflict with their previous world views (Rogers, 2002). By the same token, it is incumbent upon students to sift through their own life experiences and belief systems so that they can interrogate the knowledge they already hold within them, building upon the strongest foundations and discarding some of the shaky materials.

The second debate is a professional one which revolves around 'science versus art'. Traditionally, the professions were taught in universities on the assumption that students had to acquire scientific knowledge from experts before applying this in practice settings, so their practice teachers would simply be checking that they had applied the correct theory or research in tandem with the correct organisational rules when dealing with any given situation. Donald Schön (1987) overturned this scientific paradigm by pointing out that grassroots problems are always characterised by complexity and uncertainty so that it is rare for a particular theory or piece of research to provide a clear-cut answer to any given problem. He showed that professionals often need to develop new hypotheses to make sense of the predicament of any given individual or family, and to improvise or innovate in order to find the best-fitting solution to a unique problem. This ushers in an artistic paradigm of professional education and practice which is reflected in the recognition that skills training is just as important as acquiring new knowledge (Trevithick, 2005). It also implies that students and practitioners need to draw upon diverse skill and knowledge sources, including those derived from prior life experience which may be stored in the body–mind as intuitive or cultural ways of knowing, or as practical or kinaesthetic ways of doing (Higgs and Titchen, 2001). Ideally, 'practice wisdom' emerges from the synthesis of such diverse ways of knowing and doing.

The third debate is a political one which could be formulated as the question: 'whose side are you on?' In modern welfare states, most caring professionals are employed by a branch of the state to undertake work on terms and conditions specified by the government, and whilst it is imperative that social workers remain law-abiding citizens, it is also necessary for them to become critically reflective practitioners in relation to government policies and employing organisations. The most extreme scenario occurred in Nazi Germany when social workers, teachers and doctors followed the policies of the National Socialist government without question, helping to send Jews, gypsies and disabled people to concentration camps and gas chambers (Bauman, 1989). Although such extreme abuses are unknown in the UK, violations of human rights sanctioned by the government are not unknown, as testified by the plight of asylum seekers (Hayes and Humphries, 2004), and developing the capacity for critical reflection is central to social work education (QAA, 2008). So even if we are employed by the state, we still need to be on the side of our service users and carers, and this is the meaning of enabling and empowering practice. It is also one of the reasons why the involvement of service users and carers in the education of student social workers is so vital (Levin, 2004).

In short, this revolution means that educators need to respect what students bring to classrooms and placements, just as students need to respect the life experience of service users and carers, so that we all learn to become active contributors to our own development rather than passive recipients of whatever is handed out to us by authority figures.

Points to Remember and Questions to Ponder

- The history of social work in section 1.1 showed that it is a socially constructed response to social problems, and therefore varies across cultures and historical eras, although it will also be influenced by the identities and politics of social workers themselves. How might your own identity, politics, class and country of origin affect your approach to social work?
- Section 1.2 showed how language, policy and practice continue to be reconstructed. How do you feel about working in such complex, contentious and changing territories?
- The tables presented in section 1.3 summarised the official requirements for education and practice and will need to be revisited on a regular basis.
- This chapter also covered debates in professional education. How might you learn and be taught differently as adults in higher education compared to your time in compulsory schooling? Why is it important for service users and carers to contribute to your training?

Further Reading and Resources

For a detailed account of the development of social work in the UK and other countries, see:
Payne, M. (2005) *The Origins of Social Work: Continuity and Change*. Basingstoke: Palgrave-Macmillan.
The Heatherbank Museum of Social Work is based at the Glasgow Caledonian University. If you are unable to visit in person, there is an informative website: www.lib.gcal.ac.uk/heatherbank/index.html

Up-to-date information on social work degree programmes can be found on the websites of regulatory councils. The National Occupational Standards and Codes of Practice are virtually identical across the UK, but there are a few noteworthy intercountry variations:

www.gscc.org.uk The General Social Care Council (GSCC) based in London regulates social work education in England.

www.ccwales.org.uk The Care Council for Wales (CCW) based in Cardiff regulates social work education in Wales. The promotion of the Welsh language post-devolution means that some programmes and practice settings are bilingual.

www.sssc.uk.com The Scottish Social Services Council (SSSC) based in Dundee regulates social work education in Scotland. Its curriculum and practicum include a specific requirement that all students should demonstrate 'key capabilities in child care and protection'.

www.niscc.info The Northern Ireland Social Care Council (NISCC) based in Belfast regulates social work education in Northern Ireland. Social work degree programmes here also provide the training for probation officers and education welfare officers.

Social Work Education is the key journal for articles on social work education in the UK.

2

Students' Journeys

Introduction

This chapter offers an overview of the life journeys which brought students into social work and the ways in which the study and practice of social work changed their life worlds and life journeys. The first section examines why people choose to become social workers and how far they are supported in this choice by their family and friends, and it includes exercises to help students to clarify their own images of social workers. In the second section, we will focus upon the three major biographical routes into social work – i.e. the service user, personal carer and citizen routes – paying attention to the merits and pitfalls of each route. The final section highlights the ways in which social work training can exert powerful effects on students, their relationships and their world views. The overall theme is that becoming a social worker is a journey where personal, professional and political aspects of our identity are often intertwined and transmuted.

2.1 Choosing to Become a Social Worker

Who becomes a student social worker? Data collected by regulatory bodies in England and analysed by a team established to evaluate the new degree show that although there is a strong gender bias (80 per cent of students are female), there is also a great deal of diversity in student backgrounds. There is a wide age range so that 34 per cent of students are aged 18–25 years and 34 per cent are over 35 years; 20 per cent of students are from black and minority ethnic groups, and the profession is attracting increasing numbers of black African students; and 10 per cent of students declare a disability, the most common one being dyslexia (ESWDET, 2008: Chapter 3). But why do they decide to do a social work degree?

2.1.1 Positive Choices

Social work had been the first choice of career for 80 per cent of students[1]. They saw an umbilical cord between 'helping others' and 'helping ourselves' insofar as caring for vulnerable people can provide job satisfaction and contribute to our sense of meaning and purpose in life. At the outset, they had a strong sense of which service user groups they most and least wanted to work with, and the reasons they gave revolved around personal connectedness and principled convictions. Personal connectedness stems from our own life experiences. For example, a student who had been adopted felt a strong urge to help children in the care system, whilst another student commented that he could not contemplate working with families as he had no experience of parenting. Principled convictions stem from our own world views. Many students wanted to work with groups of people who were marginalised in society and who needed strong advocates; but a few claimed that their own moral values would prevent them from working with certain groups of people, notably those who had committed crimes of violence.

At the outset of the programme, most students did not have a clear idea of what social work was all about. But one student explained that it was precisely the fluidity of social work that attracted her to it, as it would enable her to develop her own individual approach:

S: I chose social work over other professions because by its very nature it gives you the chance to be an individual. It gives you scope to decide how you're going to practise – within certain boundaries obviously – but it should enable you to use the skills you have to help people as you see fit without somebody coming along and telling you 'No, this is how you do social work', because who is to decide that, you know? ... The idea of the *individual* approach is that you take the skills you already have and *you use yourself as a person* ... so that you *really* engage ... From beginning to end the social worker is the biggest tool for change – not theory, not policy, not procedures.

You might like to pause to ponder on the implications of this situation. If you are the most important resource for your clients, how might you need to change or grow within yourself to do your job well?

2.1.2 Constraining Factors

What about the 20 per cent of students for whom social work was not the first choice of career? Half of these students were reconciled to becoming social workers since their first choice of career had been in another caring profession. The others remained unsure of whether they really wanted to become social workers, and had been constrained in their choice of career on account of factors such as age, educational attainments and financial burdens (see Christie and Kruk, 1998). These students could harbour quite contradictory images of social workers. One man explained that he had three images of social workers in his mind and that he was unable to relate to any of them, i.e. bohemian men sporting beards and open-toe sandals; domineering policewomen who removed children from the arms of their mothers; and political activists who imposed their own vision of political correctness upon others. It is not surprising that such images continue to circulate, given the adverse publicity around social work in the UK (Aldridge, 1994). Exercise 2A will help you to clarify the images of social workers you may have internalised to date.

Exercise 2A   Images of Social Workers

1   Call to mind your image of 'the ideal social worker', or the good caring professional you hope to become. Where did this ideal come from?
2   List the qualities of this ideal social worker then compare this with yourself as you are here and now. You could put a tick beside qualities you already

(Continued)

(Continued)

possess, a cross beside those you have not yet developed, and a question mark beside others. You could share this self-evaluation with a friend or colleague. If they don't agree with you on all the points, you need to reflect upon the fact that we don't always appear to others as we do to ourselves. Our self-evaluations can be too negative if we are lacking in confidence or too positive if we are over-confident.

3   Call to mind the images of social workers portrayed in the media. These images may be quite different from the ideals in your own heart and mind. They might also be quite different from the actual social workers in your own community. If so, you could ask yourself: where do media stereotypes come from and what sustains them? You might like to note that in many countries social workers are held in high esteem.

4   Return to your image of the ideal social worker. Which one of these descriptions best matches your image: An advocate? A therapist? A community resource? A political activist? An efficient bureaucrat? A teacher? A role model? A religious leader? A combination of these? Or something else?

5   Remember that who you are now and what your ideal of social work is, as well as the social workers you encounter during your training, will influence what kind of social worker you will become. Perhaps you could make a conscious decision to become the best you can be, and to take the best of what others have to offer you. However, it is not that poor role models have nothing to offer us; they can be as crucial to our development as positive role models. It is strange but true that examples of poor practice can enhance our motivation to do things better.

Even when students sustain a positive image of social workers in their own minds, they will encounter people who hold contrary views, either within their own networks or in the wider society. Almost 50 per cent of students reported that their family and friends were very pleased that they had chosen social work; many of them could name social workers within their own social networks. Just over 10 per cent of students reported that reactions to their choice of career had been extremely hostile as a result of the stigma associated with social workers. The other 40 per cent of students had faced ambivalent reactions from friends and relatives, with some being supportive and others critical.

Dealing with prejudices against social workers from within your own network can be daunting as you will have chosen an identity which separates you from the most significant people in your life, people who in an ideal world would be supporting you or at least trying to understand your choices. Under these circumstances, you may internalise a negative image of your profession or yourself; or you may champion the cause of social work which could lead to disruptions in your networks; or you may negotiate a compromise. Exercise 2B provides concrete examples of these different responses.

Exercise 2B   Dealing with Negative Images

Read how three students dealt with the negative images attached to social work, and then reflect upon their stories and strategies. Which response(s) do you prefer and why?

1 **Distancing self from social work**. If you agree with some of the criticisms levelled against social work, or if you feel ambivalent about becoming a social worker, then you may distance yourself from the profession. A young student told himself and others that he was studying for a degree in social work rather than becoming a social worker.

> S: I don't like the bureaucracy of social services and I don't like the labelling that goes with being '*a social worker*' ... You don't want to be '*a social worker*', whether you're knocking on someone's door or going to a party! ... It's better to be ... a youth worker in the community or an advocate in a voluntary agency – you could do some of what social workers do, without having to be '*a social worker*'.

2 **Affirming social work**. The second student loved her work with drug-users and sex workers and affirmed her chosen profession in the face of hostility. She was a mature student who held a strong alternative world view in which the value of social work and the plight of service users was appreciated.

> CH: Do you find that some of the stigma rubs off on you?
> S: Oh *yes*! [laughter] 'Why do you want to work with them? They ought to be put against a wall and shot' somebody once said to me ... 'Stop wasting tax-payers' money!'
> CH: Where do these comments come from? People who don't know you very well?
> S: *No*! People who *do* know me! *Yes*! [laughter] ... Even my own *parents* make comments and say that they can't understand for the *life* of them why I'm doing it.
> CH: Has that resulted in you re-configuring your networks, as it were?
> S: No. In a way *I live with it*. I mean, this is what I do, it's what I enjoy doing, I feel I'm doing something really worthwhile. Y'know, when clients say 'thank you' – one even bought me a big thank you card [long silence]. So that's that. People around me have just got to live with it. I'm not *changing* just because *they* don't like it or can't understand it.

3 **Negotiating a compromise on the social work question**. The third student realised that social work is contentious, but also that it is subject to media distortions which do not take account of its reconstruction and diversification.

(Continued)

(Continued)

So she found a way of reflecting this back to anyone who questioned her career choice.

S: My mum's proud of me but she's also concerned ... She says 'Oh, social work is a hard job, you know – you get blamed for everything!' ... My mum just thinks that social workers go around, visit a family, take their kids and put them into a foster home ... She's 70 next year ... She just doesn't know that there are other things you can go into ... My mum's full of 'Well, in my day it was like this and social workers only came round if there was trouble' and I say 'Well, it's *my* day now, mum, and it *won't be done like that!'*

2.2 Biographical Routes into Social Work

There are three main biographical routes into social work which can be listed in order of prevalence as the service user, personal carer and citizen routes (see also ESWDET, 2008: Chapter 4). We may occupy all of these roles during our lifetime, often juggling different roles, but for the majority of students, one particular role was of primary importance in precipitating their choice of career.

2.2.1 The Service User Route

Students who travelled along the service user road are those who suffered extreme adversity in their own lives which positioned them as a service user, although not all of them had actually made use of social work services, so it may be more accurate to call them 'proxy' service users. What is important here is that they identified their specific adversity as having propelled them into a social work career (cf. Christie and Weeks, 1998). A number of students had experienced multiple trauma as a history of childhood neglect and abuse had contributed to an adulthood punctuated by episodes of mental ill health or domestic violence. The psychoanalyst Alice Miller (1994) points out that professions such as psychotherapy and social work are far more likely to attract people with troubled backgrounds than those with idyllic lives. It is not just that our own troubles are the foundation of the empathy and energy we need to help others, but also that working with other troubled people may help us to vicariously work through our own troubles whilst still helping others. Unhealthy dynamics can also occur if we work with the troubles of others in order to avoid dealing with our own

(Hawkins and Shohet, 1989) or if we are vicariously re-traumatised by working with others in crisis situations (McCann and Pearlman, 1990).

When survivors of trauma become social workers, their dilemma is encapsulated in two common phrases, i.e. the epithet of 'the wounded healer' confirms that those who have been wounded may be in the best position to heal the wounds of others, whilst the injunction 'physician, heal thyself' demands that they pay attention to their own healing before seeking to heal others. The most notable feature in the narratives of survivors was that many of them had indeed sought to heal themselves, usually because they had received little or no healing from others:

CH: You haven't really had any professional help for yourself.
S: No, I've done a lot of it myself with self-counselling.
CH: What's self-counselling?
S: For a few years I wrote a diary about things that happened. Then I read through it and saw the patterns and thought about how I felt about it all ... Then I started being more creative, painting and drawing, and from time to time I look over all these too, to check out where I am, where I've come from, where I'm going ... I make time for myself every day. I've got a room upstairs where I go and read and make cards and do some painting. I go there for about an hour after tea and shut myself away. It's therapy but it's also self-preservation. I do it to survive.

Ideally, survivors would have experience of healing relationships with professionals and others before becoming social workers, given that relationships are pivotal to human life and social work (Howe, 1995). But those who have developed a rich repertoire of self-help strategies also have a lot to offer service users, as they carry a stock of tried-and-tested knowledge within themselves. As long as they are able to acknowledge that 'what worked for me might not work for you', and are willing to explore the evidence base for a variety of methods, this represents a sound starting point.

Nevertheless, the service user route does have its pitfalls (cf. Barter, 1997). People who had travelled along this road tended to make 'absolute' decisions about their career specialisms, decisions which had a compulsory flavour to them which is usually indicative of unresolved issues. So students with a history of child abuse may feel compelled to specialise in child protection and depict this as their 'mission in life'. Unfortunately, some of the defences we have mobilised to survive traumatic situations continue to influence our life and work as they have been internalised within our bodies and psyches (Miller, 2005). For example, a student who had survived domestic violence as a child by 'shutting down' and retreating into her own inner world found that she continued to rely upon this defence mechanism when working with aggressive clients in the criminal justice system. Her supervisor had noted this apparent oblivion to risk-laden situations, urging greater awareness and alertness, but the student was unable to modify this defence and unwilling to share its origins with the supervisor.

Being a student offers an ideal opportunity to heal from some of these wounds insofar as confidential counselling services are freely available on university campuses. You might like to note that students of psychotherapy are required to undergo therapy themselves as part of their training.

2.2.2 The Personal Carer Route

Most people provide routine care for relatives and friends without becoming a professional carer. Students who travel along the carer road are those who provide extraordinary care for people with special needs and who recognise this as the springboard for a social work career (cf. Parker and Merrylees, 2002). In the case of mature students with an established career in another field, the experience of caring for a profoundly disabled child or a terminally ill parent transformed their self-concepts and world views before propelling them into a caring career.

This is exemplified by the case of a mature woman who gave up her scientific career to care for a profoundly disabled son. Initially, she had to research his condition in order to challenge medics who pronounced that there was no hope for him, a claim which proved untrue. Then she had to research the law around children's rights and to challenge the local authority in order to access mainstream education. She came to realise that carers may have as much expertise as professionals in certain respects and that people with disabilities need strong advocacy if they are to secure the most appropriate services:

> S: I challenged the Council … I gave them six months to sort out [my son's schooling], if not I would take them to court. Don't know how I was going to do it, but I knew I was within my rights. *Guess what? They did it!* … It was like a light going on. I kept thinking 'Why is it that it's only if you keep pushing people … that they get into action?' … Then I thought 'Look at all that information that you've collected, and you now know how to deal with professionals, you should go and offer it to someone else' … When the Citizens' Advice Bureau held a surgery in our village I went along and said 'Could you use me?'

Voluntary work with disabled people led to paid employment as an advocate for disabled adults, but here she discovered that her lack of official credentials constrained her ability to make a difference to the lives of service users, as she remained in a subordinate status in relation to social workers:

S: I realised that I didn't have the qualifications like the people I was challenging ... I was writing reports and handing them in to social services and they were totally disregarded ... because I was classed as the 'do-gooder' with the charity ... So I'm here to get that qualification. I want the knowledge. I love the knowledge! ... But I need the piece of paper ... *If you can't beat them, you've got to join them!*

The distinctive features of carers' narratives were that they had acquired considerable knowledge and skills in relation to service users' and carers' predicaments, welfare rights and remedies, and the roles of diverse professionals, all of which grew organically from their own life experience. Whilst they wanted to develop this knowledge and skill base in order to assist others, they were far more flexible in their career plans when compared to students from the service user camp, recognising that their expertise was transferable to a range of people in need.

Nevertheless, students in the carer camp have other difficulties to grapple with. The general predicament is that when caring responsibilities are onerous, it impacts upon the time and energy available for study. Half of the population of student social workers in England do indeed have unpaid caring responsibilities, mostly in respect of children, and a significant proportion of students also engage in part-time paid employment, but most complete their programmes successfully (ESWDET, 2008). There are three situations in which caring responsibilities can cast a shadow over students' progress. First, extraordinary care for relatives who are profoundly disabled may be more compatible with part-time studies, and if a relative suffers a serious health crisis the student may need timeout. Second, student carers whose support networks are disrupted will be operating under more stress, a situation which is particularly acute for overseas students (Bartoli et al., 2008). Third, there are young students who have been child carers in a dysfunctional family of origin and who have not yet become autonomous adults. One student had been a child carer to her disabled mother and younger siblings in a family which had required considerable social work intervention, and she straddled the service user and carer camps. Her positive experiences of social workers had convinced her that her own destiny was to become a social worker, but she realised at an intellectual level that she could not dedicate herself to social work training if she continued full-time caring in her family, so she moved across the country in order to separate herself from her family. This student exhibited all the hallmarks of what is known as 'compulsory caregiving' which is associated with people whose own needs for care have been neglected (Glaser and Prior, 2002). As soon as she arrived on the programme, she immersed herself in voluntary work with disabled adults, and when her family complained about the absence of their chief carer and breadwinner, she took on paid employment with disabled children, sending the money back to her family. By the end of the first year, she was so exhausted that she withdrew from the programme and returned to her family of origin, although she still hoped to resume a social work career later on.

Caring professionals are vulnerable to burnout, and the most enthusiastic and idealistic people are most susceptible to it (Shapiro and Clawson, 1988). Self-care is an integral part of caring for others; it nurtures our own body, mind and spirit which are the source of our capacities for caring and learning; a capacity for self-care will help you to sustain a social work career (see Chapter 12).

2.2.3 The Citizen Route

Students who travel along the citizen route are those who bear witness to poverty and prejudice in communities without necessarily suffering these problems themselves or directly caring for others, so their narratives revolve around the structural and cultural conditions which underpin human suffering rather than the specific issues in their own lives as a (proxy) service user or carer. These students may have experience of impoverished communities, as was the case with a young man brought up on a council estate who witnessed poverty, crime and drug dependency all around him. He had escaped these problems himself and wanted to devote his life to eradicating them. And they may take on some care tasks, as was the case with a woman whose best friend had died of AIDS. She was not his primary carer, but the friendship opened her eyes to the stigma surrounding HIV/AIDS and, after her friend died, she signed up to voluntary work and political campaigns in this area.

Taking the citizen road involves a broadening of our horizons and a politicisation of our world views so these students have a more radical standpoint on social work than others (cf. Gilligan, 2007). Overseas students from developing countries were most likely to adopt a radical standpoint as they had witnessed extremes of poverty and prejudice in grassroots communities as well as corruption among governments:

> S: In my country there is nothing for the people. If they don't have relatives
>   or if they've been shunned by relatives they end up on the streets ... So
>   they're suffering in silence, or they're dying, or they're committing crimes
>   to survive then being locked away and sometimes beaten up and thrown
>   out, then it starts all over again ...

CH: So what do you really want out of this course?

S: To be able to be heard. To be able to complain to the government when the people need something and have nothing. To be able to approach the right people in power and have some influence over them so that the poorest people can benefit.

CH: That sounds like a cross between professional and political work.

S: I think it's political.

Awareness of the economic, political and cultural contexts of human suffering is the greatest asset brought by these students. They are not only committed to an ethos of empowerment, but also cognisant of the need to challenge existing power elites in a manner which is highly congruent with the social justice dimension of social work endorsed by the International Federation of Social Workers (2000). Nevertheless, these students may have to face other quandaries, particularly when they hail from the camp of global citizenship, since the experience of diverse countries and cultures can give rise to conflicts in our world views.

Two examples will be provided to illustrate cross-cultural dilemmas. One example pertains to an overseas student who had undertaken social care work in the UK prior to embarking upon the programme and who found herself in conflict with some aspects of cultural norms and welfare services in Britain. In her country of origin, families retained the primary responsibility of caring for their members, so when she was required to provide services such as shopping to an elderly housebound woman who had sons living nearby, she questioned whether the state should provide such services on the grounds that this would prevent the sons from discharging their duties. The other example pertains to a British student who had spent most of her youth in the Middle and Far East as a result of her father's employment. She had been perturbed by the harsh punishments meted out to people who committed offences in these countries, which could result in disease or death, and returned to the UK determined to work with offenders in a more humanitarian manner. But when she had placements in the criminal justice system, she was shocked by the permissive nature of some regimes and regarded prisons as more akin to 'a holiday camp'. This student tried hard to adopt a middle path between these cultural extremes, endorsing punishments which did not jeopardise life or health, but from the vantage point of social work in the UK, her views would be described as closer to the conservative end of the political spectrum.

Exercise 2C is designed to help you reflect upon your own biographical route into social work.

Exercise 2C   Reflecting Upon Your Own Journey

Ponder on which role(s) propelled you into social work and address the following questions:

1 Students for whom a service user background is paramount

During the troubled times in your life, were you helped by people in the caring professions?

If so, who helped you the most, and how?

If not, how did you recover from difficulties and how do you now feel about professionals?

Do you want to work specifically with service users with similar backgrounds to yourself?

Ponder on whether and how you could draw upon your own life experiences to help others, and whether there are aspects of your life experience which might not be helpful to others, or indeed aspects of your life experience which you may still need some help with yourself.

2 Students for whom a personal carer background is paramount

When you care for a close relative or friend, what personal qualities and values are you drawing upon? And what kinds of skills and knowledges do you develop during the caring?

Which of these qualities, values, skills and knowledges are directly transferable to social work where you will be caring for strangers?

Note that whilst social care workers may be based in residential homes, most social workers are based in offices and communities and do not provide direct personal care.

3 Students for whom a citizenship background is paramount

Call to mind the specific injustice(s) you have witnessed or studied (many injustices revolve around class, ethnicity, age, gender, sexuality, disability).

Do you think that social work as a profession is in a position to alleviate such injustice?

If so, how do social workers go about challenging injustices and empowering people?

If not, which people and professionals are the key change agents?

Note that social workers may be employed by statutory or independent agencies, so you may want to give a different answer for social workers employed in different sectors.

NB If you think your own journey is different from the above, then you can draw up your own biographical route into social work. Afterwards, you can reflect upon its implications for your career, noting the strengths and weaknesses you may carry as a result of this life journey.

2.3 Transformative Journeys

Social work training is likely to change you in ways which cannot be anticipated in advance. Indeed, just over 50 per cent of students changed their career plans and/or preferred service user and carer specialisms during the programme[2]. Why was this? It usually reflected positive experiences with service user groups which had inspired them with trepidation at the start of the programme. So the lesson here for students is: keep an open mind and be prepared to go beyond your comfort zone.

But the social work journey can transform us personally and politically as well as professionally. For some people, their self-concepts as well as their conceptions of social work underwent radical changes. The student whose images of social workers were discussed in the first section had placements with elderly, dying and bereaved people so that his fears that social workers might be domineering policewomen or political activists were replaced by a strong sense that they were caring professionals more akin to counsellors. Other students reported that they applied the knowledge and skills acquired during the programme to their own everyday life worlds, by acting as advocates for friends and relatives when dealing with other professionals and their organisations.

Of course, learning about social problems and working with vulnerable people has the potential to trigger any unresolved traumas in our own lives, a phenomenon which is familiar to social work educators who specialise in child protection (Humphrey, 2007a). If students face the challenge, seeking professional help if necessary, and if they are supported by supervisors in universities and communities, then they emerge stronger and wiser from this revisiting of their past. A vivid example of resolution was provided by a student who had been brought up in a situation of domestic violence; her father suffered mental health problems and presided over a punitive regime where he treated his wife and children as 'little prisoners'. When her mother died during her first placement, the student was tempted to sever contact with her father. But when she reflected upon her university-based learning around mental health and attachment issues, she realised that there could be other ways of framing the problem and that the severance of contact might not be the only solution or even the best one. So she visited her father with an open mind and found a bereaved and broken man who wanted to confess his misdemeanours and who disclosed the abuse in his own childhood which underpinned his parenting style. The student developed a genuine relationship with her father for the first time in her life. She was able to draw upon this deepening of her life experience in her final placement where she worked with offenders with mental health problems, since she could tap into a more compassionate understanding for people who may have dealt with their own suffering by inflicting it upon others.

Young students can undergo some of the most profound changes since by definition they are still discovering themselves. One young man arrived on the programme suspecting that he was gay, but he had not dared to explore this possibility in his own white, working-class community where homosexuality was stigmatised. Over the next couple of years, he came out as gay to some of his peers who offered a more sympathetic audience and embarked upon a relationship with a black man which opened his eyes to racism in Britain. He then started to travel abroad during vacations in a quest to find a multi-cultural and gay-affirmative city, and evolved a long-term plan to emigrate. Another significant feature of his transformation revolved around spirituality. He had arrived as an atheist from a community which ridiculed all religion, but during a placement he was faced with the suicide of a child which sparked off deep questioning about the meaning of life and death. His travels abroad had brought him into contact with people of diverse faiths as well as places deemed to be sacred, and at the end of the programme he announced that he was becoming a Buddhist.

Becoming a social worker can propel you towards self-actualisation, but sometimes people stumble across obstacles en route. Figure 2A shows the hierarchy of human needs leading to the summit of self-actualisation which was developed by Abraham Maslow (1943). It is usually applied to service users as it helps practitioners to understand their most pressing needs and to aim for realistic goals. But it is equally applicable to students – it will enable you to assess your own level of development and to anticipate some of the obstacles which you may face on your social work journey.

Points to Remember and Questions to Ponder

- Section 2.1 dissected the contradictory images of social workers in contemporary Britain. These images are social constructs which can change over time, and social workers need to contribute to a positive reconstruction of their profession wherever possible. How are you going to express and enact a positive image of social work when challenged by others?
- Section 2.2 unveiled three biographical routes into social work, along with their merits and pitfalls. If it left you with worries about your own life journey and its implications for your career, you can consult a supervisor or check out the resources for self-help listed below.

- In the final section, I explained that social work training is itself a transformative journey for those who truly engage with it. The best advice is to keep an open mind and to embrace whatever opportunities come your way. But first you need to ask yourself: 'Am I genuinely open to change?' Many people have a fear of change, and this translates into resistance to new learning, as you will find when you work with some service users and carers. It is a good idea to undertake an annual review of the ways in which you have changed, so that you become self-conscious of your own ongoing development as a person and as a professional. You can then enjoy more choice and control in relation to your own 'reconstruction'.

Basic needs around survival, health and safety provide the foundation for physical and material security so that we can progress up the hierarchy. Students whose basic needs are compromised by poverty or domestic violence are likely to struggle with the social work journey which requires the development of esteem.

Love and belonging provide us with social and emotional security so that we are not dependent upon our service users or carers for meeting these needs. Students with sound partnerships or friendship networks will be able to cope more easily with the ups and downs of relationships with colleagues and clients on placements.

It is also useful to have a source of esteem outside of your educational or employment base. Caring professionals who rely upon their power over service users and carers to raise their own self-esteem are unlikely to empower others to move up the hierarchy and meet their own higher needs.

According to Maslow (1943), all human beings are seeking self-actualisation – a stage characterised by spontaneity, creativity, sensitivity, morality and spirituality.

FIGURE 2A   *Self-actualisation and Stumbling Blocks*

Notes

1   Statistics are based on a survey of BA students at the start of their programme (unless stated otherwise).
2   This finding is based upon a survey of BA students at the end of their programme.

Further Reading and Resources

Retrospective accounts about becoming a social worker by practitioners, managers and educators are provided in the following edited collection:
Cree, V. E. (ed.) (2003) *Becoming a Social Worker*. London: Routledge.

If you are unsure what social work entails, or need to counteract negative images, you should read some positive accounts by practitioners and service users:
Cree, V. E. and Davis, A. (2007) *Social Work: Voices from the Inside*. London: Routledge.

Students with unhappy childhoods may benefit from reading a short work by Alice Miller, a psychoanalyst who had to recover from her own childhood wounds:
Miller, A. (1994) *The Drama of Being a Child: The Search for the True Self*. London: Virago.

If you are daunted by the prospect of change, try reading this classic text:
Jeffers, S. (2007) *Feel the Fear and Do it Anyway: How to Turn Your Fear and Indecision into Confidence and Action*. London: Vermillion.

If you need to develop self-care, then a good starting point is to learn the art of relaxation:
Harvey, J. (1998) *Total Relaxation: Healing Practices for Body, Mind and Spirit*. New York: Kodansha. (This includes a 60-minute CD.)

3

Studying Social Work at University

Introduction

This chapter is designed to enable students to become self-conscious and self-directed learners. Section 3.1 examines the key players in university settings as well as the subject matter of modules. It shows how all of us need to adopt an integrated approach to teaching and learning where the affective and intuitive aspects of understanding are as important as the conceptual and practical ones. It explains that there are two bridges for students to cross during their degree – the bridge from surface to deep learning, and the bridge from university to community learning. Section 3.2 introduces students to models of learning relevant to both university and community settings; if you apply these throughout the programme, you will have a firm foundation for lifelong learning. The subject of section 3.3 is 'the hidden curriculum', a phrase which is used to embrace everything which goes on at universities but which falls outside of the official curriculum. Here, we will take a closer look at the peer groups formed by students and their implications for anti-discriminatory practice.

3.1 Studying at University

Student learning is influenced by the approaches to teaching and learning adopted by educators and students themselves, and these are in turn affected by our biographies and beliefs.

3.1.1 Students, Teachers and Experts by Experience

Students were adamant that teaching styles made a difference to their learning. Tutors who are passionate about their subject area are often animated speakers who can make even a dull topic come alive; tutors who are sensitive to the range of experiences and viewpoints in the audience and who are skilled in drawing out this diversity can bring silent students out of their shell; in short, students said that a good teacher forces them to 'wake up' and 'speak out'. Some of the favourite strategies to keep students awake reported by academic tutors included using case studies from their own careers as practitioners and inserting interactive media clippings into presentations to make links with current events. Other educators have encouraged students to share their own life experiences around social problems such as domestic violence (Trotter and Leech, 2003) and to adopt the role of 'devil's advocate' when debating political controversies (Balen and White, 2007).

How do the biographies and beliefs of students make a difference to their learning? Young students with recent experience of higher education but limited life experience tend to prefer didactic methods of teaching (i.e. lectures which present information) and virtual learning environments (i.e. e-learning with online materials and discussion groups), whilst mature students with a social care career behind them are more comfortable with face-to-face interactive methods (ESWDET, 2008). But students can erect defensive barriers to prevent them from assimilating new learning if this conflicts with their life experiences or beliefs, regardless of the method of teaching (Rogers, 2002). For example, a student whose close relatives were health care professionals remained wedded to a medical model of mental ill health to the end of the programme, believing that it was genetic in origin and should be controlled by medication, in spite of three years of learning about the social model which underpins the social work profession (see Tew, 2005). In other words, the influence from her family was stronger and deeper than the influence of her tutors, supervisors or peer group.

Service users and carers present guest sessions on most modules, and may be involved throughout an entire module, and they are deemed to be one of the most valuable educational resources by the vast majority of students (ESWDET, 2008: Chapters 6 and 8). Why is this? First, they present true stories of personal difficulties, societal discriminations and interactions with social workers. For young students with limited life or work experience, only such first-hand seeing and hearing will propel them towards an insider understanding which enables them to really connect with personal distress, political injustice and professional practice. When lecturers convey information second-hand – based upon research findings, theoretical models or outdated practice – students can be left with doubts about its reality or relevance (cf. SWTF, 2009: Chapter 1).

Second, educators with a service user or carer background are positive role models for the wider groups of service users and carers. Their role as educators is significant in its own right as they provide a live demonstration of their 'expertise by experience' (Levin, 2004). This operates to dismantle negative stereotypes which students may have internalised in respect of a specific group, so students are forced to recognise and redress their latent prejudices, as illustrated below:

> S: Mental health was the big thing [for me] … I think it's been a media thing. You just think 'Oh, mental health is schizophrenia, it's a person talking to themselves and they're in a straitjacket'. But it's not like that; it's the rest of us wearing the straitjacket! … [This guest lecture] challenged the picture you have in your head … When that service user came in who was suffering mental health problems, well, *he just looked normal!* Most of us thought he was another lecturer … but then he started to tell us his story. That was a real eye-opener.

Third, service users and carers specialise in interactive and creative presentations. Their life stories are conveyed in a manner which engages students, and they may be supplemented by poems and paintings which provide vivid testimonies to their distress and subsequent healing (see Advocacy in Action and Sure Search Collective, 2006). Students' capacities for empathy and imagination are awakened under these circumstances, and their motivation to help service users is reinforced. If affectivity and imagery are the primordial ground for both conceptual and practical knowledge – an argument

Practical Mode: Practical or performative knowledge crucial to placements. BUT it will be compromised if students have not mastered conceptual knowledge or if they do not connect intuitively and affectively with others.

Conceptual Mode: Conceptual or propositional knowledge at university. Language is the foundation for our theory, research and critical reflection. BUT if abstract knowledge is divorced from the other modes, it becomes sterile.

Imaginal Mode: Creative or presentational knowledge offered by service users and carers in the form of life stories, poems, paintings, personal insights. These awaken students' own intuitive and imaginal capacities. BUT these capacities must then be developed into conceptual thought, otherwise students will not be able to articulate their intuitive knowledge in essays or dialogues.

Affective Mode: Experiential or embodied knowledge from everyday life. Encounters between human beings involve the exchange of energies and emotions which is vital to empathic attunement. It should propel us to the next levels, i.e. we discover new insights, seek to make sense of them conceptually and become committed to helping people practically through their distress. BUT if we carry too much distress ourselves or if we are closed off to the distress of others, then our experiential learning will be jeopardised.

FIGURE 3A   *An Integrated Approach to Teaching and Learning*

made most forcefully by John Heron (1992) and now embraced by other professional educators (e.g. Higgs and Titchen, 2001) – then experts by experience communicate directly with this primordial ground.

Figure 3A is based upon the work of John Heron (1992). It displays four different modes of understanding, each of which is equally crucial to our development as social workers. Problems are likely to arise whenever these modes of understanding become split off from one another. One of the mistakes made by some students is to assume that the social work journey starts and ends with service user stories; these students form the impression that 'social work is just about everyday people in everyday life'. In essence, they want to leap from the affective mode to the practical mode, and to bypass the conceptual mode in particular. But critical and conceptual thought is vital to professional expertise (SWTF, 2009), and service user knowledge also transcends life stories (Beresford, 2000). One of the mistakes made by some academics is to assume that university teaching and learning revolves primarily around conceptual models of theory, policy and practice. In essence, they want to bypass the affective and imaginal modes in order to give a full exposition of the knowledge base of the profession. But this leaves some students uninterested and disconnected (CWDC, 2009a). Therefore, we all need to adopt an integrated approach to teaching and learning where service user stories are linked to theory and policy, and where academics engage with the affective and imaginal modes during lectures on theoretical frameworks and practice interventions.

3.1.2 Social Work Modules

The subject matter of modules exerts its own influence upon teaching and learning, although this will again be mediated by the approaches taken by staff and students. Students tend to learn more easily from modules which connect clearly to their own life experience or their career plans. When the subject matter of the module is the social psychology of human growth and development throughout the lifespan, there are ample opportunities for students to draw from their own life experience in order to connect with core concepts such as attachment, separation and loss (see Bowlby, 1969, 1973, 1981). Students often arrive at new understandings of their own family history at university, and this equips them to work more effectively with families on placements.

Modules which enable students to rehearse and reflect upon communication skills are also popular since their relevance to social work practice is transparent (Trevithick, 2005). Nevertheless, all aspects of the curriculum will be relevant even if their relevance is not immediately obvious to students, and part of the ethos of a university education is that students should transcend their previous horizons, including their assumptions about what is or is not relevant. For example, one student complained bitterly about a teaching session devoted to making use of play materials with children on the grounds that she had not come to university to learn 'child's play' and she had no intention of working with children. Her first placement was in a day centre with learning disabled adults and her special project was to develop a strategy for staff to communicate with a service user who had developed an idiosyncratic language with his own carer which no one else understood. She retrieved the play materials used at university and adapted them to create a communications board which enabled this service user to express his wishes and needs to staff at the day centre. The student was amazed by the fact that this 'non-relevant' learning was actually highly relevant, and by the fact that she had retrieved this memory since she believed she had discarded it. Ironically, we often recall 'bad experiences' more vividly than 'good ones', and her resentment of the 'child's play' session invested it with powerful emotions which helped to preserve it in her memory (Goleman, 1996).

Student motivation to learn is high in respect of modules which cover the substantive areas of social work practice in community care, mental health and child care, but these modules are also more complex since they combine theory, research, policy, law, practice, ethics and politics. Students offered the analogy of a jigsaw to depict their experience of these modules – it requires patience and persistence to study each piece of the jigsaw, as well as hope and faith that all the pieces will eventually fit into place. The following student is discussing a mental health module:

> S: The law I was getting to grips with ... then all the theories came along ... I was starting to make sense of the different social and medical models ... then the politics came up ... I was going round in circles! ... I was able to understand things at the time, you know, I had a bit about everything. But was it a big enough bit? How did it fit in with the other bits? And I could lose bits!

From a student's perspective, research-based modules are the least relevant to social work and their recurrent refrain is that they are training to be social workers not researchers. From an educator's perspective, research-based modules are essential to becoming evidence-based practitioners – all students have to learn how to read research in order to ascertain its relevance to their practice and apply its findings appropriately, and some programmes and placements may require them to undertake a piece of empirical research (cf. McLaughlin, 2006; Whittaker, 2009). Interestingly, after their placements, a number of students reported that the research module proved to be the most relevant to practice. One student captured this beautifully by stating that although he had not been 'taught' anything in this module, he had learned the most from it. This module included exercises where students searched for and sifted through research studies in the library and online, and then ascertained the merits and limitations of the studies including their implications for practice in the UK. These are precisely the skills that come into play in practice settings when, for example, a student is asked to initiate group work and needs to find out what kind of activities or approaches work best with a particular service user or carer group. In other words, during research modules students are learning how to learn, which is known as 'meta-learning' as it is more about acquiring skills which are transferable across contexts than about acquiring specific knowledge (cf. Gardiner, 1989; Cree and Macauley, 2000).

3.1.3 Bridges for Students to Cross

During a social work programme there are two bridges for students to cross. The first is the bridge from surface to depth understandings, a bridge which must be traversed by all students in higher education if they are to operate at degree level since it concerns our understanding of any given discipline in terms of its concepts, methods and perspectives (Biggs, 1999; Rogers, 2002). Anyone who sits in on a lecture or who skims through a book can gain a surface understanding of the subject matter, simply by this exposure to a multitude of signs such as words, pictures and charts. Surface learning is also known as passive or serial learning and it results in short-term and recognition-based memory. In other words, the student stays on the outside as a series of signs passes by their sensory organs; the signs are stored in short-term memory and will rapidly be displaced by subsequent experiences; at a later date, the student will be able to recognise that they have been exposed to a particular sign such as the name of a theory, but they will not be able to recall anything significant about this theory. Depth understanding can only be gained by taking an active approach to learning, by concentrating on any given sign and questioning its meaning, by discussing a topic with other people, by following up clues and doing further reading. It is also called holistic learning since the student will be making links between whatever they have learned today and whatever else they may have learned through other life experiences. Investing energy into new learning and forging links with other learning enables new ideas to be stored in long-term memory where they can be recalled at a later date, and there is a richness to this recall since the student has already found their way onto the inside of the material and made it significant to their own pathway in life and learning.

Table 3A provides an example of the difference between surface and depth understandings in relation to the concept of anti-discriminatory practice. Once you get a sense of the process of critical thinking, you can apply it to other concepts in social work. Don't despair if there are more questions than answers – this is typical of critical thinking – rest assured that each set of questions and answers will take your understanding to a deeper level.

The second bridge to be crossed is that from university to community learning, which requires that conceptual or propositional knowledge is translated into practical or performative knowledge. This bridge is peculiar to students on professional programmes who are training to be social workers, nurses or teachers (Higgs and Titchen, 2001). A university is akin to a virtual learning environment insofar as it teaches about phenomena 'out there in the

TABLE 3A   *Surface and Depth Understandings*

Concept	Surface Understanding	Depth Understanding
Anti-Discriminatory Practice (ADP)	Being non-discriminatory, non-judgemental and keeping an open mind. This results in 'neutrality' which does not always fit with our humanity or the concept of ADP or the role occupied by social workers in statutory settings. So it is a starting point but there is further to travel …	It isn't enough to simply not discriminate; the term 'ADP' asks us to actively challenge discrimination. How can I do that in my everyday working life? What if my managers are the source of discrimination – is it safe to challenge them? What if the discrimination is caused by the wider community or government policies? How does 'being non-judgemental' fit with legal duties to safeguard vulnerable people? Would I remain neutral when meeting a child sex offender? If not, would I run the risk of discriminating against someone in need?

real world' by reference to law, theory, research and methods of intervention, but these are second-order representations of those phenomena summarised in the form of concepts, models and statements ('propositions'), i.e. you do not witness domestic violence itself or even social work practice in a lecture theatre. Students reported that although university modules were indispensable for making sense of practice, they had to 'start all over again' when they got out into practice. You can learn all about community care legislation and needs assessments of vulnerable adults at university, but this will not equip you to take referrals on duty in an adult care team or to undertake a community care assessment. Why not? Just taking a referral presupposes familiarity with procedures, paperwork and information technology systems in a specific setting; doing a community care assessment requires skills in observation and interviewing as well as knowledge of local resources. Of course, this does not mean that university learning is redundant; it simply means that you must convert your abstract knowledge into 'performative' knowledge, by *doing* the job as opposed to reading, writing or talking about the job! You need to embody and enact social work values, skills and knowledge; you have to internalise them, perform them and even 'become' them. It is not surprising that placements can also be the chief catalyst for moving from surface to depth understanding for many students.

3.2 Models of Learning

There are several models of learning, but they can be categorised into three types, depending upon whether they relate to a cycle of learning or stages of learning or styles of learning. They are all based upon research with students and practitioners in higher education and the caring professions. If you understand the learning process, and yourself as a learner, then you will travel much further.

3.2.1 Cycles of Learning

Figure 3B outlines the cycle of learning initially articulated by David Kolb (1984) and subsequently applied to student learning on professional

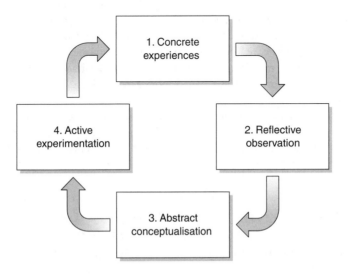

You should apply this learning cycle to something significant in your own life.

You can start with a concrete life experience. Have you reflected upon it and what materialised from your reflections? How does your experience relate to abstract concepts or ideas which you have read about in books or heard about in lectures?

You could also start with an abstract concept or idea and track it around the circle. If you travel clockwise, you need to ask: how can it be applied in a practice setting? If you go counter-clockwise, the question is: how does it connect with your reflections on life experience?

Some social work students struggle with the entire notion of 'an abstract concept'. But our language is brimming with abstract concepts; we use them every day, often without realising this, and often with an intuitive rather than conceptual understanding of the relevant theory. 'Attachment', 'separation' and 'loss' are concepts drawn from attachment theory and research, i.e. they are abstract representations of the actual experiences of human beings, and they are designed to take us beyond our own concrete experiences of being a child, parent or partner. 'Person-centred practice' is also a concept which refers to a particular kind of practice; it is an abstract representation of that practice, and not the practice itself; but our understanding of the language and our understanding of the practice are intimately bound up with each other.

FIGURE 3B   *The Learning Cycle*

programmes in education, health, social work and counselling (e.g. Heron, 1992; Johns, 2000). This is how it works:

1   The starting point of adult learning is concrete life and work experience. This gives rise to experiential and embodied knowledge – but it is raw knowledge and needs to be refined.
2   We refine our knowledge by reflecting upon experience. Reflection presupposes observation, i.e. if we don't stand back and survey things from a distance, we remain too immersed in them. But, rather paradoxically, the result of reflection is to take us deeper into things. As we ponder on experiences, we discover their significance for us – we compare and contrast them with other events in our lives so that the experience becomes embedded in a wider narrative; and metaphors and images may spring to mind which take us into the imaginal mode of understanding.
3   Higher education propels us further along the road as it adds abstract conceptualisation to the equation; this covers theories, research studies, legal frameworks and the like.
4   Practice placements complete the cycle by encouraging students to actively experiment with the application of knowledge; this becomes the source of more experiential and embodied knowledge; and it even generates its own practical knowledge ('practice wisdom').

This is a continuous cycle which must be repeated in respect of all new learning. Over the course of a professional career, it becomes akin to a spiral insofar as each turn of the cycle can bring us to deeper understandings of relevant phenomena and higher stages of the learning process itself.

3.2.2 Stages of Learning

Students should be progressing to higher stages of learning during their degree, and you can check out your own current position and subsequent progress by reference to the following two models.

The first is a model of learning stages discussed by the medical educator Colin Coles (1998) and it foregrounds the beliefs about knowledge held by students. The views of students at Stage 1 are characterised by a polarisation between right and wrong; these students assume that there are right answers to every problem and that their teachers possess all these right answers which students must assimilate. By Stage 2, students are becoming aware of the complexity of social problems and the relativity of knowledge; during this stage, all the claims made by teachers and textbooks appear to be 'mere opinions' which the student is free to accept or reject. Ideally, students will move beyond this to Stage 3 where they realise that some knowledge is 'better' by virtue of robust theories or research studies or by virtue of its congruence with their own chosen vocation. At this stage, they are able to make choices and commitments in respect of knowledge and world views. For example, in social work we prioritise the social model of understanding the predicaments suffered by service users – such as depression and domestic violence – since these are often rooted in the wider environment, i.e. family relationships, gendered cultures and even the global political economy.

The second model derives from research by the social work educator Derek Gardiner (1989). It depicts three levels of learning which are distinguished by the student's approach to mastering new material. Level 1 is when a student focuses upon the content of the material, trying to make sense of it and memorise it. Level 2 is when a student broadens their horizons beyond the content and considers wider contexts and processes. This is a higher level of learning since the student is actively making links between the specific content of one module and other relevant material from other modules and from life experience. Level 3 is the highest level of meta-learning reached by students who have understood their own learning processes and developed a variety of strategies to master new learning in different settings. So meta-learning is also linked to versatility of learning styles.

3.2.3 Styles of Learning

Different styles of learning have also been identified, and your preferred learning style will affect your capacity to master different kinds of skills and knowledges and to operate in different kinds of settings. Peter Honey and Alan Mumford (2000) proposed a fourfold typology of learners whom they called activists, reflectors, theorists and pragmatists, and they also developed a learning styles questionnaire so that students could test their own learning styles. This typology is linked to the learning cycle in Figure 3B since each type of learner is understood as travelling between two sites:

* Activists travel from 'concrete experiences' to 'reflective observation' since life experiences form the primary subject matter of their reflections.
* Reflectors are most comfortable moving between 'reflective observation' and 'abstract conceptualisation' since ideas provide the axis around which their reflections revolve.
* Theorists walk cautiously along the bridge between 'abstract conceptualisation' and 'active experimentation'; they take time to make sense of theoretical models in their own minds before venturing into experimentation.
* Pragmatists leap between 'active experimentation' and 'concrete experience'; they love to translate life experiences into experiments without reading or thinking too much about it.

Exercise 3A illustrates the ways in which these four learning styles typically manifest themselves in university and community settings and will help you to identify your own preferred learning style. Since a social work degree is weighted equally between university and community learning, students need to develop versatility in learning styles and to engage with all parts of the learning cycle.

Exercise 3A   What Is Your Preferred Learning Style?

Learning Style	University Setting	Community Setting
Activist Walks the bridge between experience and reflection	Activists enjoy classroom debates about life experiences and sessions with practitioners, service users and carers. But they can soon switch off in lectures.	They are eager to visit service users and to shadow other professionals, but they struggle to connect these new experiences to broader issues around theory or policy.
Reflector Walks the bridge between reflection and conceptualisation	Reflectors engage equally in lectures and debates, and read widely around theory, research and practice. They often find role plays difficult.	They need to prepare themselves for practice by reading and discussing issues with colleagues. So they take longer to arrange visits, but once they are in the field they easily see the links between service user stories and wider social work issues.
Theorist Walks the bridge between conceptualisation and experimentation	Their priority is to develop an overview of theory, policy and practice from books and lectures. Once they have mastered a conceptual framework, they will be comfortable with most interactive exercises.	Theorists will be reading relevant books and agency policies prior to supervision sessions or community visits. So again it can take them longer to settle into a placement, but by the end of it they are usually creative and critical practitioners.

Learning Style	University Setting	Community Setting
Pragmatist Walks the bridge between experience and experimentation	They prefer sessions presented by service users, carers and practititioners to standard lectures. They relish practice skills modules which include role plays.	Pragmatists can be creative as they are not afraid to draw upon their own life experience or to try out new ways of working. But they are not always critical, so they may struggle if asked to explain their methods of working or any relevant theory or research.

3.3 The Hidden Curriculum

The hidden curriculum refers to all the informal teaching and learning which does not appear on the official curriculum, an area which has been studied extensively in medicine and nursing, but which has unfortunately been neglected in social work (Barretti, 2004). Here, we will take a closer look at peer group formation among social work students – this will reveal significant things about social divisions which have implications for anti-discriminatory practice.

The diversity of students' profiles along the dimensions of age, gender, ethnicity, sexuality and disability should provide ample opportunities for working with diversity which is so central to the social work ethos of anti-discriminatory practice (Thompson, 2006). But peer groups can also reflect and reinforce segregations in the wider society, and during the first year when university life is novel and strange, many students choose to socialise exclusively with peers who are most similar to themselves as this creates a sense of security and familiarity. Some young students were shocked to find themselves studying alongside mature women whom they regarded as similar to their own mothers, pointing out that they had embarked upon a university education to get away from the influence of their mothers, and they tended to avoid these women. The mature women were acutely aware of these dynamics; some worked hard to dissolve the barriers by asking young students for advice on assignments; one of them used the joke that 'I'm only 16 on the inside, you know!' as an ice-breaker. But during practice placements, young students regularly turned to mature students for advice on dealing with complex problems where they felt out of their depth. By the end of the programme, they had developed a genuine collegiality which transcended age-related social barriers and associated stereotypes.

There are a number of distinct minority groups in social work programmes, but the extent to which they perceive themselves as forming a group is highly variable. At one extreme, there are overseas students who may form a separate group when they originate from the same continent or belong to the same church or face the same kind of discrimination in a predominantly white British community (McNamara and Harris, 1997; Bartoli et al., 2008). Unfortunately, this limits the opportunities for cross-cultural learning in the university, although these dynamics often shift during placements when home and overseas students may be placed in the same agency so that they form close bonds. At the other extreme, there are men who avoid same-sex peer groups. Men reported that they enjoyed the company of women and that they felt 'special' on account of their minority status; they managed to be both socially integrated and special since only one man would be attached to a large group of female students. Interestingly, women in male-dominated professions often feel excluded or subordinated (Grimwood and Popplestone, 1993) and male students could also suffer a sense of isolation on placements if they were the sole man in a team or agency (see Chapter 4: Exercise 4A).

Lesbian and gay students are another minority group, although a lesbian or gay student may form a minority of one on some social work programmes. Lesbian and gay students are often 'invisible' unless they choose to 'come out' of the closet and declare their sexual orientation to their peers or supervisors, an undertaking which carries risks of discrimination, ostracism and gossip (Equality Challenge Unit, 2009). This hiddenness means that they are more reliant upon educators to provide positive role models. For example, a lesbian parent explained how empowered she felt after a teaching session delivered by a lesbian couple who were foster carers. But homosexuality remains stigmatised in a number of cultures and religions, and other students complained about such teaching on the grounds that it normalised homosexuality and ran contrary to beliefs in their own communities. This contentious issue is the subject of the research report *Love Thy Neighbour* (Hunt and Valentine, 2008).

It is not surprising that teaching and learning about anti-discriminatory practice can be controversial (Chand et al., 2002). Social divisions associated with age, ethnicity, gender, sexuality and disability are written into our bodies and psyches; and beliefs about such divisions are central to our own identities and communities. Students should be open to new learning rather than wedded to past learning, and they need to appreciate the socially constructed nature of identities, communities and world views. There is an important question of values here, so when you are faced with conflicting world views, you would benefit from asking: which is most congruent with social work? And it is difficult to champion some kinds of anti-discriminatory practice at the expense of others, given that the discourses which legitimate different types of oppression are remarkably similar, as Anna Marie Smith (1994) demonstrates so vividly in relation to racism and homophobia in Britain.

The social reconstruction of identities was most apparent for students with specific learning difficulties. Some were shocked to find themselves assessed as having a learning difficulty, which placed them in the camp of 'disabled students'; they needed time to adjust their self-perception, and their self-esteem could plummet as they wondered whether they were capable of completing a degree. But, as a result of specialist technology and tuition, they could make tremendous leaps forward in terms of their grades and their confidence, to the point that they ceased to perceive themselves as 'disabled students' by the end of the programme (cf. Swain et al., 1993). Some students with specific learning difficulties have indeed been awarded First Class Honours degrees.

Points to Remember and Questions to Ponder

- The first section emphasised the need for an integrated approach to teaching and learning. Experts by experience play a significant role here, but students should remember that they also have their own expertise by experience as a result of their life journeys to date.
- Section 2.2 should have enabled you to identify your own learning stage and preferred learning style. How are you going to put this learning to good use?
- The final section highlighted informal processes around peer group formation. Next time you arrive for a lecture, think about who you have chosen to sit next to and why, as well as which individuals or groups you may have avoided, and ponder on whether these choices are likely to limit or extend your learning opportunities. You should relate peer group dynamics to wider social divisions and the concept of anti-discriminatory practice, i.e. if social work students replicate segregation by age or 'race' within their own peer groups, how then are they going to gain a deeper understanding of anti-discriminatory practice?

Further Reading and Resources

Undergraduate students should access the following text on study skills which also contains
sound advice on the practical, social and psychological aspects of university life:

Burns, T. and Sinfield, S. (2008) *Essential Study Skills: The Complete Guide to Success
at University*. London: Sage.

There is an introductory guide to studying social work:

Thompson, N. and Thompson, S. (2008) *The Social Work Companion*. Basingstoke:
Palgrave-Macmillan.

More complex material to promote deep learning includes:

Cree, V. E. and Macauley, C. (eds) (2000) *Transfer of Learning in Professional and
Vocational Education*. London: Routledge.

You can download a learning styles questionnaire from Peter Honey's website: www.
peterhoney.com

4

Practising Under Supervision in the Community

Introduction

This chapter provides an overview of practice education. Section 4.1 surveys the arrangements for placements in different UK countries and the arrangements for supervision in different agencies. Under the new degree programmes offered from 2003, the technical term for placements has been 'Practice Learning Opportunities' which is usually abbreviated to PLOs in speech and writing. Section 4.2 provides a tour of the different models of supervision used by practice teachers. Again, you should note that in the implementation of the new degree programmes a new technical term was coined to refer to practice teachers who became 'Practice Learning Assessors', which was again abbreviated to PLAs for convenience. In England social work education is already undergoing another raft of reforms, and the term 'practice educator' will be increasingly used in the future. Students can become confused when they move between placements and find that different practice teachers adopt very different approaches to supervision, so this section will help you to clarify where your practice teacher is coming from. The final section is devoted to 'the hidden practicum', the counterpart of the hidden curriculum which we encountered in the last chapter. Case examples will demonstrate that the most powerful learning experiences are those which force us to revisit aspects of our own identity or biography.

4.1 Community-based Learning

Community-based learning is delivered through partnerships between universities and welfare agencies, and there are staff dedicated to managing student placements in the university and in local authorities who are usually called 'Practice Learning Coordinators' or 'Placement Coordinators'. The current requirement is that students must undertake at least two placements with two different service user or carer groups which should amount to a minimum of 200 days (DH, 2002a). The stipulation as to the number of days is under review as a result of pressures upon placement providers and the realisation that quality of practice learning is more important than the sheer number of days spent in the community (SWTF, 2009). The practice learning landscape is so diverse that it can look daunting to students, but it is vital that you make sense of your own local landscape.

4.1.1 Progressing Through Placements

Although students are guaranteed placements, they are asked to complete application forms and attend interviews at one or more agencies so that all parties can do the requisite reality checking to promote a good 'match' between the student, agency and staff. This is a useful exercise for students as they will be rehearsing some of the skills needed for job interviews (see Chapter 12).

Placements are progressive in two senses, i.e. students must pass the first placement in order to progress to the next placement, and each placement is more demanding than the previous one. Many programmes in England have two placements, each lasting 100 days (or 20 weeks) which are dubbed PLO1 and PLO2 (Doel et al., 2007; ESWDET, 2008). But placement arrangements vary across the UK as illustrated in Tables 4A, 4B and 4C. Social work programmes in Scotland, Wales and Northern Ireland (as well as

TABLE 4A   *Practice Learning in Wales*

A three-stage progression:

1   20-day placement

2   80-day placement

3   100-day placement

Note that some placements may be Welsh-speaking.

Source: Care Council for Wales website: www.ccwales.org.uk

TABLE 4B   *Practice Learning in Scotland*

A three-stage progression:

1   Assessed preparation for practice learning

2   Direct work under supervision

3   Direct work under supervision

Note that Scotland is developing a number of innovative multi-agency placements as well as Practice Teaching Units.

Source: Scottish Practice Learning website: www.scottishpracticelearning.com

TABLE 4C   *Practice Learning in Northern Ireland*

A multi-layered progression:

Level 1: Foundation – preparation for direct supervised practice (25 days)

Level 2: Application – direct supervised practice (85 days)

Level 3: Integrated Application – direct supervised practice with integration and critical analysis in respect of knowledge, skills and values (100 days)

Plus: Individualised Practice Development – all students to undertake projects to advance their skills and knowledge in a specialist area of their choice (30 days)

Note that there are APEL (Accreditation for Prior Experiential Learning) arrangements so that students with significant work experience in social care may be exempt from practice learning at Levels 1 and 2.

Multi-layered progression is conducive to rich and robust practice learning, but it can also give rise to difficulties in juggling all programme demands (for students) and differentiating the levels of placements (for practice teachers).

Source: NISCC (2003b, 2009)

some in England) incorporate an initial short placement to prepare students for practice learning so that they can observe social workers in the field without assuming direct casework responsibilities. Students in Northern Ireland also undertake one or more specialist projects in addition to their main placements to consolidate expertise in an area of their choice.

As a general rule, students progress from one or more initial placement(s) in the independent sector to a final placement in the statutory sector. There has been a tremendous diversification in respect of independent sector agencies. Some offer a wealth of opportunities for advocacy, community projects and therapeutic casework as they fill in the gaps left by over-stretched statutory safety nets (King et al., 2002). Others continue to provide traditional social care services in day centres so that some students may be undertaking more routine social care work (Barron, 2004). There are also voluntary agencies specialising in such complex work that they may be reserved for final placement students, notably drug and alcohol services and hospices. But most final placements are undertaken in statutory settings in child care, community care, mental health, civil and criminal justice teams.

Agencies are required to offer induction programmes to students which may vary in length from a few days to a few weeks. Standard topics include health and safety policies, ICT and duty systems. Additional training will be agency-specific and could include child protection policies or specialist intervention techniques. A student's workload is a rich tapestry woven from several different strands. First, there will be casework where students work directly with service users and carers. Second, there is participation in the routine life of the agency which ranges from attending team meetings to engaging in duty work – this may be office-based duty taking telephone referrals or community-based duty going out on urgent visits. Third, students take on specialist projects in order to meet all the Units of their Key Roles, which may include group work or evaluation research. Fourth, students have regular 'timeout' from their placements to fulfil the academic requirements of their degree, i.e. there are recall days when they are required to return to the university and study days when they will be reading, writing assignments and putting together a portfolio of evidence to demonstrate that they have met their Key Roles.

The move from PLO1 to PLO2 is akin to a quantum leap for most students. Why is this? In the independent sector, they were working with service users and carers who had requested assistance and the application of relevant skills and knowledge typically yielded successful outcomes, but in the statutory sector they were faced with some involuntary clients with chronic problems so that progress was far more elusive. They also had to devote considerable time and energy to navigating the complex bureaucracy of statutory agencies in terms of paperwork, procedures and ICT systems which could detract from direct work with service users and carers (cf. CWDC, 2009a). Nevertheless, there are students who thrive on these challenges, and many students only feel like 'proper social workers' after a final placement in a statutory setting.

4.1.2 Making Sense of Supervision Arrangements

There are two types of supervision arrangement:

- A 'singleton' arrangement is when your supervisor in the agency is also qualified as a social worker or practice teacher so that (s)he can occupy the role of PLA in assessing your progress and writing the report which enables you to pass the placement. This applies to most placements in statutory settings and some in the independent sector.
- A 'split' arrangement is when there is a separation between an agency-based supervisor and a long-arm PLA. It is common in the independent sector where agency-based supervisors may not have social work or practice teaching qualifications so that a long-arm PLA has to be appointed to oversee a student's progress. Long-arm PLAs may be practitioners in another agency, or self-employed social workers who specialise in practice teaching.

What happens in a split arrangement? A student meets with their agency-based supervisor one week and then with their PLA the next week and this continues throughout the placement. The agency-based supervisor supports the student in day-to-day practice and ensures that casework follows agency protocols (a 'first-order' role) whilst the PLA checks that the student is meeting their Key Roles and applying the theories and values of the profession (a 'second-order' role). Many practice teachers enjoy a long-arm role since it gives them opportunities to explore social work across diverse agencies. But they are unlikely to be experts in relation to all the different types of practice which their students are undertaking, which may compromise aspects of their teaching. Many students value a split arrangement since they believe that they have 'the best of both worlds' with ample time to explore a range of issues and perspectives. But if there are tensions in a student–supervisor relationship, then a three-party situation can make matters worse since triangles are often associated with game playing (Metson, 1998). In these situations the involvement of a more independent party, notably the Practice or Placement Coordinator, can help to resolve matters.

Students have reported that they do not always have adequate access to qualified social workers to act as role models, co-workers or supervisors (ESWDET, 2008; NISCC, 2009; SWTF, 2009). Why does this occur and what difficulties can it cause?

- Some agencies in the independent sector are staffed entirely by unqualified social care workers. Here the student has to develop the social work role in a virtual vacuum and then defend their conception of professional practice if it differs from traditional custom and practice in the agency. This challenge was relished by some students with lengthy social care careers behind them, but it could be overwhelming for novices who were more likely to follow the established custom and practice and then describe it as 'social work'.
- Some multi-professional teams in the statutory sector are staffed mainly by professionals with other backgrounds. In mental health nurses and psychiatrists outnumber social workers, and in criminal justice police and probation officers outnumber social workers. If a professional from a non-social work background has practice teaching credentials, then (s)he may act as a PLA for a social work student in a singleton arrangement. Given that different professionals may have distinct roles as well as conflicting perspectives, this can create difficulties for students seeking to acquire the practice wisdom of a social worker.
- Some social work teams in the statutory sector have had difficulty in releasing staff to act as PLAs on account of work pressures, and have therefore employed long-arm PLAs in a split arrangement. But here the student is still surrounded by qualified social workers who should be able to offer themselves as role models and co-workers.

Regulatory bodies are seeking to address the issue of access to qualified social work staff. In the meantime, students should check out the arrangements for accessing qualified social workers at the point of drawing up a Learning Agreement between themselves, their university and the agency prior to the placement, and should be prepared to raise concerns with their Practice or Placement Coordinator if they are experiencing difficulties during the placement.

4.2 Models of Supervision

This section unpackages the four models of supervision which emerged from discussions with practice educators and students. Apprenticeships and person-centred dialogues are traditional models, whilst evidence-based assessments and professional pedagogy are modern developments. Each model has its merits, but it is the degree of 'fit' between the approach adopted by a practice educator and the learning needs of a specific student that matters most. Some practice educators may be 'eclectic' in their willingness to draw upon different models at different times, whilst others are wedded to a single model. The position of the practice educator can also be influential – 'pure' versions of apprenticeships and professional pedagogy were most common among on-site practice educators; 'pure' versions of person-centred dialogues and evidence-based assessments were found among long-arm practice educators; and managers in the statutory sector favoured evidence-based assessments regardless of their location on-site or off-site.

4.2.1 Apprenticeships

One traditional approach to practice teaching is to treat the student as an apprentice of the trade and to assume that he or she will acquire the necessary knowledge, skills and values through a kind of osmosis, i.e. the student is expected to absorb social work practice in the course of observing others at work just as a plant absorbs its nutrients from soil and sunshine (Shardlow and Doel, 1996). Practice teachers do not have to 'do' anything other than go about their everyday practice as social workers; they simply have a student sitting next to them on a duty desk or accompanying them on home visits; they will be discussing concrete practice issues with students but they may not engage in more critically reflective discussions about theory, research or policy. The student is then expected to go out into the community and do unto their own service users whatever they have witnessed the practice teacher doing unto his or her service users. The following excerpt captures this approach nicely:

CH: Do you have a particular style as a supervisor ... ?

T: Yeah, chaotic I would say. I don't know. I guess you'd have to ask the students what my style is! What I tend to do is role-modelling ...They do duty with other people, they come out with me ... I don't know that I'm academic enough to give it a name and I trained before we put labels on things, but I think it's about being hands-on, being shown how to do something ...

CH: That's what we call a traditional apprenticeship approach.

T: Yes, it's probably that then.

There are merits in this approach as the practice teacher is continuously available to the student and the skills of excellent practitioners often need to be witnessed directly by trainees (Schön, 1987). But students reported that their broader learning needs were frustrated by this approach since these practice teachers can be resistant to conventional supervision sessions. They may see no need to dedicate a one- or two-hour slot to student supervision when they can discuss issues during a car journey or a lull on the duty desk. Many agencies are starting to monitor supervision practices in order to ensure that all students have access to dedicated supervision sessions, and this can include observing the sessions. One student explained that her practice teacher had to rehearse a supervision session with her before their observed session because he needed a trial run himself, but that after the observed session he reverted to his usual custom and practice. Students are reluctant to express their concerns, especially when they have a good working relationship with their supervisor and are on track for passing the placement, but those who experience a traditional apprenticeship without opportunities for dedicated supervision should report this to their Practice or Placement Coordinator.

4.2.2 Person-centred Dialogues

The other traditional approach to student supervision stems from person-centred counselling (Rogers, 1951, 1961). These practice teachers explore the personal–professional interface in becoming a social worker during supervision sessions. Since it is a non-directive approach, students are invited to share their journeying with the supervisor rather than being pressurised into disclosing sensitive issues, although practice teachers in this tradition get worried if students fail to engage at a personal level. Supervision consists of in-depth dialogues about casework and its contexts, which range from what the student is bringing to their practice from their own biography to what kinds of value conflicts have arisen in specific cases. If the student needs to acquire a specific casework tool, then the practice teacher will often encourage the student to apply this tool to themselves before using it with service users or carers. For example, child care social workers often use ecomaps to enable children and parents to map out their current life situation in terms of stresses, supports and significant relationships (Ryan and Walker, 2003). A practice teacher in the person-centred tradition would ask a student to draw up their own ecomap and discuss it in supervision before doing such an exercise with a client.

Person-centred dialogues are indispensable in the personal social services where a holistic approach needs to be taken in respect of staff, students and service users alike. So many students hail from service user and carer backgrounds themselves that practice teachers are right to anticipate that biographical issues will be triggered by social work training (see Chapter 2). A vivid example of this is provided by the following practice teacher:

> T: [Students] come very tigerish, you know … 'I want to make people's lives better' … but by the end of the placement there is at least one person that's made them feel like crap … where they come and say to you 'I don't like that person. They make me feel horrible.' And then you say 'Why do they make you feel horrible?' And then they might have to own up to something quite personal on this score … Our motto is: *there is always a reason, you've just got to dig*

deep enough to find it ... At some point in the placement there will be a service user whom they absolutely adore, a service user to whom they say 'Call me at any time ... whatever time, I'll come and see you' ... [So I say] 'Why are you giving that person more time than anyone else?' ... It's usually because they remind them of somebody in their family who helped them or who they wanted to help ... It makes them feel good ... and everyone feels happy when they're rescuing. But what if you've got 25 of them? Who are you going to rescue first? So I talk to them about survival and stress and what they're going to do to save themselves.

There are clear benefits to this approach, but there are also some built-in risks on both sides. Students may find themselves treated as quasi-clients since the boundary between supervision and counselling is rather blurred, although practice teachers refer students elsewhere if they believe that specialist counselling or therapy is required. Students may also become confused by non-directive dialogues in which they are supposed to discover the answers to predicaments for themselves:

> S: I sort of felt as if I was working in a cloud. I mean, not that the practice teachers weren't helpful ... but I always felt as if they wanted you to work things out for yourself rather than telling you what to do ... Sometimes I came out [from supervision] more confused than when I went in!

The risks to the practice teacher stem from the fact that their democratic dialogues with students set the stage for an egalitarian relationship which may subsequently backfire on them if they lose their professional authority as assessors of student progress. Most practice teachers maintained boundaries around their role by not engaging in mutual self-disclosures with students, but one practice teacher had not been able to maintain these boundaries when faced with a very assertive student, and claimed that she had subsequently been harassed at home by the student and forced to remove critical observations on the student's practice from her assessment report.

4.2.3 Evidence-based Assessments

The model of evidence-based assessments is a modern approach to supervision which emerged from the competency approach to practice (O'Hagan, 2007). These practice teachers are very demanding of students and very directive in their teaching. They may set homework for students even before the placement commences, instructing them to read up about relevant law and policy so that they arrive with a sound knowledge base and are left in no doubt about their responsibilities as adult learners. They require students to bring evidence from case records and reflective journals to all supervision sessions so that they can see material evidence to support the student's claims about their casework, and they will tick off the Key Roles and Units one-by-one when they are satisfied that the student has demonstrated the relevant learning. In other words, these practice teachers embraced the primacy of their assessment role and identified strongly as the new breed of practice learning assessors rather than as traditional educators who would provide nurturing, counselling or role modelling.

The rationale for this approach goes beyond evidencing student competencies; these practice teachers are also acutely aware of their own role in safeguarding service users and indeed the public reputation of the social work profession:

> T: If a student comes back and says 'I've been out to see Mrs so-and-so; she says she is absolutely fine and she doesn't need anything', well, we can't force services on people, but I have to check it out ... What I worry about is if we find out later that they were confabulating because they had dementia. So nobody comes to visit them, and they don't cook, and they can't get out of the house, and then they're found three days later after they've fallen and broken a hip. And [the local press] and everyone else will want to know who was the last practitioner who saw them and who was supervising that practitioner and who double checked the information? ... So it's our job to double check information so things don't slip through the net. The worst-case scenario is that a service user dies or is harmed because we've not picked something up.

Some students are very appreciative of this approach since the expectations of them are clear and their own progression through the Key Roles and Units is transparent. Other students can become apprehensive when nothing that they say is taken at face value and they are continually required to justify their words and deeds. One PLA was aware of this dynamic:

> T: I'm very meticulous around *evidence*. If someone has told me a story, I say 'Evidence it for me. I want copies of your diary sheets ... I want a copy of the care plan' ... I can be a little bit *in your face*. I don't do it in a nasty way but I say '*Why* have you made that decision? ... Is there *another* way you could have dealt with that?' ... *I'm not prepared to just listen to their story!* ... One of my students is very wary of me and thinks that I'm trying to get them to make a mistake, and I keep trying to reassure them that I'm *not*.

Another potential danger with this approach is that practice teachers may concentrate so hard on the material evidence around casework that they bypass both the inner world of the student (thus neglecting the personal–professional interface) and the wider contexts of practice (thus neglecting the professional–political interface).

4.2.4 Professional Pedagogy

Some practice teachers are wedded to professional pedagogy; they love learning and are continuing on their own learning journeys; they love teaching and delight in facilitating students' growth; they will also be trying to embed a learning culture within their own organisation (Hawkins and Shohet, 1989; Gould and Baldwin, 2004). They offer a rich induction as part of a broader practice curriculum developed specifically for students placed in their own agency. If they have a solo student, they may ask the student to read through the case file of a particular service user in order to draw out the theoretical perspectives implicit in the work undertaken to date or to comment on what alternative interventions could have been considered. If they have a group of students in the agency, they may experiment with role plays around the typical scenarios which confront staff and students on a day-to-day basis, starting with the easiest scenarios around advice giving and building up to challenging scenarios with distressed or angry service users. Supervision sessions are characterised by the liberal use of pedagogic techniques drawn from practice wisdom as well as textbooks (e.g. Doel and Shardlow, 2005). These practice teachers ask students to complete learning styles questionnaires (Honey and Mumford, 2000) and they are prepared to adapt their own teaching style accordingly. They also make good use of visual diagrams such as the drama triangle which helps us to make sense of unhealthy relationship dynamics – this is explored further in Figure 4A.

Professional pedagogy was most highly developed in the independent sector, particularly in agencies which housed Practice Learning Units or Practice Teaching Units taking several students at a time. Students based in these units expressed the highest levels of satisfaction with their placements as they had formed a cohesive peer group, enabling them to learn from and support each other. They enjoyed two streams of supervision since group supervision was used to supplement individual supervision (Hawkins and Shohet, 1989; Morrison, 1993). Group supervision can take different forms. Sometimes one member of staff meets with all of the students to draw out and deal with cross-cutting issues which all students are likely to be grappling with. Sometimes the entire staff team and student group meet up to discuss a few complex cases, and staff may also bring their own casework quandaries to these meetings. Group supervision can be very empowering for students; when one member of staff acts as group facilitator, they

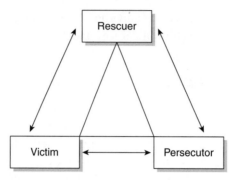

The drama triangle was developed by Stephen Karpman (1968) and is used extensively in the training of professionals.

Difficult situations often trigger our own unresolved baggage which can propel us towards a 'victim', 'rescuer' or 'persecutor' role. In turn, this propels other people in the situation to adopt one of the other complementary roles. The triangle is then complete and people can switch their positions as indicated by the arrows. So a persecutor may claim to be victimised by a victim who has dragged in a rescuer to save them from the persecutor, and so on.

Victims assume a helpless child position: 'Poor me – this is a dreadful situation and there's nothing I can do'.

Persecutors operate from an authoritarian parent position: 'It's all your fault'.

Rescuers seek to be a good parent but if their efforts backfire they fall back into a victim or persecutor role, i.e. 'I wanted to help, and this is how you've treated me!' (Victim) OR 'You've just made your situation much worse; now no one will bother to help you' (Persecutor).

The drama continues until at least one person refuses to play the game by returning to an 'adult' position and recalling the other parties to adulthood.

Can you apply this to a difficult situation in your own life or work? Or do you know a friend or colleague who may have been ensnared by such a drama triangle?

FIGURE 4A   *The Drama Triangle*

overcome their inhibitions in asking questions; and when a member of staff presents a casework dilemma, they appreciate the nature of life-long and multi-directional learning, i.e. the experts are still learning, and even novices can have insights which can help the experts to resolve casework dilemmas.

Students were unanimous in their preference for an approach rooted in professional pedagogy. By the end of their placements, these students had become teachers to incoming students, since the ideal of a learning culture is that everyone is positioned as a learner *and* as a (potential) teacher:

S: So you sit down [with the new students] and *that's when you get to know it yourself!* ... I was now using my own knowledge to help them settle down and then I realised what I had learned, with them asking me questions and me help-ing them and showing them this and that, from what [my practice teacher] had taught me. It was good that [the agency] was happy to give me the opportunity to do this, you know, *teaching* them as part of *my* learning.

Professional pedagogues are likely to be in the forefront of reforming practice education in the future, and may represent a new breed of practice educators, who incorporate vital aspects of traditional practice teaching whilst going beyond this in significant ways. Nevertheless, there is no perfect model, and professional pedagogy has evolved in the independent sector which specialises in initial placements, and would need to evolve further in the direction of evidence-based assessments if it is to be sufficiently robust for students on final placements in the statutory sector. This is because its focus is primarily upon students as learners rather than as future practitioners (see Chapter 11).

4.3 The Hidden Practicum

There is a hidden practicum in community-based learning analogous to the hidden curriculum in university-based study. Students' biographical trajectories as service users, carers and citizens, along with aspects of their current identities and life situations, typically surface during placements and demand attention in their own right. Students may work through these matters by themselves, with peers or partners, in supervision sessions or through a counselling service, but this work is the source of their most profound insights and therefore crucial to their development. It is unfortu-nate that the hidden practicum has not been studied explicitly in social work, although the role of emotions in practice learning has been acknowledged (cf. Barretti, 2004; Barlow and Hall, 2007).

Practice teachers reported that unresolved issues were most frequently triggered for students with service user backgrounds. But people who have occupied a carer role in their personal lives can face similar issues. For exam-ple, one student explained that a boy she was helping reminded her of her brother; he had been the scapegoat in her family and she spent her child-hood trying to shelter him from beatings from their father; on her placement she realised that she had spent her entire life in a carer–rescuer role and she reappraised her approach to life and work as a result. When we do not acknowledge our own baggage we are not only more vulnerable to dynam-ics of transference from service users but we may also instigate dynamics of counter-transference. Transference occurs when service users project their own baggage onto social workers, treating them 'as if' they were a loved or loathed person from their own past, often casting them into the role of rescuer or persecutor. Counter-transference occurs when professionals project their own baggage onto service users, and surreptitiously make use of service users to meet their own needs to occupy a certain role or to enhance their own sense of self-importance (Grant and Crowley, 2002).

Practice learning raises issues for all students, including those with no significant troubles in their own background, who may be faced for the first time with issues of domestic violence, homelessness or death as manifested in the lives of their service users. A young student on a placement with older people had formed attachments with her service users and was devastated when one of them was diagnosed with terminal cancer. She spent the final month of the placement dealing with issues around disability, dependency, death and bereavement, issues which had simply been absent from her own life experience to date. In her portfolio, she reported that she was deeply distressed by the realisation that death is built into the human condition, adding that she was also shocked by her failure to have appreciated this beforehand. Her reflective journals were full of questions such as: 'Who will look after my parents when they get older? What will happen to me when they die? How will I cope when I'm old and disabled? Who will look after me?'

In the above example, the age dimension of identities predominated as a young student worked with elderly service users and came to see her own life very differently. But any dimension of our identities can come to the foreground in practice learning. Exercise 4A provides a vivid example of the hidden practicum in relation to gendered identities as well as the dynamics of transference and counter-transference in the helping relationship.

Exercise 4A   Identifying Transference and Counter-transference

The dialogue below is from an interview with a mature student who had just completed a placement in a hospice. He is discussing a day dedicated to bereaved children which included a number of exercises around love and loss; he developed a particularly close relationship to one girl and he was quite distraught at the end of this working day.

CH: Was this the little girl that reminded you of your daughter?
S: Yeah ... At the end of that day, when I knew I'd never see her again, I felt bereaved myself. I was in bits on the night ... Yeah, this little girl was the same age as my little girl, she'd lost her dad and ... she was with me all day,

holding my hand ... [In a group exercise] the children got these balloons and they had a love heart card which they tied to the balloons and then they let them go. And they had to write a message on the card – I guess it signifies that, you know, the balloons are going up to Heaven and the message will be sent up there. But she kept her card, the love heart card, and she drew another heart on it and then put a line through it and gave it to me to keep. She said 'Oh that's my broken heart'. What do you do or say to that?

CH: Gosh.

S: So yeah, it did impact on me. I think I needed counselling after that!

CH: It was symbolic, you were holding her broken heart.

S: Yes. And getting back to the gender differences, I was the only male member of staff there that day ... At the end of the day [when the children had gone] all the women were having a cuddle and were crying, and even my practice teacher was crying ... It was a very emotive day but kind of difficult for a man to do that.

CH: Yes. Were you able to shed tears – or were you – ?

S: I did on the night time.

CH: What – when you'd gone home?

S: Yeah.

CH: When you'd gone home – with your family or by yourself?

S: By myself.

CH: By yourself.

S: Yes.

You should be able to identify clear examples of transference and counter-transference in the student's account of his relationship with this child. You could ponder on gender differences in socialisation and how they influence our self-concept and self-expression. Male students would benefit from accessing the work of Alistair Christie (2001, 2006) on men in social work. Emotions are explored further in Chapter 9 of this text.

Points to Remember and Questions to Ponder

- Placements and supervision arrangements were covered in sections 4.1 and 4.2. You should be able to identify the model of practice learning which underpins your own programme and the model of supervision used by your own practice teacher.
- If you are experiencing difficulties on placement, remember that there are dedicated Practice Learning or Placement Coordinators whose job is to advise and assist students in the community.
- The hidden curriculum was the subject of section 4.3. What aspects of your own biography or identity could surface on placements? Are there any issues you should deal with now?

Further Reading and Resources

Students should consult their own programme handbooks as well as the websites of the relevant regulatory council to check out practice learning requirements. In Scotland there is a separate website devoted to practice learning: www.scottishpracticelearning.com

There are some excellent texts on learning and teaching in practice settings:

Beverley, A. and Worsley, A. (2007) *Learning and Teaching in Social Work Practice.* Basingstoke: Palgrave-Macmillan.

Doel, M. and Shardlow, S. M. (2005) *Modern Social Work Practice: Teaching and Learning in Practice Settings.* Aldershot: Ashgate.

Lishman, J. (ed.) (2007) *Handbook for Practice Learning in Social Work and Social Care: Knowledge and Theory.* London: Jessica Kingsley.

Also see the *Journal of Practice Teaching and Learning.*

Part 2

Integrating Knowledge, Skills and Values

5

'Why Do We Need Theory or Research?'

Introduction

This chapter is devoted to an appreciation of the academic skills and knowledges underpinning social work practice. Many students underestimate the importance of this foundation for practice, questioning whether they really need a high standard of literacy or numeracy to do social work, and whether they really need to study theory or research. Section 5.1 outlines a model of the different types of knowledge which inform practice, showing how these combine to form tapestries with common professional strands and unique personal strands. Section 5.2 demonstrates that skills in literacy, numeracy and information and communication technology (ICT) are vital for effective and evidence-based practice. Section 5.3 clarifies the ways in which sociological and psychological theories have shaped social work perspectives and practices, and explores how students and their educators engage with (or disengage from) the welter of theories around them. Summaries of theories and their embeddedness within practice are provided in tables and diagrams, and there are exercises on working with numbers and concepts. The final section examines the role of research in social work and gives examples of students undertaking research on the Internet and on placements.

5.1 Tapestries of Knowledge

Social work knowledge is akin to a tapestry of many strands. Figure 5A illustrates the different types of background knowledges which have to

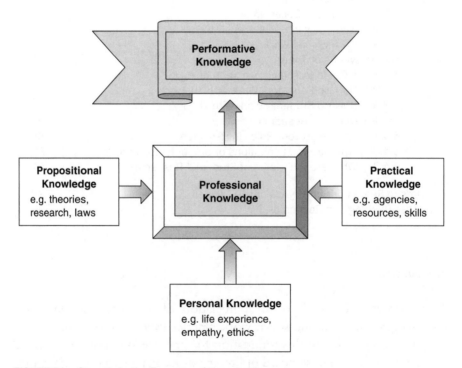

FIGURE 5A   *Strands in the Tapestry of Knowledge*

be woven together to create professional knowledge, i.e. propositional knowledge from theory, research and legislation which is acquired at university; practical knowledge of agencies and resources, along with practical skills, which are consolidated in the community; and personal knowledge stemming from our own life experience (cf. Higgs et al., 2001; Trevithick, 2008). During social work practice, we have to draw upon the most relevant strands of all these knowledges to create 'performative knowledge', i.e. we perform our knowledge in our words and deeds and even in our general demeanour, our ways of being with others. Although many background knowledges will be common to the social work profession, some strands may be unique to an individual or an agency. At the end of the programme, each student emerges with a distinctive tapestry of knowledge as a result of the ways in which unique life experiences and individually tailored placements are intertwined with the generic strands of social work knowledge. Ultimately, your practice wisdom will reflect your skilfulness in the art of weaving your own tapestry. You will need to cultivate each strand of knowledge with patience and persistence; to integrate different strands so that your growing body of professional knowledge is coherent; and to reflect upon the ways in which you perform your knowledge in practice settings, taking on board feedback from other people. Here, I would like to highlight two pitfalls in weaving the tapestry of knowledge which result from what I shall call 'torn' and 'worn' tapestries respectively.

A tapestry becomes torn when there is a failure to integrate different strands of knowledge into a coherent pattern which is congruent with the social work profession. Torn tapestries can be found among students who are placed in a non-social work agency such as a school or clinic, but they can also occur when students work closely with a senior member of staff from another profession. Such students may acquire and apply an alternative set of concepts to make sense of the predicaments of their service users, concepts which reside outside of the legitimate knowledge base of social work, concepts which may also conflict with social work values. For example, a student in a Youth Offending Team was writing a court report on a teenage girl who had been remanded for criminal offences and who had a history of sexual abuse and substance misuse. The student had initially deployed social work knowledge around attachments and abuse to understand the behaviour of her client, but later on, a clinical psychologist claimed that such risk-taking behaviour and failures of self-regulation stemmed from frontal lobe damage in the brain. The student subsequently adopted this bio-medical framework without any attempt to challenge its evidence base, its compatibility with social work knowledge or values, or its implications for the work of the Youth Offending Team (see Tew, 2005). It is not easy to challenge professionals who enjoy a higher status, particularly when you are still in training, but it is important to ask critical questions and to stay connected to social work.

A tapestry becomes worn when it is used so frequently in everyday life that it is no longer subject to conscious and critical reflection. Worn tapestries are common among practitioners who are experts at performing their knowledge, but who may have trouble in explaining the theory and research underpinning their performances (Osmond and O'Connor, 2004). In other words, they learned the theory and research many years ago and it continues to shape their performative knowledge, but they rarely discuss theory and research in practice settings so these become relegated to the subconscious mind. However, students can also develop worn tapestries, particularly towards the end of a placement when they have become habituated to certain ways of seeing, thinking and doing and may be operating on auto-pilot. It is true that the more our professional knowledge is converted into performative knowledge, the less conscious and critical we become of the diverse strands which make up that professional knowledge. Nevertheless, expertise should never be divorced from conscious and critical reflection, particularly among trainees.

5.2 Literacy, Numeracy and ICT

All too often we take these everyday life skills for granted, but even if your literacy, numeracy and ICT skills are adequate for everyday life purposes, they still need to be refined for the purpose of becoming a social worker, so please don't succumb to the temptation to skip this section!

5.2.1 Literacy in Social Work

Literacy skills are equally important in the university curriculum and the community practicum. Whilst the spoken English language allows for diversity of dialects, the written English language operates in accordance with standardised rules of spelling and grammar (Payne, 1993), an observation which applies to other languages in the UK and elsewhere. There are also specific conventions which apply to writing in specific contexts, so that additional rules apply to academic writing and court reports respectively (cf. Greetham, 2008; Brammer, 2010: Chapter 4). Academic writing includes specialist terminology, along with appropriate references to theories and research studies, and is typically impersonal ('As a result of research it has been established that …'). Court reports are written in the language of everyday life so that they can be easily understood by lay magistrates and clients themselves, and they include many paragraphs written in the first person ('When I visited Ms X I discovered that …').

Academic tutors highlighted the irony whereby students from overseas and students with dyslexia could produce superb written work, while some home students with no special needs could hand in work littered with errors of spelling and grammar. They attributed this to the fact that these students were more resistant to learning about language:

> T: If you talk to someone who is 28 or so, and you start telling them that their English or their mathematics is not very good, it's the same as telling them that they're not very good as a parent … They are most indignant … They use all the defences – denial, rationalisation, minimisation … Some come to tell me that other staff have criticised them unfairly for mixing up their e's and i's, or accept and except, and they say 'I can't see what the difference is'. If you point it out they say 'What's that got to do with social work? I came here to be a social worker, not to do a degree in English Literature!'

Practice teachers also expressed concerns about standards of literacy among students. A capacity to express things with clarity and coherence, and in accordance with the logic of rules and conventions, is integral to the performative knowledge embedded in case records and court reports. Case records may be read at a later date by other workers who have picked up the case, or by government officials who are inspecting recording practices in the agency, or by service users themselves who have accessed their file under data protection legislation, so it is important to ask the question: 'Is this sufficiently clear to be understood by a future reader?' Court reports will be read by magistrates and lawyers, and their contents will be shared with clients, and any lack of clarity may impact adversely on the decision-making process or generate a prolonged cross-examination in the witness box. More generally, any report destined for a multi-agency meeting which falls short on the literacy front can call into question the competence of the author and adversely affect the reputation of the agency.

5.2.2 Numeracy in Social Work

Social work students come across numbers in research-based modules and some IT software packages such as Excel. But they need to do more than simply recognise a few numbers – they need to understand where those numbers came from, what they mean in a specific context and how they might be presented in visual charts or graphs. A capacity to grasp the logic of quantitative methods of data collection and to read graphic displays of statistical data is vital when reading research studies for the sake of evidence-based practice (see Smith, 2004).

Social workers need to be able to communicate with other professionals who utilise numerical data and statistical charts. During a multi-professional meeting, you may be presented with height and weight charts in respect of a neglected child which will have to be deciphered rapidly in situ. Risk assessments in child protection and youth justice presuppose a capacity to assign numerical values to risk factors, to add them up and, most importantly, to interpret the resulting figure. But this can become a superficial exercise in the absence of understanding some of the controversies around statistical data in relation to the prediction of risks (see Chapter 8: Table 8.2). In community care settings, social workers require numeracy skills when assisting service users with debt management and costing out care packages for respite or residential care. Exercise 5A has been taken from the portfolio of a student working in a drug and alcohol agency and is designed to provide a practical test of your numeracy skills.

Exercise 5A   Working with Numbers

Students working with people in drug and alcohol agencies have to be able to calculate the quantity of intoxicating substances a person is taking as this guides their assessment of needs and risks, as well as their advice and intervention plan.

The formula used to calculate units of alcohol is as follows:

$$\frac{\text{ABV [= Alcohol by volume of drink or \% proof]} \times \text{Volume of drink}}{1000}$$

In other words, it is ABV (or % proof) multiplied by the volume of drink (measured in millilitres) and divided by 1000.

If you follow this formula, you will see why a pint of lager (500 ml) at only 4% proof (ABV) has more units of alcohol than a shot of whisky (25 ml) mixed with soda when whisky is 40% proof. Try it for yourself before turning to the end of the chapter to see the formula in action.

5.2.3 ICT in Social Work

Students become conversant with information and communication technology (ICT) very rapidly. At university, they will be typing essays in

Word, producing PowerPoint presentations and participating in online discussions in a virtual learning environment. During placements, they will be using computers during office duty and for case recording, e-mailing colleagues in other agencies, checking the ContactPoint database in respect of children at risk and submitting online applications for funding to Commissioning Panels in respect of service users who require a costly care package.

But the art of utilising ICT needs to be balanced by the art of recognising its limits. There is evidence that social workers in statutory settings may spend longer with their computers in their offices than with their clients in the community (CWDC, 2009a) and that virtual communications more generally may undermine social and emotional intelligence in everyday life (Goleman, 2007). ICT can be an educational resource when working with some service users, particularly disabled people. But many older service users and their carers have no access to a computer, and although young people are often highly computer literate, it is easy for ICT to be overused or misused. For example, a student was working with a girl who expressed a strong desire to 'do some art' during their sessions. The student responded by bringing in a laptop, asking the girl to choose some pictures in Clip Art, then printing them out for her to take home. This is more akin to shopping for art than doing art. Art is a vital element in therapeutic work where people are encouraged to express their inner worlds in drawing, painting, poetry and sculpture (Oaklander, 1998). It enables people to get in touch with their bodily senses, emotions, intuition and thoughts, and to share these with someone who cares about their struggles to communicate and create. Clip Art is useful for developing a PowerPoint presentation, but it is not a therapeutic tool for working with service users.

5.3 The Relevance of Theory

Theory has generated more confusion among students than any other area of the curriculum. In a large-scale survey of newly qualified social workers, they listed a total of 80 theories and theorists which had been taught during social work training (Marsh and Triseliotis, 1996). This is a by-product of the multi-disciplinary curriculum and multi-professional practice whereby social workers borrow from the theories and traditions underpinning other disciplines and professions. But of course the more theories we encounter, the more superficial our understanding is likely to be.

5.3.1 A Guide to Theory and Terminology

Malcolm Payne (2005b) proposes the following distinctions to clarify terminology around theory:

- Theories provide explanations for the origins and operations of social phenomena such as inequalities and attachments; theories propose cause–effect relationships between different concepts or variables, and ideally they should be tested by large-scale empirical research.
- Perspectives are ways of perceiving and interpreting social phenomena which can be steeped in political ideologies such as liberalism, conservatism, socialism and feminism.
- Models are descriptions of phenomena or processes which lend themselves to visual diagrams and which can be found in most social work textbooks. Examples include the personal–cultural–structural model of oppression (Thompson, 1998) and the learning cycle (Chapter 3: Figure 3B).
- Techniques are practice tools developed by experts in specific professions for working with individuals, families or groups.

Most students and educators use the term 'theory' to apply to all of these things without making distinctions between theories, perspectives, models and techniques. There are a few theories specific to social work such as attachment theory, but as a general rule practitioners rarely make use of pure theory. They adopt perspectives upon the social world (usually critical rather than conservative); they adhere to models which guide their practice (sometimes these are also policy frameworks); and they apply therapeutic techniques when working with service users. Most of these perspectives, models and techniques have evolved from theories, and therefore cannot be fully understood or properly utilised without a basic-level understanding of the parent theory (or the supporting body of research evidence where appropriate). So social workers do not need to be theoreticians as such, but they do need an accurate and adequate understanding of the core concepts which underpin practice. If we want a generic term to cover models and techniques as well as the theories and perspectives which have influenced their development, it would be more apposite to refer to 'approaches to practice' (Trevillion, 2008).

Tables 5A and 5B illustrate the ways in which we have borrowed from the disciplines of sociology and psychology to develop theoretical knowledge which is applicable to social work. Anti-oppressive practice is rooted in critical sociology and its understanding of inequalities such as class, 'race' and gender, whilst person-centred practice is rooted in humanistic psychology. But sociology and psychology are academic disciplines which do not provide specific techniques for practice. So social workers have to

TABLE 5A   *The Relevance of Sociological Theories to Social Work*

Sociology tends to start from grand theories around global inequalities and works down to lower level theories pertaining to specific institutions and environments:

Level 1: Inequalities, e.g. between states, classes, ethnic groups, genders

Level 2: Institutions, e.g. welfare, workplaces, schools, courts, media

Level 3: Ecology, e.g. cities and communities

But there are a variety of theories in respect of the workings of all these phenomena, and here we find that perspectives count for just as much as theories. Functionalist theories are underpinned by a conservative perspective – they assume that existing inequalities and institutions are useful (functional) to the healthy workings of society. Critical theories are underpinned by a radical perspective – in Marxist theory, class inequalities are exploitative of ordinary workers, and in feminist theory, gender differences are construed as functional for men but often dysfunctional for women.

How do social workers make use of sociological theories?

Level 1: The critical theories about inequalities are the cornerstone of anti-oppressive practice (see Chapter 10).

Level 2: A blend of functionalist and critical perspectives have shaped our understanding of welfare institutions – we use the policies and resources of our institutions to help service users and carers function better in society, but we remain critical of their limitations.

Level 3: Ecological theories are important to understand the material and social environments inhabited by groups of people. Community-based models of practice seek to empower disadvantaged communities to improve their environments. Assessment frameworks in child care and community care are designed to be ecological and ask us to take account of factors such as housing and transport (see Chapter 7).

TABLE 5B   *The Relevance of Psychological Theories to Social Work*

Psychology tends to start from theories about individual development and works up to dealing with groups:

Level 1: Individuals, i.e. dimensions of human development across the lifespan, e.g. biological, behavioural, cognitive, moral, social, sexual

Level 2: Significant relationships, i.e. attachment, separation, loss

Level 3: Systems, i.e. families and groups

Again, there are many theories, particularly in respect of individual development. They may be complementary insofar as they deal with different dimensions of development. But they may be conflictual if they stem from different perspectives, e.g. behaviourists claim that only observable behaviours matter, but psychodynamic theories are built around internal and often unconscious processes.

Psychological theories have been translated into various therapeutic traditions – behaviourist, humanist, cognitive, psychodynamic and systemic – and social workers borrow heavily from these therapeutic traditions in direct work with service users.

Level 1: Humanist psychology is vital to social work principles around person-centredness and self-actualisation but it yields few practical techniques. Techniques from cognitive and behavioural traditions are used to help people to change problematic patterns of thinking and behaving (see Chapter 6).

(Continued)

TABLE 5B   *(Continued)*

Level 2: Psychodynamic theories have been most influential here. Applications include play therapy for children, bereavement counselling and an understanding of transference and counter-transference in the helping relationship itself.

Level 3: Systemic theories are essential when dealing with groups where difficulties in one person or subsystem tend to reflect difficulties in the wider system, and any changes in one person or subsystem will reverberate across the rest of the system (see Chapter 8).

develop their own techniques (e.g. life story work) and borrow from sibling professionals such as community activists (who convert sociological understandings into practical methods of consciousness-raising and empowerment) and bereavement counsellors (who convert psychological theory and research into talking therapies which promote the recovery process). But you cannot simply bypass sociology and psychology, since to utilise practice tools without appreciating some of the parent theory is to risk misunderstandings and misapplications.

Figure 5B provides a fourfold typology of approaches to practice adapted from the early work of David Howe (1992) so that readers can see how theories and techniques are linked together, and how different approaches to practice are shaped by different professional concerns. But what determines how we frame professional concerns in the first place? This is where our perspectives come into play, perspectives which reflect practical constraints, personal choices and political convictions. Statutory agencies require a pragmatic approach which tends to be conservative since they are funded and regulated by governments which demand low-cost or quick-fix solutions where possible. Most students and practitioners have a strong preference for humanistic and systemic approaches which promote healing within and between individuals and groups but which are more resource-intensive. Community activists and academics subscribe to critical perspectives which are oriented towards wider cultural and political change. The problem in social work is that we may be seeking to do all of these things simultaneously. It is not surprising that social workers describe themselves as 'eclectic' insofar as they are trying to be all things to all people, but the term eclecticism can be a reflection of confusions and contradictions rather than a coherent approach to practice in its own right (Payne, 2009a).

5.3.2 How Do Educators Work with Theory?

Academic tutors are acutely aware of the dangers of confusing theory with terminology. The key theoretical terms in social work – such as

1. Pragmatic approaches	2. Humanistic approaches
Professional concern: how can we ensure a better fit between the individual and their environment?	**Professional concern:** how can we make sense of what's going on in the inner world of this person?
Theoretical foundations: functionalist sociology and behaviourist psychology	**Theoretical foundations:** humanistic psychology and psychodynamic theory
Therapeutic applications: task-centred approaches crisis intervention cognitive-behavioural techniques	**Therapeutic applications:** person-centred approaches narrative therapies play and art therapies
3. Systemic approaches	4. Political approaches
Professional concern: how can we help this group of people to convert problems into possibilities for change?	**Professional concern:** how can we contribute to social justice and how can oppressed people empower themselves?
Theoretical foundations: ecology and systems theory	**Theoretical foundations:** critical sociology
Therapeutic applications: family therapy group work community work	**Practical applications:** anti-oppressive practice collective (self) advocacy social movement activism

FIGURE 5B   *Approaches to Social Work Practice*

attachments, addictions, crises and classes – are routinely used in everyday language with commonsensical meanings. The result is that it is all too easy for students to use some of the relevant terminology without understanding the relevant theory or research base; their intuitive understanding of these concepts from everyday life may be in accordance with theory and research, but it may also be dissonant from this knowledge base. So students can easily call situations 'crises' without understanding the theory and research around crisis intervention (Roberts, 2000). Professionals bring additional meanings to concepts which can disrupt common sense – the term 'addictions' is controversial so that some specialists in substance misuse regard it as a metaphor deriving from a medical and moral world view rather than a 'real condition' (Booth Davies, 1997).

Practice educators were located along a wide spectrum in respect of their understanding and use of theory. At one extreme, there were some who confessed that they did not really understand or use theories at all but rather relied upon students to tell them which theories they were using. As long as they could recognise the labels provided by students (such as 'person-centred' or 'systemic'), they would endorse these; but they were not in a good position to educate or assess on the theory front. This situation occurs when off-site practice educators are supervising students across several agencies. At the other extreme, there were others who insisted that students had to understand and use all relevant theories. These practice educators drew up theory grids with the theories listed along one axis and the service users allocated to the student listed along the other axis; students filled this in during supervision, explaining which theories they had used for which service users and why. This occurs in specialist agencies where therapies are strongly rooted in theories.

The majority of practice teachers eschewed both these extremes. They had a well-worn tapestry with all its advantages and disadvantages. Its advantages are that theories have been thoroughly integrated into practices, so that practitioners working in child care teams routinely draw upon attachment theory and understand it from the inside-out in practice settings. And its disadvantages? The knowledge base has descended to the subconscious regions of the mind and is not updated, so when these practitioners take on a student, they may struggle to explain their practice wisdom to a novice and they may not be familiar with recent terms or theories taught at the university. If we do not explicitly revisit our knowledge base, we can lose significant chunks of whatever knowledge we had once acquired, resulting in a fragmentation of frameworks. For example, one practice teacher claimed to make use of 'the three circles of oppression' in student supervision; she recognised that this stemmed from the work of Neil Thompson (1998) but she was unable to recall the entire model, describing it as 'the individual, the societal and something else' (the three circles of oppression are actually called the personal, the cultural and the structural – see Chapter 10).

By the end of their programme, many students commented on the schism between theory and practice in social work, and some complained that academic tutors had taught them theories but practice teachers had subsequently told them to discard theories[1]. It is true that some practice teachers harbour a dislike and distrust of theories which will be conveyed implicitly or explicitly to students. The dislike stems from their own sense of being out of their depth in relation to theories, whilst the distrust stems from their humanistic approach to practice:

> T: It's important to see people as human beings, to see them sometimes as *not* fitting theories, and to live with that … It's an easy trap for students to fall into … 'This is perfect! I've got this person … I can put this theory to them and *Oh, they fit perfectly!*' [Laughter] … Someone might be perfect for a theory, but they're human beings in the first place, and so keeping them as human beings, and not as theoretical guinea pigs, that's very important.

This is a valid criticism which may apply to a few students, but most need to become better acquainted with the theoretical foundations of practice. This presupposes stronger partnerships between all social work educators – including service user and carer groups – so that we can engage in dialogues about substantive matters at the curriculum–practicum interface.

5.3.3 How Do Students Work with Theory?

Students were also located along a wide spectrum in respect of their understanding and use of theory in practice, and their position is determined by the interaction of several factors:

- The preferred learning style of the student sets up certain parameters around their ability, aptitude and motivation in respect of theoretical work (see Chapter 3: Exercise 3A).
- Practice educators – how far they understand and use theories themselves and how far their model of supervision sanctions theory talk (see Chapter 4: section 4.2).
- The agency – how far theories are embedded in practices and how far the culture of the agency is conducive to reading, reflection and debate.
- The stage of the placement – there is far more scope to undertake theoretical reading and reflection in the early stages of a placement.

All students start placements with an awareness of the approaches to practice in Figure 5B. The reflectors and theorists among them will deepen their knowledge over the course of the placement, with positive spin-off effects on their casework and multi-professional practice as well as academic assignments. One student explained that as a result of ongoing reading, she had realised the difference between a person-centred approach and a service user-led approach, resulting in a subtle but significant shift in her own casework as she foregrounded the empowerment of service users. Others reported that they only made sense of disputes in multi-professional meetings when they reflected upon the ways in which different professions were rooted in different academic disciplines and ideological perspectives. Somewhat ironically, the most dedicated theorists can experience the most confusion around theory and terminology due to their ongoing reconstruction. They asked legitimate questions about the relationships between different therapeutic approaches. At what point does a person-centred approach become a psychodynamic approach? Are all talking therapies necessarily narrative therapies? Is play therapy with children also a form of narrative therapy and/or a person-centred approach and/or a psychodynamic approach? Often, they were left without answers, perhaps reflecting the paucity of pure theoretical research in social work (Dominelli, 2009).

Activists and pragmatists tend to resist theories. When they are required to specify which aspects of their knowledge base they have applied in reflective journals, they usually manage to invoke correct terminology around being person-centred or task-centred or working in an empowering or systemic manner, but their substantive understanding is often limited. So they may depict any session where two or more family members are present as evidence of their systemic approach to practice, even though there may be no evidence that they have worked in a systemic manner by using concepts or techniques from this tradition (see Chapter 8: Table 8A). But if your understanding of theory is flawed, then your understanding of practice may also be flawed, and sooner or later this will manifest itself in a misappropriation of terminology. For example, a student who was working with a group of disabled service users to improve leisure facilities in the community dubbed this as 'play therapy' on the assumption that leisure facilities for adults are equivalent to play for children, so that she was enabling disabled adults to enjoy their leisure/play. This betrays a lack of understanding of play therapy which is rooted in psychodynamic theory and intended for troubled children and adolescents (Ryan, 2002). But it also misrepresented the agenda and activities of the disabled service users. They had challenged the Council on the accessibility of leisure facilities and they campaigned for funding to redesign public parks, so theories of oppression and empowerment were far more appropriate in this case (Oliver and Sapey, 2006).

The agency also makes a difference to student learning. A student with an activist or pragmatist learning style will acquire theoretical knowledge if placed in an agency where all staff deploy the same theoretical approaches

and therapeutic tools in their everyday working lives. For example, motivational interviewing in drug and alcohol agencies is underpinned by the
cycle of change (Miller and Rollnick, 2002); bereavement counselling in
hospices draws upon theory and research into stages of grief and tasks of
mourning (Weinstein, 2007); and adoption agencies rely heavily upon
attachment theory when assessing prospective adopters and matching
children to approved adopters (Howe, 1995). Conversely, even students
with an avid interest in theory can fail to grow on the theory front if
their agency is under extreme pressure. A student working in a statutory
child care team explained that although she was continually working in
the arena of domestic violence, she had not had a chance to consider
any of the theory or research around patterns of domestic violence and
their ramifications for children which had been taught at university, since
the team had been inundated with referrals (up to 70 in one week) and
all her time and energy was consumed by sifting through referrals and
visiting high-risk families where immediate intervention was required.
Since students are entitled to a protected workload, you may need to
challenge agency managers, with support from a Practice or Placement
Coordinator.

Most agencies are neither so specialist that they promote an excellent
theory–practice integration, nor so overwhelmed with referrals that theory–
practice links disintegrate. In more typical settings, students tend to short-
circuit the theory–practice integration in two ways. The first short-circuiting
occurs around the mid-point of a placement when some succumb to the
temptation to abandon theory on the grounds that it fails to 'fit' neatly with
the infinite permutations displayed by real people in real life. Students
working with victims of bullying claimed that the causes of bullying were
so numerous, and often unique to each victim, that it was impossible to
acquire and apply all potentially relevant theories around sexism, racism,
disablism, family feuds, etc. Instead, they focused upon techniques to
enable victims to understand the dynamics between bullies and victims
and to rehearse different ways of dealing with incidents. Their techniques
revolved around cognitive–behavioural interventions, but they did not
always appreciate that these are also underpinned by theories from cognitive and behavioural psychology (Sutton, 2000). Paradoxically, it is when
you are tempted to discard theory that you should look for opportunities
to delve further into it.

The other short-circuiting occurs towards the end of a placement when
students develop a worn tapestry. The following excerpt is typical of
reflective journals in the final month of placements:

P: I have used various theories … I must confess that I sometimes do it subconsciously … Task Centred practice is a theory I tend to anticipate in advance if I feel a person requires positive encouragement … to do more for themselves … I use Person Centred practice without realising it as it is somewhat second nature to me … On occasions I have made the transition to Psychodynamics, again without conscious effort.

The only solution to the worn tapestry syndrome is to become more self-conscious and self-critical. Chapter 6 will be helpful on this score. In the meantime, read Exercise 5B which shows how our everyday language and commonsensical understandings should be subject to critical analysis.

Exercise 5B   Working with Concepts

Read the following dialogue from an interview with a student who had just completed a placement in an impoverished inner-city area:

CH: What about the class front – did you find you were mostly dealing with deprived families?

S: Define deprived for me! People say I'm deprived because my nearest McDonald's is 20 minutes away, along with my nearest supermarket. They say where I live is 'deprived' but there's a house up for sale in my village for over half a million pounds. So define deprived!

CH: You live in a nice rural village by the sound of it … So I'm saying: did you find yourself among people from a different class background?

S: Right, I see what you mean now. Yeah. But I wouldn't say they were 'deprived' … One lad had a coat with a hole in it, his shoes didn't fit him properly and his trousers were too short, so to me that could be a deprived child because the parents couldn't nip out to the shops – they haven't got that spare kind of money … But he was an astute child, a very astute child – so no, I wouldn't say he was deprived.

Try to disentangle the different conceptions of 'class' and 'deprivation' which are at work in this dialogue before you turn to the end of the chapter for some suggested answers.

5.4 The Relevance of Research

Why is research important to social work? Pure or basic research is the source of our theory, whilst applied or empirical research is the source of our evidence base, and we need more rather than less of both of them if we are to justify our status as professionals in a knowledge economy. Of course, students are training to be social workers rather than academic researchers, but the boundary between academics who undertake original research and practitioners who read the research of others is becoming blurred, and future practitioners will be more actively involved in research.

5.4.1 A Guide to Your Roles in Research

Students and practitioners will occupy three roles in relation to research during their careers. First, they are consumers of research insofar as they undertake literature searches and Internet searches in order to find out what has emerged from the research studies conducted by academics in relation to their own area of interest (Payne, 2009b). Students need to cite research studies for their academic assignments, and practitioners need to check out the evidence base for the interventions they are using, particularly when experimenting with techniques outside of their usual repertoire.

Second, they can be participants or subjects in relation to other people's research. They may be invited to participate in research conducted by university staff or service user groups. Beyond this, statutory agencies are the subjects of regulatory research undertaken by reviewers appointed by the government (Humphrey, 2003). You can be required to present your case files for inspection or to be interviewed about your work in order to provide officials with evidence about the performance of the agency, evidence which is then collated into a report and published.

Third, students and practitioners are increasingly involved in evaluating practices or services. There is a tradition of practitioner research whereby some social workers have evaluated their own work with service users – if it is sufficiently pioneering, it will be published in academic journals (Robson, 1993). Agencies in the independent sector are increasingly evaluating their work since their funding stream from the statutory sector often depends upon their ability to prove that they are delivering value-for-money (cf. Frost, 2009). Students were often approached to carry out these evaluations by managers on the grounds that they would have more time for such work than employees with full caseloads, and on the assumption that they had the benefit of research modules behind them, unlike other staff who trained many years ago. But research modules may be designed to enable students to make sense of and make use of research rather than to do research projects or produce research reports, so managers should check out such assumptions and tailor their expectations of students accordingly. Students' capacities to undertake evaluation research also vary in accordance with their stage of learning on the programme – such projects caused far more problems to PLO1 students who were still grappling with practice than to PLO2 students.

5.4.2 What are the Limitations of Students' Research?

Students who are 'stuck' in their work with service users are increasingly turning to Internet searches for casework and group work interventions, particularly when they have been placed in a non-social work agency. It is easy to download self-esteem exercises for individuals and therapy kits for groups. But it not easy for novices to determine the relevance of these materials for their own role or their own service users, and Internet pages do not provide guidance on important matters such as how to respond when a particular exercise triggers trauma for an individual or disputes within a group? Searching the Internet is superficial at best and misleading at worst if the search for interventions is divorced from research into their professional relevance, theoretical foundations and evidence base, and many practice teachers are now monitoring such searches more closely.

When students are asked to undertake evaluation research by managers, they can stumble across difficulties at all stages, i.e. designing the project, conducting the research, compiling a report and making recommendations. The most common flaw in both designing the project and presenting the report stems from students' struggles with quantitative data. This is somewhat ironical given that their projects are often small-scale ones where qualitative methods of data collection and qualitative reports on the findings would be more apposite. For example, a student was placed in an agency which had recruited ten volunteers to supplement the work of staff, and she was asked to evaluate the support provided to volunteers and the training needs of those volunteers. The student designed a tick-box questionnaire and presented the results in a long series of pie charts on the assumption that quantitative data is the gold standard of all empirical research, without considering the merits of qualitative methods such as interviews and focus groups (see Shaw and Gould, 2001).

Another student was forced to deal with a large sample which generated a higher volume of data, but soon became overwhelmed by the sheer amount of information to be analysed and displayed, until she lost sight of the original aims of the project. She was based in a day centre for learning disabled adults and the managers had been advised that their services needed to be modernised, so they asked the student to evaluate the effectiveness of services and make recommendations for their improvement. The student developed lengthy questionnaires for service users and their carers, which was appropriate given that there were over 100 respondents, but she then found herself 'drowning in the data' and struggling to master new software packages which could convert the data into a variety of charts and graphs. She became so immersed in the statistical data and so exhausted by her efforts to master new ICT skills that she forgot about the original rationale and remit of her project. The final report consisted of a plethora of statistics presented in beautiful diagrams, but it was devoid of any qualitative analysis of the findings or indeed any recommendations to managers.

Of course, students need to be forgiven for flawed research. It is not just that it takes years to train an academic researcher – and research by experts is not immune from criticism. It is also that students' capacity to discharge these tasks and reflect upon their mistakes is hindered by the lack of research expertise in the community. In effect, practice teachers and agency managers may not be competent to provide research supervision, so that when students are required to develop research projects, they may be left to their own devices. Clearly, there could be a role for academic tutors to act as consultants in respect of projects undertaken by students on placement.

5.4.3 What are the Merits of Students' Research?

Internet searches in respect of national policies and local resources can be very fruitful when providing advocacy for service users or assisting a group with its own collective self-advocacy. Students have downloaded information about anti-discriminatory legislation and the accessibility of local facilities and summarised it in the form of fact sheets for disabled and minority ethnic service users – education is almost always the prerequisite of empowerment (cf. Humphries, 2009).

Two students in a drug and alcohol agency were asked to evaluate the involvement of service users in social work education, which was clearly a pertinent topic where both the students and service users could claim legitimate expertise. The students embarked upon a participatory research project by convening a series of meetings with service users, with both parties doing 'homework' in the form of reading and reflection in between meetings (cf. Banks and Barnes, 2009). This resulted in the development of new forms used in students' portfolios, i.e. a new service user feedback form (where service users are asked to comment upon the care and competence of student social workers) and a new consent form (where service users give consent to anonymised items from their case files being included in student portfolios). They also discussed how service users could contribute to the education of students in the agency, and service users produced a list of workshops which they could offer to students in order to enlighten them as to the experiential realities of being (or being labelled as) an 'addict' or 'alcoholic' and recovering with (or without) the assistance of professionals. The students presented a PowerPoint report to the senior management team with clear results and recommendations, and were highly commended for this participatory project.

In another agency which worked with drug-dependent service users, managers were concerned at the rising drop-out rate of service users and asked two students to investigate. One of the students specialised in the quantitative side of the research. He analysed the case files of all service users who had been involved with the agency in recent months and developed demographic profiles of service users in terms of their age, gender, ethnicity, residence, etc., in order to establish whether or not there were significant differences between service users who stayed in contact with staff and those who dropped out suddenly. The other student was more comfortable with qualitative research. He made telephone contact with service users who had disengaged in order to find out the reasons for their disengagement, a task which was particularly onerous since he realised that these people might not want to talk with a representative from the agency and that they might be under the influence of intoxicating substances at the point of the telephone call. The students' report included references to other research into client disengagement and recommendations for a follow-up study, and again it was presented to and highly commended by senior managers.

These examples suggest that students can undertake good-quality research and that some evaluation projects are eminently suitable for students to carry out. They also suggest the benefits of undertaking such projects in pairs since the students can support each other and may provide complementary skills and knowledges.

Points to Remember and Questions to Ponder

- Students were invited to take responsibility for weaving their own tapestries of knowledge in section 5.1. Is your own tapestry intact or torn? Or is it already becoming worn?
- You were reminded that competence in literacy, numeracy and ICT is an integral part of professional competence. How did you fare with Exercise 5A on working with numbers?
- The theoretical foundations of practice were the subject of section 5.3, and you may need to re-read the tables to consolidate your learning. Which approach to practice do you prefer in Figure 5B and why? During placements, you should try to identify not only the models and techniques you are using but also their theoretical foundations.
- Section 5.4 demonstrated the relevance of research to students and practitioners. When you read about research studies, try to reflect upon their broader methodology (i.e. sample, methods, displays of data, interpretations of findings), just in case you are called upon to undertake your own research project sooner rather than later in your career. If you are asked to do evaluation

research on placement, check whether you could do this work jointly with another student or practitioner, and request consultancy from an agency manager or academic tutor who can help you to stay on the right track.

Exercise 5A   Solution

A pint of lager = 500 ml of alcohol at 4% ABV: 4 × 500 ÷ 1000 = 2 units
A shot of whisky = 25 ml of alcohol at 40% ABV: 40 × 25 ÷ 1000 = 1 unit

Government health and safety guidelines specify 2–3 units of alcohol per week for women and 3–4 units of alcohol per week for men. You might like to calculate your own consumption of alcohol per week, or that of a friend or relative.

Exercise 5B   Suggested Answers

The interviewer understood 'class' in accordance with critical sociology, i.e. capitalism generates inequalities of income and wealth which in turn generate inequalities of life chances. The student had a sense that people come from different class backgrounds which could be measured by their level of material poverty or affluence. But the concept of deprivation complicated matters:

1 Geographical deprivation: people living in rural villages may be deprived of access to facilities such as supermarkets, especially if they cannot afford transport.
2 Material deprivation: people who cannot purchase things essential for health such as adequate food or clothes; this results from poverty or class inequality.
3 Social-psychological deprivation: people who lack the knowledge and skills essential for social survival; this can be caused by various factors such as neglect and abuse, insecure attachments, low self-esteem, poor education or learning disabilities.

The confusion arose in part because people can be 'privileged' in some ways and 'disprivileged' in others. The student believed that the child's astuteness provided him with the resilience essential for social and psychological survival and that this outweighed the material disadvantages stemming from lack of money.

There is another kind of confusion in relation to capitalism and consumerism. Late capitalism generates a society in which consumption is highly valued (this is what keeps the capitalist wheels in motion) and students brought up in a consumer society may associate class inequalities with differences in purchasing power and proximity to shopping centres. But the upper classes invest most of their money rather than spending it, and they live the furthest away from shopping centres.

There is an official classification of social classes in the UK discussed on the Social Research Update website http://sru.soc.surrey.ac.uk/SRU9.html

Note

1   This finding emerged from a survey of BA students at the end of their programme.

Further Reading and Resources

The most accessible textbooks on theory are:

Adams, R., Dominelli, L. and Payne, M. (eds) (2009) *Critical Practice in Social Work*. Basingstoke: Palgrave-Macmillan. (Part 2 covers approaches to theory.)

Howe, D. (2009) *A Brief Introduction to Social Work Theory*. Basingstoke: Palgrave-Macmillan.

Lishman, J. (ed.) (2007) *Handbook for Practice Learning in Social Work and Social Care: Knowledge and Theory*. London: Jessica Kingsley.

The most accessible textbooks on research are:

Adams, R., Dominelli, L. and Payne, M. (eds) (2009) *Practising Social Work in a Complex World*. Basingstoke: Palgrave-Macmillan. (Part 3 covers approaches to research.)

McLaughlin, H. (2006) *Understanding Social Work Research*. London: Sage.

Whittaker, A. (2009) *Research Skills for Social Work*. Exeter: Learning Matters. (This is designed for students embarking upon their own empirical research.)

Your Internet searches will be far more economic and effective if you consult the best websites. These include online library catalogues and government departments as well as the following:

Research in Practice contains studies relevant to child and family workers – www.rip.org.uk

Research in Practice for Adults contains studies relevant to adult care staff – www.ripfa.org.uk

The Social Care Institute for Excellence contains literature reviews – www.scie.org.uk/index.asp

If you undertake empirical research, then you should consult the Code of Ethics for Social Work and Social Care Research. This can be accessed via the following link: www.juc.ac.uk/swec-res-code.aspx

6

'What Do They Mean by Practice Wisdom?'

Introduction

Practice wisdom is at the heart of becoming a good social worker and being recognised as such by others. The first section offers a general account of the development of practice wisdom, and the rest of the chapter examines the practical skills and knowledges associated with wise practitioners. Such practitioners adapt their communication repertoires to the needs of service users and carers, and are able to identify and dissolve defences which distort communications. They understand general approaches to practice and specific intervention techniques so that they can select and apply them correctly. Guidance on how to combine approaches and choose techniques will be summarised in tables. Beyond this, you will find that wise practitioners regularly take time out of concrete practice for reflection, reading and dialogue – becoming a wise practitioner is inseparable from becoming a reflective practitioner. So the final section includes case examples and exercises to help you to become reflective practitioners.

6.1 The Joy of Practice Wisdom

'Practice wisdom' is the fruit which emerges from a prolonged period of studying, practising and reflecting upon any given human endeavour, in this case the profession of social work. There is a certain mystique about any practice wisdom, given that it emerges from within a social practice and within an individual practitioner, so people located outside of the practice may be sceptical about it. Some social scientists have suggested that the term practice wisdom in social work is so nebulous that it may reflect a certain delusion among practitioners – perhaps they are simply conforming to local customs rather than pursuing creative or critical practice? (Jamrozik and Nocella, 1998). Challenging this scepticism will only be successful if we can articulate the nature of practice wisdom and the difference it makes to practice itself, preferably with reference to ethnographic research grounded upon the voices of insiders (e.g. Fook et al., 2000; Cree and Davis, 2007; Beresford et al., 2008).

Developing practice wisdom is about becoming at one with yourself, others and your profession; it is about being at home in social work, discovering your true identity in this vocation, connecting with your service users, carers and colleagues, and channelling your energies into serving them. Excellent practitioners are those who can enter into a difficult situation and sense what is going on and how they need to respond in the here and now, so that they say and do the right things to alleviate tensions and facilitate a resolution. Service users and carers recognise sensitive and skilful practitioners; those who are ready to be helped will blossom, although they may express painful emotions in the process; some involuntary clients may still resist engagement, but they will be left in no doubt about the care, competence and convictions of their social worker.

The capacity to be 'in the flow' so that you produce what is known as 'a peak performance' arises spontaneously when you have acquired the relevant knowledge, skills and values and amassed sufficient practical experience so that these are embedded in your cognitive schema and embodied in your entire way of being with others. On the one hand, you have to establish the right conditions for this capacity to emerge by fully engaging with all aspects of your training; this is time-consuming and labour-intensive as you need to acquire and apply a variety of knowledges, skills and values in a variety of settings; your progress may be slow and offset by mistakes and setbacks, leaving you with doubts about whether it is all worthwhile. In other words, you may feel that you are crawling along on the ground like a caterpillar in the dark. On the other hand, patience and persistence invariably bring about the integration of knowledges, skills and values; then there are moments of profound insight and interactions where everything flows perfectly, so that you experience the sheer joy of making breakthroughs and making a positive difference to people's lives. In other words, integration is the catalyst for the emergence of a brightly coloured butterfly. And there is a domino effect so that each breakthrough paves the way for the next and peak performances can become the norm rather than the exception. Testimony to this process comes from studies of caring professionals as well as artists, scientists and athletes; indeed, it is the hallmark of self-actualisation (Maslow, 1964; Csikszentmihalyi, 1990; Heron, 1992).

A few students display practice wisdom during their first placement, but others may have to wait until their final placement to experience the joy of practice wisdom. You will recognise it when it happens and it will transform your relationships with service users and carers:

> S: [In PLO1] I didn't bring any emotion into my work because I wanted to get it so right; I couldn't do that and put emotion into it at the same time, I was just concentrating on getting it right … [In PLO2] I brought emotion into it … I would be talking to the children not just about official things but I would also be bringing in conversation about what music they liked, what sports they liked, what they were doing with their mates the night before … A lot of the children I worked with were abused, they were kicked out of home at very young ages, they've never really had parents, they've had placement breakdowns … I wasn't just someone in a suit from an office who was there to do a job and that's it. I was there as their social worker, I was there as their friend, I was there as their rock for them, and that's what they channelled into. It didn't take me very long using that method to form a good, strong, solid, trusting professional relationship with those children and *it was fantastic!*

Relationships are indeed the foundation of social work and its sibling professions (cf. Howe, 1993; Wilson et al., 2008). If you do not establish the right kind of relationships with service users, carers and colleagues, then everything else can start to crumble, no matter how solid it appeared to be.

But establishing the right kind of relationships with a variety of vulnerable people itself presupposes a high level of knowledge, a wide repertoire of skills and a strong commitment to humanistic values. It is also more difficult in statutory than in voluntary agencies (cf. Trotter, 1999; Beresford et al., 2008).

6.2 Developing Communication Repertoires

Extending your communication repertoires is a vital component of becoming a competent social worker. All students learn to become multilingual in a metaphorical sense insofar as they adapt their native language to different audiences. In a child care placement, you may be communicating on different levels and in different ways to toddlers, teenagers, learning disabled people of all ages, highly educated carers, legal and medical experts. Many students start to become multilingual in a literal sense as they work with people with specific communication impairments or people with a different native language. Facilitating the chosen form of communication of service users and carers is a practice requirement (see Chapter 9: Table 9A), and this is why students in some Welsh communities where Welsh is the preferred native language need to be bilingual.

6.2.1 Verbal Communications

Social workers align their communications to the needs and preferences of service users where possible. A student working with a mental health service user found that she had to greet birds and fish before the service user would talk to her, since the service user had developed strong attachments to these pets and would not trust anyone who did not greet her companions. But it is not feasible to acquire a variety of complex languages, so students working with asylum seekers often rely upon the services of interpreters when people arrive in the UK from many different countries.

Our capacity to use verbal communications is mediated by our sensory and intellectual faculties. Visually impaired people are heavily dependent upon verbal communications. Life story work with blind children should be recorded on audio-tape so that they can listen to their life story, and agencies can supply information on services for blind adults in Braille. Conversely, hearing-impaired people struggle with verbal communications. Students working with elderly people found themselves changing their speech style to take account of the hearing loss common in older age, by slowing down their speech, elongating their words, checking out what had been understood after every point and repeating it as required. People with cognitive impairments need verbal communications to be simplified and supplemented by non-verbal communications.

Differences in speech styles often reflect differences in class, culture and status, and mismatches between professionals and service users can occur. On the one hand, service users and carers may not understand the terminology associated with social work agencies. Pamela Trevithick (2005: 54) reports on a study by the Social Services Inspectorate which showed that service users did not recognise a number of terms frequently used by social workers, and misunderstood the meanings of other terms. For example, in community care settings, we refer to 'eligibility criteria' in determining whether a person is a vulnerable adult in accordance with law and policy and therefore entitled to services. But service users in the study did not know what 'criteria' meant at all and they believed that 'eligibility' referred to some form of marriage matchmaking. On the other hand, social workers may be uncomfortable with some of the language used by some service users. Students were often shocked at the prevalence of swearing among young people and asked whether such forms of communication should also be facilitated, or whether they could be challenged without being discriminatory? A compromise was to accept the swearing-in-general as part of youth culture but to challenge specific incidents of swearing at specific individuals (including students).

Versatility in verbal communications underpins therapeutic ways of working. Students need to develop expertise in eliciting the full story from their service users, decoding these stories, reframing aspects of their narratives which are likely to be detrimental to them, reinforcing aspects which are helpful, and sometimes encouraging them to re-author their lives with a new set of stories which emphasise the positives in their past, present and future (Parton and O'Byrne, 2000). Additional skills are required when students move from working with individuals to working with families (see Chapter 8: Table 8A).

6.2.2 Non-verbal Communications

Face-to-face conversations with a social worker can be threatening to children and vulnerable adults alike. They reinforce the power imbalance between adult and child, or between authority figure and vulnerable adult, and there is nowhere to hide for a person who is not ready to look at, listen to or talk with this stranger from social services. Working around a third object is an ideal way of defusing the threat of a stranger's gaze and providing a safe refuge for service users. Children will relax if you sit on the floor with them drawing pictures or playing a game, and then they may start to talk spontaneously about what matters to them. Adults also respond well to invitations to draw a map of their family (a genogram) or current situation (an ecomap) or cultural background (a culturagram). For examples of these mapping activities, see Congress (1994), Ryan and Walker (2003) and Chapter 8: Figure 8A.

Non-verbal communication is more wide-ranging than novices appreciate, as indicated by the following list provided by Pamela Trevithick (2005: 56):

- presentation, i.e. clothing and make-up as well as home and office decor
- chronomics, i.e. time-keeping for appointments
- paralinguistics, i.e. the way we speak in terms of volume, speed and emphasis
- kinesics, i.e. bodily postures, facial expressions and hand gestures
- proxemics, i.e. the distance we maintain between ourselves and others
- contact, i.e. our use of physical contact in handshakes and hugs.

Students become hyperconscious of non-verbal communications as a result of feedback from staff who observe their sessions with service users and carers. There is a symmetry in non-verbal communications insofar as they always operate in both directions, i.e. for every piece of non-verbal information we pick up from others, there will be a corresponding piece of non-verbal information which they are picking up from us. But there is an asymmetry insofar as we are often highly sensitive to non-verbal communications emitted by others whilst remaining oblivious to some we are emitting ourselves, especially if they are part of our habitual way of being. It is difficult to change our habits. One student was told by her practice teacher that she had to make radical changes in her body language since she was continually fidgeting and fiddling with her hair during meetings with service users, which could be distracting and which could be interpreted as a signal of her own discomfort. But she found it almost impossible to sit still! She claimed that she was more uncomfortable when following her practice teacher's prescriptions, and questioned whether her discomfort in adopting 'artificial' postures would be even more obvious to service users than her spontaneous movements?

Students may develop their own communication impairments which promote an expansion of their repertoires and greater empathy with service users. The umbilical cord between growth in our personal and professional knowledges, skills and values is palpable in the following portfolio extract:

P: I had laryngitis ... I have had to revisit different methods in order to communicate with my family and friends – such as writing things down, sending mobile phone texts and e-mails – which was very time-consuming. At times I could sense impatience from my family and friends and I felt quite lonely and depressed ... I feel that this unfortunate experience has given me a greater understanding of how disabling it is not to have a voice ... The client group which I am working with may have difficulty in communication on a daily basis due to memory impairment or hearing problems ... I have a greater understanding of how important it is to facilitate each individual's use of language and the form of communication of their choice. I have also recognised that the person's use of communication may not be a choice when they don't have any alternative methods.

Makaton is the most common alternative language acquired by students on placement. Although simple forms of speech are included within Makaton, they are heavily supplemented by non-verbal communications – i.e. facial expressions, bodily movements and picture cards – and when these are all strung together, it can work as an entirely non-verbal language. Makaton was originally developed for people with learning disabilities and then extended to people with sensory and speech impairments. It is a living language with a growing vocabulary so that social workers and police officers can now interview learning disabled children who may have been sexually abused via Makaton (Kennedy, 2002). The other main non-verbal language is British Sign Language, but social workers who work with deaf people need specialist training in this, unless they are already members of the deaf community and fluent in this language.

6.2.3 Defensive Communications

Defences are erected in response to threats to our self-esteem or well-being from within or without and often result in distorted communications. A classic threat from without is when we have been accused of a misdemeanour or even a crime, and we know that we are guilty but we also know that to confess our guilt could result in punishment. Children and adults alike are tempted to deny their deeds, and may blame others to divert attention from themselves, and in some cases they will even convince themselves that they are innocent so that events are repressed to the unconscious. Threats from within pertain to negative emotions around fear, prejudice, hostility and envy; again we are tempted to disown such emotions as they suggest that we are not as caring or capable as we would like to be; but if these emotions continue to circulate in our unconscious, then they will impact upon our relationships with others and our self-understandings will become distorted. Professional helpers need to recognise not only the defences used by service users, but also their own defences, which can form part of what Gerard Egan (2002) calls 'the shadow side of helping', i.e. negative defences can undermine our capacity to help others, especially when we remain oblivious to them.

An understanding of defence mechanisms takes us into the territory of psychodynamic theory since many defences are mediated by unconscious processes. Table 6A summarises some common defence mechanisms, but for a more detailed account, see Fonagy and Target (2003). Defences serve a positive function in the short term by enabling us to avoid dealing with

TABLE 6A *Some Common Defence Mechanisms*

---

1   Some defence mechanisms are manifested in verbal communications:

- Denial: the outright denial of events or emotions. Sometimes people remain conscious of the truth (in which case they are lying). Sometimes they have repressed memories to their unconscious (in which case they are telling their subjective truth, but this is not the objective truth).
- Projection: the attribution of one's own negative deeds or emotions to others.
- Reaction formation: the repression of the truth to the unconscious and the reversal of this truth in the conscious mind. A clear example is when some homophobic people have strong homosexual proclivities.
- Rationalisation: the invention of a plausible story to explain one's own decisions and deeds in a manner which will be more acceptable to the audience. Professionals can be experts in this.

2   Some defence mechanisms manifest themselves non-verbally:

- Somatisation: the conversion of psychic pain into physical ailments. The person may only be conscious of the bodily symptom, not the original problem.
- Regression: the return to ways of thinking–feeling–acting which belong to an earlier stage of development. This is a common response to stress.
- Dissociation: the splitting-off of events and emotions which accompanies trauma. In extreme cases, it can result in splits between different aspects of one's personality associated with 'multiple personality disorder'. Significant chunks of experience are buried in the unconscious.
- Displacement: the deflection of aggression from the source of the problem and its redirection towards others. This occurs when we dare not challenge the person who 'caused' the problem on account of their status or power, so we take it out on a more vulnerable person. Children and vulnerable adults are often the victims of such displaced aggression.

3   Some defence mechanisms can be positive and even healthy:

- Suppression: the bracketing of difficult events and emotions which may interfere with our current activities, with the intention to revisit them later.
- Sublimation: the transformation of suffering into creative works, which can be found among artists, scientists and caring professionals.
- Humour: the conversion of a dreadful situation into a joke which paves the way for laughter as a form of release. This is common in social work teams.
- Idealisation: the maintenance of a positive image of a significant other in a way which disregards their human weaknesses.

---

painful aspects of reality; most become increasingly dysfunctional over the longer term; but some defences have an overall positive effect upon our communications, coping capacity and creativity. You should try to find further examples of each defence mechanism from your own life and work experience.

Social workers often find themselves treading a tightrope between respecting and challenging defences. On the one hand, if a person is suffering a mental health breakdown characterised by delusions, then it is unwise to inform them of the erroneous nature of their perceptions. On the other hands, if a person claims that they did not commit a crime when all the evidence indicates that they did, then challenging their denial and supplying some of the evidence may be essential. The sense of treading a tightrope is most acute when practitioners are seeking to work anti-oppressively with minority ethnic groups. Child sexual abuse is a taboo topic in many Asian communities, and asking the authorities for assistance in such matters can be regarded as bringing shame upon the family and community, so practitioners have to tread carefully if they are to avoid outright denials from adults and retractions of allegations from children (Gilligan and Akhtar, 2006). Identification and interpretation of defences can also be problematic. Young asylum seekers frequently present stereotyped stories of their flight and plight, but are these false stories which have been designed to improve their chances of becoming refugees and rehearsed on the journey, or true stories which come across as stereotyped on account of their limited language skills or the ongoing effects of trauma? (Kohli, 2006). Wise practitioners will treat their suspicions about the operation of defences as hypotheses which require further checking with respect to the evidence for the client's story and their own interpretations of the client's psychology.

6.3 Applying General Approaches to Practice

Reading students' portfolios indicated that all of them made use of four approaches to practice, i.e. task-centred, person-centred, crisis intervention and anti-oppressive practice. These terms provided useful descriptive labels which could be easily transported across agencies and service user groups, and students could represent their work as involving a seamless merging between approaches. For example, one student was based in an agency which provided legal advocacy for people served with an eviction notice by their landlord on account of non-payment of rent. She presented her work as task-centred insofar as it was essential to complete specific tasks to pre-set timescales in order to allow the court hearing to take place. It was person-centred insofar as people were distressed and had to be treated with care, and the task of completing court paperwork had to be adapted to the communication capacities of each individual – some of them had limited English language or literacy. It could involve crisis intervention if a person had a drug or alcohol problem and arrived at the court in an intoxicated state. And it exemplified anti-oppressive practice insofar as the agency was seeking to prevent people becoming homeless and destitute.

Nevertheless, there can be conflicts between these approaches to practice since they have been spawned from different theoretical and therapeutic traditions (see Chapter 5: Figure 5B). Let us explore this with reference to the task-centred and person-centred approaches.

The person-centred approach originates from the work of Carl Rogers (1951, 1961) who pioneered a new approach to counselling and psychotherapy revolving around the 'core conditions' of congruence, genuineness, empathy and unconditional positive regard. He believed that if the therapist can create these core conditions by being true to themselves and real with their client, by accurately understanding the situation facing the client as the client experiences this, and by sustaining a positive attitude towards the client no matter what the client may have done, then the client will find the courage from within to change themselves and their situation for the better, and to move towards self-actualisation. This is an open-ended process of growth which was well-suited to middle-class professionals who had chosen to pay for their personal development. However salient the core conditions remain in all caring professions, the general approach cannot be neatly transposed onto statutory social work with high caseloads and involuntary clients.

Task-centred practice emerged as an alternative in the 1970s. It was pioneered by researchers who demonstrated that time-limited interventions were often just as effective as prolonged counselling (Reid and Epstein, 1972), a message which was music to the ears of social work managers. This approach is most useful when service users or carers are confronted with practical problems in connection with housing, finances, education, employment and life skills. They can be helped to prioritise problems and to list the tasks which need to be done to overcome each problem; a contract will be agreed between the social worker, service user and/or carer specifying who will complete which tasks by which date; then they meet to evaluate progress. The professional provides a safety net but service users and carers are expected to do as much as possible for themselves, and those who acquire new skills as well as new beliefs about their own competence are less likely to become clients in the future (Marsh and Doel, 2006). This approach depends upon the cooperation of service users and carers, and may not work so well with involuntary clients or those with deep-rooted trauma or strong psychological defences.

Person-centred and task-centred approaches can be fruitfully synthesised, and the adoption of person-centred planning in community care is a clear attempt to do this (Dowling et al., 2006). But there are tensions between them, and practice wisdom is about achieving the right balance between being task-centred and person-centred and knowing which approach should be prioritised and why. If students simply adopt their preferred approach without reflecting upon the case in its context, they are likely to make errors of judgement. You might like to ponder on the following two case examples. In the first example, a student placed in a fostering and adoption agency depicted her work with one prospective carer as entirely person-centred on the grounds that she was providing counselling to help the prospective carer to resolve her own childhood problems. But the student's task was to undertake an assessment of the suitability of this woman to care for vulnerable children, not to provide counselling, and her deep-rooted problems did not bode well for her suitability. Here, the core task as prescribed by the agency was downplayed in favour of a person-centred approach. In the second example, a student working with an elderly housebound woman who had recently been bereaved depicted her work in terms of task-centred practice and closed the case as soon as services had been provided according to the agreed contract. But the elderly woman had wanted the student to continue visiting as she remained isolated and depressed. In this case, a task-centred approach was pursued at the expense of a person-centred approach – and even in a task-centred approach, there is scope for generating a further task around promoting social networks.

So we need to find a way of being person-centred and task-centred which is compatible with the remit of our agency and which can connect people to networks in their community. Table 6B has been adapted from the work of Gerard Egan (2002) in order to indicate which approach typically needs to be prioritised at which stage of the helping process in social work.

6.4 Applying Techniques in Practice

Techniques need to be applied with care, competence and comprehension. Care provides the relationship context in which social workers seek to sustain the core conditions of counselling; competence ensures that techniques are applied appropriately in accordance with a working hypothesis

TABLE 6B   *Combining Approaches in Social Work*

Stage 1: What is the problem?

A person-centred approach is paramount since we want service users (and their carers, where appropriate) to tell us their stories about their difficulties. The core conditions of counselling help people to open up to strangers and to dissolve defences.

But other factors may also come into play at this first stage:

- Tasks: are there multiple problems which need to be prioritised?
- Agencies: is the problem within the remit of our own or another agency?
- Networks: do we need to check this story with others in the network?

Stage 2: What is the solution?

The role of the agency and the resources in the community are paramount here. If the main problems are practical ones, the social worker can access relevant services. If the main problems are personal or interpersonal, this calls for therapeutic interventions, and significant others in the service user's network may be included.

Anti-oppressive practice is also valuable here to ensure that professionals do not 'impose' their preferred solutions upon service users. This will result in resistance. We can only impose solutions when protecting people from harm under the law.

Stage 3: How do we move from problem to solution?

Task-centred practice comes to the forefront since the social worker and service user need to create a contract specifying timescales and tasks to implement the solution. Contingency plans are helpful since plans may go awry – what will the social worker do if funding for services is denied? Or if the service user does not attend a training programme they have signed up for? Or if the chief carer is no longer able to cope?

Stage 4: How can you sustain progress?

Networks are vital here. The social worker prepares to disengage after the resolution of the problem, but if the service user does not have access to supportive networks then they will be more vulnerable to relapse or further difficulties in the future. Networks include families, neighbours, self-help groups and other professionals.

NB Crisis intervention may be required at any time if the service user suddenly discloses a different and more serious problem such as domestic violence.

about the nature of the problem and the level of skill of the practitioner; and comprehension is about our understanding of the theory or model underpinning the techniques.

All social work techniques require skills in listening and talking. Careful listening to others promotes talking which is attuned to them, and a clear comprehension of theory promotes educational and empowering dialogues. Consider the following example from a student who was working with a mother and her young son. The boy was developmentally delayed, and the student was appalled when the mother repeatedly referred to him as 'stupid' in his presence, but her request that the mother refrain from such negative talk had no effect. So she arranged a one-to-one session with the mother where she discovered that the mother had been labelled as 'stupid' by her own parents, a label she had internalised until fairly recently when she had successfully completed a training course in computing. This enabled the student to talk with the mother about labelling theory (Eyben and Moncrieffe, 2007) and intergenerational cycles (Egeland et al., 2002). The student explained that labels can have self-fulfilling effects insofar as we often live up to the labels and expectations of significant others, but that negative labels are harmful and may not be fair or true in any event, as the mother herself was discovering. She also explained that parents often say and do the same things to their own children as had been said and done to them by their parents when they were children, but that if their parents did not provide the best role models then this would involve recycling problems from one generation to the next. This sensitive and skilful sharing of knowledge proved to be a moment of enlightenment for the mother who subsequently changed the ways she thought and talked about her son. Her own story had been heard and understood; she saw the parallels between parenting across the generations; she no longer perceived her son to be 'stupid' at all, but simply in need of sensitive and skilful parenting; and she rose to this challenge.

An earlier study of student social workers found that the most competent students were those who were able to share their working hypotheses and the theoretical rationales of their interventions with service users and carers (Secker, 1993). Of course, it is not always appropriate to discuss these matters, particularly with children, people with profound cognitive impairments and people in crisis. Furthermore, the extent to which we adopt an explicit educational role varies in accordance with techniques and traditions as well as the capacities of service users and carers. Practice wisdom is about knowing which technique to select, how to apply it, when to explain it and how best to do so.

Tables 6C and 6D are designed to help you to develop practice wisdom in this area. Table 6C summarises techniques from cognitive and behavioural traditions; these traditions have very different origins, but they are often combined in social work and psychotherapy; detailed case studies can be found in Cigno and Bourn (1998) and Neenan and Dryden (2002). Table 6D summarises techniques which have emerged from psychodynamic and Gestalt traditions; these are also distinct traditions but they share a lot of common ground; detailed case studies can be found in Oaklander (1998) and Briggs (2008). Even before you ask yourself 'Which technique should I use?', you should pose the question 'Which tradition is most appropriate here?', since if you can work out the answer to the second question you are closer to answering the first question. Cognitive and behavioural

TABLE 6C   *Techniques from Cognitive and Behavioural Traditions*

These techniques are used when patterns of thinking and/or behaving are problematic. Cognitive-behavioural work with an individual is about enhancing their understanding of how their mind–body works, how they interact with others and their environment and how they can alter habitual patterns which have become harmful to themselves or others. Ultimately, it gives them the freedom to regain control over their lives. It is possible to incorporate emotions as well, and work with children tends to be described as cognitive–affective–behavioural work. But sometimes it suffices to use purely cognitive techniques; and at other times it is necessary to resort to purely behavioural techniques:

- Motivational interviewing – this is a technique used to assess whether or not a service user is ready to change problematic behaviour patterns. It was first developed in relation to people with a dependency upon drugs or alcohol.
- Diaries – service users may be asked to keep a diary in relation to their moods, worries or destructive habits. This helps them to become reflective observers of the patterns in their lives and the triggers for bad moods or behaviours.
- ABC charts – social workers can explore critical incidents with service users by drawing up a chart of Antecedents–Behaviours–Consequences. This shows how problematic Behaviours are triggered by Antecedents and then have adverse Consequences. They can then consider ways of avoiding the antecedents, or interpreting and responding differently to unavoidable antecedents. This is effective with young offenders and parents who over-chastise their children.
- Positive reframing – this is a purely cognitive technique used when thought patterns are the primary problem, particularly when people are stuck in self-defeating thoughts such as 'I can't do anything right!' A positive frame could be 'But you've turned up for our session and you've decided to make changes, so you are already doing something right!'
- Behaviour shaping – this is a purely behavioural technique used when the cognitive capacity of service users is not strong enough for cognitive-behavioural work, particularly with young children or severely learning disabled adults. Professionals and informal carers have to reward and thus reinforce good behaviours, but they must be wary of dispensing punishments for bad behaviours. Strategies such as 'time out' or withdrawal of privileges are much safer alternatives to punishment. Some institutional regimes operate in accordance with behavioural principles, particularly in the secure estate, and they can become abusive regimes if punitive measures consistently outweigh positive ones.
- Skills training – rehearsing new skills or alternative ways of responding to difficult situations is vital. People with learning difficulties benefit from skills training. Group work with victims of bullying often entails role plays of scenarios.

approaches are most appropriate when people need to change their assumptions, thoughts or behaviours, but psychodynamic and Gestalt approaches are far better if people need to make sense of trauma or life transitions and express their emotions.

If you are using purely cognitive techniques, you should be prepared to share your knowledge explicitly; these techniques will not work unless service users understand their predicaments and the methods of curbing negative thought patterns; here you have an explicit educational role. Purely behavioural techniques are reserved for situations when a person's behaviour is causing harm to themselves or others but when they are unable or unwilling to change it themselves – this can be the case with

TABLE 6D   *Techniques from Psychodynamic and Gestalt Traditions*

These traditions focus upon the inner world of the psyche, i.e. emotions, memories and internal representations of our relationships with significant others. The inner world of the psyche includes unconscious phenomena which may be so traumatic that they have been split off from consciousness. Therapy seeks to bring some of this to consciousness in order to heal the splits and to make people whole again. The term 'psychodynamic' refers to the dynamics within the psyche as well as dynamics in our relationships with others, whilst 'Gestalt' is a German word for 'whole'. Trauma results in the hyper-activation of stress responses in everyday life, so techniques for managing stress by regulating the body–mind–breath are also important. But sometimes it suffices to teach stress management techniques without delving deeply into the original trauma.

- Narrative techniques – service users are encouraged to make sense of their lives through story-telling. This can include creating a life story book with photo albums, and keeping a journal of events, emotions and dreams. Specialist books are also available to deal with issues around being adopted, growing up gay and coping with bereavement.
- Play therapy techniques – play therapy was developed for children but can be used with adolescents as well. Some agencies have a dedicated play therapy room with games, puppets, a punch bag, a sand tray, dolls' houses and dressing–up clothes. Social workers take child-friendly materials in the car so that they can use simple play techniques with children during home visits. Parents can be invited to join in since an inability to play with children is a common feature of poor parenting. Children express their inner worlds through play so that to tune into the child's play is in effect to tune into the child. They relive past stories and rehearse new stories through their play, but they need a therapeutic companion, i.e. someone to witness their struggles and to help them make sense of their situations.
- Art therapy techniques – art is valuable for adults with mental health difficulties and learning disabilities as well as children. Art includes poetry, drawing, painting and sculptures. People can be encouraged to draw or paint self-portraits, family portraits and family trees; these can be included in life story books.
- Body-based techniques – drama therapy encourages people to express themselves through the body and the voice, and to interact more authentically with others. Yoga and t'ai chi are practices promoting a calm, controlled and coordinated body. You will not be trained in these so you will need to refer service users elsewhere.
- Mind-based techniques – meditation and creative visualisation help people to calm their mind and to change their internal representations. Students who acquired these techniques through life experience have used them with service users.
- Breath-based techniques – stress management involves regulating the breath which links body and mind, and this is common to both body-based and mind-based techniques. Simple breathing exercises can be learned by practitioners and taught to others.

some disturbed children and some habitual offenders. In these situations, you apply techniques which are known to 'work' without explaining their rationale. A cognitive–behavioural approach with a family may involve explaining some of the theory to the parents but not the child if you are helping the parents to change the behaviour of a child who is beyond their control. Enhancing the consciousness of clients is central to psychodynamic and Gestalt approaches, but you are not in the role of an educator explaining a pre-given theory or method to the client; rather, you are a facilitator who helps the client to express themselves, and an interpreter of the client's stories, poems, pictures and play activities. The work of intuiting your client's inner states and interpreting their creative self-expressions does, however, require care and caution (see Oaklander, 1998).

6.5 Becoming a Reflective Practitioner

Practice wisdom is fuelled by the development of reflection, critical reflection and reflexivity. These terms sound similar and it is not surprising that they cause confusion among students (and even among educators) so we will examine each of them in turn.

6.5.1 Reflection

Early research into reflection found that it is triggered when we encounter phenomena which are different to anything we have hitherto experienced or different to anything we might have expected (Dewey, 1910). Students on social work programmes will encounter a welter of new ideas and situations giving them ample opportunities to reflect, but the extent to which they actually make use of reflection depends heavily upon their access to a repertoire of techniques of reflection. Some students arrive on the programme with a rich repertoire of techniques; but for others reflection itself is a new and strange activity, and they need educators to prescribe models and methods in order to start the process (see Johns, 2000).

Reflection is about acquiring new insights in relation to any given phenomenon, including ourselves, other people, theories and cultures. It involves an inward journeying as we need to process these new insights within our own minds, and also an outward journeying insofar as we discuss these new insights with other people including peers, supervisors, service users and carers (Humphrey, 2009a). Exercise 6A will help you to expand your own reflective repertoire.

Exercise 6A   Extending your Reflective Repertoire

1 Below is a list of techniques which social work students told me they used when reflecting. Put an asterisk (*) beside the ones you use regularly when you reflect.

> Keeping a journal to write down your thoughts and feelings
> Re-living the encounter over and over again in your mind
> Writing up a 'critical incident' analysis
> Going for a long walk to clear your head

Drawing a diagram or map to help make sense of the situation
Meditating in silence
Praying to God
Doing some art work (e.g. painting or poetry)
Switching off with another activity (e.g. sports or socialising)
Telling someone you trust about the problem (e.g. friend or relative)
Arranging to meet with your supervisor
Consulting with other students or staff in a group setting
Discussing the incident directly with the people involved in it

2   Introverts tend to process difficulties inwards, dealing with them in solitude, whilst extroverts tend to process difficulties outwards, usually with other people. There is merit in doing *both*, since doing one at the expense of the other can cause further difficulties. Introverts often develop excellent capacities for critical analysis and creative reflection *but* they may become 'out of touch' with other people and fail to take on board other perspectives. Extroverts are good at staying in touch with other people *but* they may become over-reliant upon others at the expense of developing their own independent judgements.

3   Review your own preferred ways of reflecting with a view to ensuring a balance between inner-directed and outer-directed strategies *and* with a view to enlarging your repertoire. Go on – try out something different from the list! And if you have other ways of reflecting, share them with your peers and educators.

There are three phases in the development of reflection among students new to this activity. The first phase is when reflection is a foreign language which students are forced to acquire and apply. Every week during placements, they have to complete a reflective journal providing examples of theories they have used, value conflicts they have faced and a critical incident analysis. Essentially, they are doing what is known as reflection-on-action after the event (Schön, 1987). They may not have consciously used any theories in their practice at the time, but they have to find a suitable theoretical label after the event. They may not have thought deeply about a critical incident at the time, but by the end of the week they will have to provide not only a description of the incident, but also an analysis of the underlying causes or conflicts of the incident and an evaluation of the role of their own beliefs, emotions, actions or omissions in facilitating or hindering a resolution. But students may be mimicking the words of others and following rituals prescribed for them:

S: Reflection on PLO1 for me was more forced than anything … I knew I had to complete my portfolio … Obviously there was a little bit of reflection there in terms of 'Oh, did I handle that situation well?' but it would be just a few seconds then I'd forget about it … The words that I used … came from the reflective practice module that was taught at Uni and the way that my peers would talk about it … But it was just words, it was meaningless, hollow, transparent words … It didn't mean anything to me … I felt that I was just repeating myself over and over again on the reflection from week to week, journal to journal … I thought '*Oh God, is this really worth it? They drill this into you but it's rubbish!*'

In the second phase, reflection is internalised and starts to arise spontaneously within the student. Here, students find themselves reflecting on theories and interventions when travelling to and from the homes of service users, request-ing extra discussions with their supervisors and buying notepads which they carry with them everywhere in order to capture new insights in words or diagrams. Once reflection is internalised, they start to reflect-in-action during interactions with service users and carers (Schön, 1987). Their prac-tice is then characterised by fluidity as they are capable of theorising, hypothesising, improvising and innovating within the situation itself. Essentially, they have discovered or developed a space within their own minds which enables them to process information from others and to operate as reflective observers of their own practice. The forementioned student conveys his own breakthrough in the following manner:

S: Looking at my reflection through PLO2, *wow, what an absolute difference!* … As the placement went on I would be in the situation, *physically* in the situation, reflecting as I go along, and the reflection-in-action would inform, would actu-ally *inform* that situation if you understand me … In PLO1 I would go into a situation with the firm, solid structure in my head and I would stick to it, but in PLO2 I would go into a situation with no structure … I would shape my practice to the situation through reflection-in-action … It helped me test theories … and if they didn't fit then I would try a new theory.

In the third phase, reflection is naturalised so that students depict it as 'sec-ond nature' to them. But there are three pitfalls awaiting students at this point of their reflective journeying. The first pitfall is that reflection may take on its own life force which intrudes into every waking moment and which can prevent restful sleep. Some students reported that their reflec-tion had become an obsessive-compulsive habit which they were unable to switch off, as they perpetually relived the encounters of yesterday, and rehearsed encounters scheduled for tomorrow. The creative force at the heart of reflection will atrophy under these circumstances, so it is crucial for students to learn relaxation techniques where they can let go of exces-sive worrying. The second pitfall is that reflection may be relegated to subconsciousness; several students claimed that by the final placement they were 'reflecting unconsciously'. This is rather paradoxical, given that reflection revolves around the conscious processing of new insights, and it may be that these students had simply become habituated to applying the same set of theories and techniques to situations so that they were no longer reflecting on new material at all. The third pitfall is that students may be tempted to believe that their reflective journeying is over when reflection becomes second nature, but this would be to derail the reflective process – there is always further to travel.

6.5.2 Critical Reflection

Critical reflection requires that we stand back from any given situation and analyse it from an alternative standpoint from which it can be reframed and critiqued. It presupposes that we have access to alternative standpoints or alternative ways of framing a situation; students will find that theories, ideological perspectives and ethical codes provide a rich source of standpoints and frames. When we become aware of the short-comings of a situation and when we have access to an alternative stand-point which illuminates how the situation could and should be very different, we need to be able to argue our case with the people who are maintaining the status quo in order to change it. So critical reflection, when pursued to its logical conclusion, results in practical reform (cf. Fook, 2002; Humphrey, 2009a).

Critical reflection is often easier to sustain when we are outside the situation being critiqued. Students may start to reflect critically upon the welfare state from socialist or feminist standpoints whilst at university, but they may not be able to sustain these critical reflections on placements where they are immersed in delivering welfare services in accordance with agency policies since they are almost inexorably drawn into the system. The most common type of critical reflection during placements occurs when students become aware of the gap between the ideals taught at university and the realities in social care organisations. For example, one student was horrified to find that a group of older women who always sat together at a day centre had been labelled 'The Mafia Table' by staff; their main 'crime' was to 'do their own thing' at the day centre rather than follow scheduled activities, and to do so vociferously in a manner which could unsettle staff and new service users. The student's questions were: 'Is this oppressive practice? If so, how do I challenge it?' (see Chapter 10: Exercises 10A and 10B).

6.5.3 Reflexivity

Reflexivity is the final stage of the reflective journey where reflection and critical reflection come together and are propelled onto the higher level of meta-reflection where we understand our own reflective journeying. One of the hallmarks of reflexivity among students is the capacity to comprehend the interfaces between the personal, the professional and the political (Ruch, 2000).

Exercise 6B shows how different types of reflection were combined for one student in a single session with a client. He applied the Four-strand Reflective Approach (Fish et al., 1991):

- The Factual Strand – this is a factual description of the situation which can include reference to reflection-in-action during the situation itself.
- The Retrospective Strand – this is about reflection-on-action after the event.
- The Substratum Strand – this pertains to underlying factors which are not immediately visible in the situation itself and which need to be explored with reference to theories, ideologies and ethical discourses. Consequently it requires critical reflection.
- The Connective Strand – this is where we connect the personal, the professional and the political. Consequently it involves reflexivity.

Exercise 6B   Developing a Multi-layered Reflexivity

Read the following account of the Four-strand Reflective Approach taken from the portfolio of a student on his final placement. The reflection revolves around a critical incident during his initial session with a man who had just been released from prison for drug-related offences and who needed a relapse prevention programme.

1   The Factual Strand – the critical incident occurred when the client explained that his most difficult problem after his release from prison was his discovery that his partner had ended the relationship and wanted to deny him access to their children. The student was thrown off balance as the client's situation resonated with his own – he had recently separated from his partner and he was having to fight for access to his own child. The student used these few seconds of shocked silence to do some reflection-in-action which took the form of an inner dialogue. He reminded himself that his focus needed to stay on the client's predicament, so that he had to shelve his own thoughts and feelings. He then resumed dialogue with the client.

2   The Retrospective Strand – after the session, the student returned to this critical incident and did some reflection-on-action. He realised that he had successfully contained his own predicament so that the client had not become aware of his inner turmoil, and that he had made good use of his own experiential knowledge insofar as he had been able to advise his client

> on child care law and couple mediation services as a direct result of dealing with his own situation.
>
> 3 The Substratum Strand – the student embarked upon critical reflections on ideologies around gender and parenting and the ways in which traditional assumptions about the primacy of mothering were embedded in legal systems, sometimes to the detriment of the father–child relationship.
>
> 4 The Connective Strand – the student appreciated the need to connect *and* separate the personal, the professional and the political. He could make good use of his own life experience to help his client, but he had to guard against over-generalising too much from his own experience – we all have unique experiences, even when facing similar situations. He chose to challenge traditional ideologies in his own life, and he could raise the consciousness of his client, but he had to refrain from politicising his work and sharing his own political views with his client.

Another hallmark of reflexivity is a capacity to contribute creatively to our own and others' reflective journeying. The above student was a Buddhist and he went on to create his own model of reflection which incorporated his own spirituality. He called it 'A Path to Reflective Nirvana'; it contained stages of contemplation and concentration associated with the development of compassion and wisdom respectively; and its summit was the enlightenment of Nirvana (cf. Sangharakshita, 1996). Although much practice wisdom will be shared by all competent practitioners, there is a signature tune unique to each practitioner, and this will be highly developed among excellent practitioners.

Points to Remember and Questions to Ponder

- You should now have a clearer sense of practice wisdom. If not, re-read this chapter after you have completed a placement – that's when the pieces of the jigsaw usually fall into place.
- Communication repertoires were explored in section 6.2. When you have a particularly difficult encounter with a service user or colleague, you should ask yourself: Who was using which defences and why? How can I dissolve negative defences used by myself or others?
- General approaches to practice were covered in section 6.3. Why might both task-centred and person-centred approaches be problematic when dealing with involuntary clients?
- Specific techniques were considered in section 6.4. Remember that the effectiveness of techniques depends upon care, competence and comprehension.

(Continued)

(Continued)

Get the relationship right first, before you try out any specialist techniques. But if you do use specialist techniques, then make sure you have a sound grasp of the underlying theory.

- The final section outlined the development of different types of reflection. Did you learn any new techniques of reflection from Exercise 6A? How would you explain to a fellow student the difference between 'reflection' and 'critical reflection'? If a student claims that reflection is now 'second nature', why might a social work educator be worried about such a claim?

Further Reading and Resources

Resources to develop your communication skills include:

Collett, P. (2003) *The Book of Tells*. London: Doubleday. (An illustrated text about body language.)

Egan, G. (2002) *The Skilled Helper: A Problem-management and Opportunity-development Approach to Helping*. Pacific Grove, CA: Brooks/Cole.

Trevithick, P. (2005) *Social Work Skills: A Practice Handbook*. Maidenhead: Open University Press.

The British Sign Language website – www.britishsignlanguage.com

The Counselling Channel website – www.tcc.tv

The Makaton website – www.makaton.org

There is also an excellent resource for your reflective journey:

Fook, J. and Gardner, F. (2007) *Practising Critical Reflection: A Resource Handbook*. Maidenhead: Open University Press.

7

Mastering Key Roles on Initial Placements

Introduction

On initial placements, students have to demonstrate their competence at the Key Roles around assessments, partnership working and agency account-ability in accordance with the National Occupational Standards for Social Work (see Chapter 1: Table 1B). These Key Roles also have to be met on final placements, although final placements require additional competence at the other Key Roles. So this chapter includes material relevant to assessments, partnership working and agency accountability from students in both initial and final placements.

7.1 Assessments

Assessment is the first stage of a cyclical process of Assessment–Planning–Intervention–Review–Evaluation which has the acronym ASPIRE (Parker and Bradley, 2003). Assessment is the first stage since the quality of assessments will determine the appropriateness of interventions, but it is not a discrete stage insofar as advice and assistance may be offered during the intitial assessment (so assessments shade into interventions) and subsequent reviews may show that needs and circumstances have changed (so reviews yield re-assessments and the cycle recommences).

7.1.1 Preparing for Initial Visits

Preparation for social work involvement consists of finding out information which will be helpful for the initial visit to a service user or carer. This information comes from the referral form, conversations with other involved professionals and existing case files when the person has already been known to the agency. Case files tend to have a major psychological impact upon students, since they make people and problems 'come alive' in a way that textbooks do not. Even those with considerable social care experience behind them confessed that they suddenly felt 'out of their depth' by the thought of doing 'social work' rather than social care work. Perhaps the best advice is to follow the maxim 'feel the fear and do it anyway' (Jeffers, 2007) since all new accomplishments require that we take a mini quantum leap into the unknown, and practice learning is learning-by-doing so the more times we do something, the easier it gets:

> S: Just the thought of going in to do *social work*, that was the daunting part … And you're given case files and they scare you to death basically, you think '*Oh my God!*' You know, you're supposed to go out and *see* these people! … You know how much you've learned by the end [of placement] because by then when you're getting these case files it's just like 'Okay then' and you've got so much confidence and you just think 'Yeah, it may be like this' and 'I could do that' … and you just go out and *do* it.

Students soon learn that service users can present as different from what they would have predicted on the basis of referrals and case files. For example, criminal justice agencies may refer teenage offenders for family support services and depict them as aggressive, but a sensitive approach can reveal aggression to be a mask covering up pain, and such teenagers often disclose a history of bullying. Some practice teachers use these situations to explain the concept of labelling, and ask students to bracket whatever they have read or heard about a client just in case it constitutes a 'client mythology' which could prevent the student from meeting the real person (cf. Eyben and Moncrieffe, 2007). There is a tightrope to walk between accepting and acting on information about a service user provided by others, and 'bracketing' information which could contribute to the formation of harmful stereo-types. The best advice is to keep an open mind about a person and to double check the evidence base of claims made about that person by others.

Refraining from making assumptions about the abilities of your service users is also beneficial. On the one hand, people diagnosed with a specific disability may exhibit a range of life skills which also need to be acknowl-edged. On the other hand, non-disabled people may have a restricted repertoire of everyday life skills. One student became very frustrated when a young offender failed to turn up to initial appointments since she had clearly specified times, places and dates of these meetings in her letters. When she did eventually meet him, she discovered that he was unable to read, write or tell the time, so that her own methods of communication had been flawed. She ensured that subsequent appointments were made by telephone and taught the young person to tell the time herself, whilst arranging for literacy skills to be taught at a local education centre. Similarly, students working with adults could be mortified when asking a service user to read through their assessment report only to be told that the service user was illiterate. This is where agency paperwork can make a significant difference to practice – some agencies incorporate icons into their assessment and review forms so that it is easier for service users to 'see' the areas which are being covered, i.e. a large £ sign denotes discus-sions of finances, a bus signals questions about public transport in the com-munity, etc. Such paperwork itself reminds students that not all service users can relate to the written word.

The only set of assumptions which should be built into your practice concerns the role and remit of your agency which will influence the type of assessment you will be undertaking. For example:

- Needs assessments are common to the statutory and independent sectors and focus upon the needs of disabled or disadvantaged children and adults. In complex cases they will be multi-agency assessments so that reports are collated from different professionals.

- Suitability assessments can also be found across all settings. These enquire about the suitability of members of the public to provide befriending services, night-sitting services, respite care and permanent substitute care for children or vulnerable adults.
- Risk assessments are reserved for statutory agencies working in child protection, adult protection, mental health and criminal justice. In complex cases they include reports for another statutory authority such as a tribunal, civil court or criminal court.

We will examine needs assessments here as these are the most common types of assessment conducted by students on initial placements; risk assessments will be covered in the next chapter.

7.1.2 Assessments in Child Care

Table 7A outlines the official guidance for assessments in social work with children and families. It is referred to as 'the assessment triangle' since it

TABLE 7A   *Official Guidance on Child and Family Assessments*

Assessments in child care must abide by the Framework for the Assessment of Children in Need and their Families (DH, 2000a). Information is gathered in relation to three substantive domains, which are further subdivided into more specific dimensions:

1   The Child's Developmental Needs, i.e. health, education, emotional and behavioural development, identity, family and social relationships, social presentation and capacity for self-care (in the case of older children).

2   Parenting Capacity and Adaptability, i.e. capacity to provide physical care, safety, emotional warmth, stimulation, guidance and boundaries, and stability of family life, including the capacity to adapt to the changing needs of this particular child over time.

3   Family and Environment, i.e. the history of this household unit and its links with the extended family and community, as well as information on material well-being in terms of housing, income and employment.

This is designed to be a holistic framework so that information from all domains must be linked together before intervention plans are drawn up. Economically deprived families with secure parent–child attachments may simply need assistance with accessing welfare benefits, rehousing or community facilities. But if the child's developmental needs are being frustrated by poor parenting, this calls for more direct therapeutic work.

This assessment framework underpins all child care social work. In England, it has been incorporated into the Common Assessment Framework so that child care professionals across all agencies are expected to abide by it (CWDC, 2009b).

In statutory agencies, assessment of need is closely linked to assessment of risk. Under the Children Act 1989, 'children in need' include those whose health or development is likely to be impaired without the provision of services (as well as disabled children). Resource constraints can result in services being restricted to cases where there is an identifiable risk to a child's health or development, creating a blurred boundary between 'children in need' who receive services on a voluntary basis and 'children at risk of significant harm' who are subject to child protection measures (DH, 2001a).

concerns the way in which three domains interact to support or undermine the child's welfare (DH, 2000a; Horwath, 2001; Calder and Hackett, 2003). It was developed originally for social work in statutory settings, but is now used by all child care professionals across all settings.

Of course, practice is more messy than our models. If assessments are to be holistic in understanding the child within their family and environment, we must make sure that we spend time with the child who is the subject of the referral as well as parents, siblings and other carers. Making mistakes is part of the learning curve, and there are two kinds of potential traps awaiting novices. The first is when they are too ambitious in trying to work with 'the whole family' at the outset. Here, students could find themselves overwhelmed by the amount of information conveyed by different family members, or by conflicting stories about the nature of the problem, or by negative emotions which can permeate family relationships. Even to communicate with several people of different ages and abilities can be fraught with difficulty:

> S: I remember my very first visit. It was terrible, it was absolutely terrible. I went at half three, the kids had just come home from school, there was [sic] seven children running about that house. I couldn't even get a conversation going! I was sat on the edge of a chair at one end of the dining table, and a little boy sat at the other end of the table. He was in tears and I wanted to cry. Oh, I felt like – [silence]. I didn't do anything that was planned … It was just nothing was going the way I wanted it to and I felt like I couldn't salvage the visit … I got through a confidentiality sheet, and luckily I got mum to sign the consent form … I said, 'Oh, thank you very much, I'll be in touch, bye' … Then I ran for the door! [laughs] … Literally, I wanted to get out of the house.

The solution to this first trap is to undertake a multi-stage assessment whereby different members of the family are seen separately over a series of visits before a whole family session is attempted; separate visits will also prepare everyone for a whole family session if this is necessary. It may be that dyadic or triadic work would be more effective than whole family sessions in any event – a dyad is a two-person unit (usually a parent and child) and a triad is a three-person unit (a carer and two children or two carers and one child). If a whole family session is unavoidable at the outset, then a co-working arrangement with a colleague is advisable.

The second trap is when students embark upon a series of one-to-one sessions with a parent or child which prevents them from seeing the whole picture or working with the dyad or triad that is at the heart of the problem. The most common scenario reported by students was that parents were happy for them to undertake one-to-one work with a child since this implied that the child was the problem, but when students suspected that the child's problems could be symptomatic of other problems in the family and suggested that they meet with the parents as well, the parents would reject this and could close the door on the agency altogether so the child was also denied help. This can be avoided by allocating two students to a family at the outset so that one works with a child (or children) and the other works with a parent (or parents). This can be 'framed' in a way that is acceptable to parents – there is evidence that they often need and want support in their own right (Quinton, 2004) – and it can pave the way for whole family work later on.

7.1.3 Assessments in Community Care

Table 7B outlines the official guidance for community care assessments which apply to adults with a range of disabilities (i.e. learning, physical,

TABLE 7B   *Official Guidance on Community Care Assessments*

Practice guidance issued under the NHS and Community Care Act 1990 (DH, 1991) specified five substantive domains for assessment in relation to adults:

1   Personal care needs, i.e. how far can the person look after themselves in terms of washing, dressing, toileting, cooking and getting around the house?
2   Health care needs, i.e. are there specific physical disabilities, sensory impairments or mental health problems which should be addressed?
3   Finances and housing.
4   Education, employment and recreation.
5   Transport, i.e. access to shops, places of work or worship, day care facilities.

Subsequent guidance in England, Wales and Scotland has promoted a single assessment process to ensure that different professionals do not repeat their assessments in relation to any given service user (Northern Ireland already enjoyed an integration of health and social care).

If the service user is dependent upon an informal carer to sustain them in the community, the carer is also entitled to an assessment of their own needs and official guidance on conducting carers' assessments has been issued (DH, 2001b).

In statutory community care agencies, assessment of need is closely linked to assessment of risk on account of resource limitations and eligibility criteria. In England, there is a policy of Fair Access to Care Services (DH, 2002b) which defines eligibility for services in terms of fours levels of risk to independence:

1   Critical risk, i.e. the person is at risk of developing very significant health problems or suffering neglect or abuse.
2   Substantial risk, i.e. the person cannot carry out basic personal or domestic routines.
3   Moderate risk, i.e. the person cannot sustain their education or employment, or some of their social support systems are in jeopardy.
4   Low risk, i.e. the person cannot undertake one or two personal tasks or social roles.

In practice, statutory agencies often restrict services to people who are assessed as facing critical or substantial risks, and signpost others to the independent sector.

---

sensory, mental health or age-related disabilities) who require services if they are to maintain their independence in the community (DH, 1991; MacDonald, 2006). This is also designed as a holistic approach to the person-in-their-environment, and informal carers are entitled to assessments of their own needs as well as service provision in their own right (Wilson et al., 2008: Chapter 14). Again, this is a statutory framework which can be used by social workers in other settings; the areas of assessment are relevant for all vulnerable adults, although the eligibility criteria for services will vary greatly between the statutory and independent sector.

Students expressed qualms about using the term 'assessment' with adults, asking 'How would it make us feel if a stranger came round and said they were "doing an assessment" on us?' Some abandoned the term in their dealings with service users on the grounds that it has connotations of authority and bureaucracy which can trigger anxiety, and reserved it for official meetings with other professionals. Younger students also wondered whether asking for information on sensitive topics such as finances and toileting could be seen as overly intrusive or disrespectful by their elders? They discovered that if they can enhance their observational skills, they can often find out the answer without asking the question. Here is an example from a student working with older people:

> S: If you can get the observing right then you make the assessment a lot easier … From the minute you walk up the path, you're observing … There's the pavement outside: is it a big step? … Inside it's the rugs, handrails, and stuff like that. Do the rugs slip? Can the person move around okay? … The toilet is a sensitive topic … You can't say to them 'Can you get on and off the toilet?' If they can get on and off the chair okay and if there's a grab rail in the toilet you can kind of assume that they're able to get on and off the toilet.

In adult care settings, there is often a palpable tension between the wishes and needs of service users and their carers. Sometimes service users are asking for opportunities to participate in education, recreation or employment when their carers are commenting negatively in the background to the effect that such activities are 'too risky'. In these cases, students have negotiated a compromise whereby a service user attends a college course or work experience on a temporary basis to reassure the carer that their adult son or daughter will return home safe and well. Sometimes carers are asking for services on behalf of a person who does not need or want them. One student followed up a referral from a man requesting services for his wife only to find that his wife objected strongly to this; she had been diagnosed with a progressive disease and she felt that it was important that she continued to manage her personal care and domestic chores for as long as possible. Other complications arise when a carer needs respite from caring but the service user refuses to accept care from a stranger. Clearly, there are advantages in meeting separately with service users and their carers to ascertain their distinct wishes and needs, and to consider how to handle potential conflicts of interest (Heron, 1998).

It is not just that there may be different needs, wishes and interests in a household, but also that needs, wishes and interests are quite distinct categories. There may be a gulf between 'needs' and 'wishes' (we do not always want what we need, or need what we want), and people require time to reflect upon what is *really* in their 'best interests'. The following student accepted a request for residential care made during her initial visit to an elderly woman and her daughter, but her practice teacher questioned the wisdom of such a draconian intervention:

> S: I didn't question it at the time, I just thought 'Well, that's what she wants and at a hundred and one, nobody's going to deny her it'. So my practice learning assessor said 'Does she know what it's going to be like in residential care – have you discussed that with her?' I said 'No' … So she sent me back the following day to have a discussion about the reality of it for her, because at 101 years, giving up her own home wasn't going to be so easy … This was one of the better moments where the light bulb came on, you know. Although I was there to do assessments, I had to help people look at the options. And although people know the options, they may not know the reality of them. To be honest I hadn't thought about this stuff until then.

The student discovered that the elderly woman had been up all night fretting about giving up her home and going to live with strangers, and that the decision about residential care had really been made by the daughter who was exhausted with looking after two households and worrying about her mother. A package of regular home care and occasional respite care solved all the predicaments in a manner which was cost-effective for the agency and congruent with the needs, wishes and best interests of both mother and daughter.

7.2 Partnership Working

Partnership working harbours two main meanings, i.e. partnerships with service users and carers which entail relationship-based social work and advocacy-based services; and partnerships with other professionals and their agencies which involve contributing to multi-professional meetings and integrated service delivery. The National Occupational Standards for Social Work refer to 'working together' rather than 'partnerships' (TOPSS, 2002), but these terms are used interchangeably in practice and in policy guidance (e.g. DH, 2000b; HM Government, 2010).

7.2.1 Relationship-based Social Work

Partnership working is grounded upon a capacity to relate to others, and practice wisdom is about matching the ways we relate to the needs of others. The terms 'interactions' and 'relationships' are used interchangeably in the National Occupational Standards for Social Work (TOPSS, 2002) but your practice wisdom hinges upon your ability to distinguish between them. Interactions may be occasional encounters governed by an instrumental agenda (i.e. 'You want X service and I have access to it'), but relationships have to be deepened over time so they develop their own independent dynamic with more intrinsic meaning for both parties (i.e. 'I know life is dreadful right now and you don't want to see anyone, but I'm here and I care about you, and we can sort this out together'). There is room for both instrumental interactions and intrinsic relationships in social work; the former can suffice for practical problem solving, but only the latter can heal psychosocial wounds. It is unwise to establish a therapeutic relationship with someone who simply wants welfare benefits advice, or to remain in the role of a neutral needs assessor when another human being is suffering acute grief. You could also consider the ways in which you relate to other professionals in terms of a continuum between the instrumental ('I need this from your agency') and the intrinsic ('I really respect you and enjoy working with you').

Professional relationships are quite different from personal relationships, even if they come to feel like personal relationships (cf. Beresford et al., 2008). They can even be the mirror image of our everyday life relationships, as if the logic of relationship formation itself has gone into reverse. On the one hand, we sometimes have to engage with service users or carers who do not wish to engage with us at all. On the other hand, we disengage when there is a satisfactory resolution of problems, just at the point when strong and secure bonds may have been forged between all parties. Exercises 7A and 7B illustrate the nature of engaging in and disengaging from relationship-based social work.

Exercise 7A   Relationship-based Social Work: Engaging

Read the following account by a male student working in a leaving care team:

S: I was working with a young male, he was 18 years old, he'd been abused, his mum got killed in a car accident ... He ended up in a children's home ... He was in trouble with the police a lot. He was very withdrawn, looked down, didn't wash, didn't shave ... He'd been moved from social worker to social worker, so he hadn't even formed an attachment to a worker ... In that instance I think it was me that initiated the spark of the person in him, you know ... I remember the first visit. His house was damp, it was smelly, musty, he had the curtains closed, he was very closed in on himself. The first thing I noticed was all these computers around the room, just in bits, so I thought 'Okay, let's try and channel into this' ... I said, 'Oh, I see you've got a lot of computers around here. Are you a bit of a whizz with computers? Well, if I ever need mine repairing I know who to contact!' and he just looked up like that and from the initial eye contact I could see he'd never had that before ... He's probably just had people getting the job done basically, but not spending time with him ...

CH: But that breakthough ... it just took a minute, didn't it?

S: Yeah, it was in a split second ... It was the start of a ... rolling process, getting the relationship going, and each visit he would open up a little bit more. He would have his off days, you know, sometimes he wouldn't answer the door because he'd be having an off day. But at the start he would not even leave the house ... It took about three weeks, you know, to get him out, to get him into the car, to get him to the café for a coffee, to have a walk around town, to take him clothes shopping, food shopping ...

CH: And in response to this developing attachment ... did he come to see you as ... a father figure, a friend, a mate, a brother or any of these things?

S: I'd have said more as a friend ... I wouldn't have liked to have said a father figure or brought family into it because he was detached from his family ... It was his family that had abused him. So I'd have said more of a kind of a friend. He enjoyed me going to see him. He started to ring me ... Then he would text me or pop up to the office and see me ... I'm probably the only friend he's ever had really.

Why did this care leaver have difficulty with forming attachments?

How did the student manage to break through the defences of this young man?

A discerning judgement is required in each case as to whether it is beneficial to become (or be seen as) a 'friend' or 'family member'. See Chapter 9 for further guidance.

Exercise 7B   Relationship-based Social Work: Disengaging

The stronger our engagement with service users, the more complex the task of disengagement becomes. The student in Exercise 7A continues his story:

CH: How did you actually leave that case out of interest ... ?

S: Well, it went from him being unemployed and on anti-depressants with his curtains shut, locked up in a basement floor flat, and when I left my placement he was working with the council as a road sweeper with the little barrows, he was more outgoing, he could speak to people, he would do his shopping himself and he would keep regular appointments with the GP himself. Silly things like he would have his curtains open in his flat, he would hoover up, he would make himself proper meals ... I'd had to show him how to cook pasta and clean up, you know, because he really didn't have independent living skills at all ... And that's what I think social work is all about ...

CH: So ... how did he feel about you moving on ... ?

S: Six weeks before I left I sat down with him and I spoke to him about that ... I felt that this subject would maybe put him back a few steps, you know, knock him back off the rails ... He was upset.

CH: How did he show that?

S: Through aggression ... He got upset, he shouted, he swore. That's the way he channelled the way he was feeling, you know, through his anger because I was going and he was getting another worker ... I wouldn't have actually said it was against me, I think it was against the situation ... [He said] *'Oh, it's fucking happening again to me, isn't it?'* ... and I would explain 'No ... you're more independent now so you won't need as much input from another worker' ... I built his confidence up. I said *'You're your own person now'*.

Why is it a good sign that this young man became upset when his social worker left?

How is his relationship to the new worker likely to be affected by these events?

Since social workers do not stay in the lives of their clients forever, it is crucial that we help people to develop social networks as well as independent living skills.

7.2.2 Advocacy with Service Users and Carers

Robert Adams (2008) highlights two major contrasting types of advocacy:

- Advocacy by professionals on behalf of a service user or carer who occupies the role of client. Traditionally, this applies to lawyers advocating for clients in court, but now there are a variety of professional advocacy schemes. There are independent advocates for adults who lack capacity to make decisions about their own lives under the Mental Capacity Act 2005, and there is a National Youth Advocacy Service for young people in care.

- Advocacy by service users and carers themselves who occupy the active role of citizens. This includes self-advocacy by a service user; parental or peer advocacy by a carer or fellow service user speaking up on behalf of a specific service user; and collective self-advocacy by a group of service users or carers who may wish to complain about service provision or contribute to the policy-making process.

The social worker's role as an advocate is often characterised by ambiguity. We may not always be able to act as independent advocates insofar as we are employed by the agency whose policies or practices may be part of the problem from the service user's or carer's point of view so we may have split loyalties. But we may be able to facilitate self-advocacy by service users and carers and thus indirectly support them in challenging agencies including our own.

There are two stumbling blocks to effective advocacy for students on initial placements. The first stems from their tendency to defer to the views of other professionals, illustrating the tension between partnership working with service users and partnership working with other professionals. For example, one student accompanied a depressed woman to her appointment with her doctor; the woman wanted to access counselling services and was afraid of being placed on medication and they had agreed that the student would act as her advocate. The doctor prescribed anti-depressants and made no mention of alternatives but the student remained silent; she justified this afterwards by stating that she had no right to interfere with the work of another professional and no expert knowledge of mental health or medication.

The second stumbling block stems from students' sense that as professionals-in-the-making they should be doing things *for* their service users, illustrating the tension between professional advocacy and self-advocacy. Service users themselves can teach students the real meaning of empowering practice, as occurred when one student accompanied a woman with mental health problems to a job centre:

P: As she is known for being volatile, I expected her to cause problems in the Job Centre. The security guard at the Job Centre had also come up with the same preconceived expectation and chose to communicate with me rather than the client. I went along with this … [but] the client picked up that she was not being included and immediately became angry. She told me she could speak for herself and did not need me to speak for her. This was a big learning curve for me … I need to stop rushing in and taking responsibility for clients, but empower them to take control of their own lives. Speaking on behalf of clients when they do not require me to do so could lead to clients believing that they are inadequate or incapable of dealing with their own situations.

Good examples of advocacy vis-à-vis individual service users suggest that it hinges upon developing an attunement to a service user and sustaining this in multi-professional meetings. This could be dubbed 'dialogic advocacy' insofar as we foreground our dialogue with the service user, even when we are having to advocate for them in the presence of others. It is ideally suited to the role of social workers as it operates in a liminal space in between the polar extremes of professional advocacy and self-advocacy and allows flexibility in moving between these positions. For example, one student accompanied a woman to a multi-professional planning meeting where the aim was to decide how best to look after her children and how to facilitate her contact with them if she received a custodial sentence for drug-related offences. His description of dialogic advocacy in action is as follows:

> P: I sat beside her, both to allay some of her fears and to ensure that when I was advocating for her I could look to her for confirmation of what I was saying on her behalf. If I felt the point was crucial I would use reflective discussion, i.e. if I made a point, I would ask her if I had that information correct or if my interpretation of her feelings was right. I felt that by doing this I was not only acting in the client's best interests, but I was also ... showing respect for her experiences and perspectives.

But there is also advocacy vis-à-vis groups of service users. Students placed in day care and residential establishments reported that when they organised outings for people with learning difficulties, physical disabilities or mental health problems, these outings could have backfired badly in the absence of advocacy skills. Why is this? Their service users were often visibly 'different' in terms of their disability or demeanour so that service providers in charge of libraries, restaurants and shops could be reluctant to allow entry – even when prior agreements had been made – and when access was granted, ordinary members of the public could vacate the premises or make offensive comments. Students were successful in challenging service providers who apologised for their unwarranted stereotypes as well as their near breaches of anti-discriminatory legislation. It was more difficult to challenge members of the public and students' priority here was to alleviate the distress that service users could suffer as a result of ostracism or offensive jibes.

7.2.3 Partnerships with Other Professionals

Although social workers should be in an ideal position to form partnerships with other professionals on account of their remit in 'working the social' (Howe, 1996), this can be hampered in practice by a lack of clarity about the social work role and the relative lack of status of social workers compared to some other professionals such as doctors (Wilson et al., 2008: Chapter 12). Students are in a more invidious position on this front, and some depicted themselves as located on the bottom rung of a long inter-professional ladder.

Although some mature students with experience of interprofessional working behind them functioned effectively in multi-professional meetings at the outset, the majority of students were faced with a steep learning curve and passed through four distinct phases. In the first phase, they sought refuge in neutrality when attending multi-professional meetings. They witnessed disagreements among professionals in relation to diagnoses, interventions and belief systems but felt unable to adjudicate between competing viewpoints or to contribute to the debate in any way. Emotionally they felt overwhelmed, and intellectually they decided to remain neutral and non-judgemental. In the second phase, they moved towards a reflective relativity. Although they continued to be silent during multi-professional meetings, they created a safe, reflective space within their own minds in which they could ponder on the reasons why different professionals saw the same situation so differently, and they realised that each view could have its own validity. In the third phase, they moved towards an expressive inclusivity as they came to see themselves as members of this multi-professional community whose views could be just as valid as those of other members, and they started to express their views. The following student is in transition between the second and third phases:

> P: [In multi-professional meetings] I discovered that what I consider to be unethical and what a Doctor or Nurse may feel to be unethical are two different things ... I listened to the opposing views and took note of what was said, but on this occasion I did not feel qualified to make a comment ... In future I shall express my views ... even if I do not know what the correct answer is or even if there is no correct answer. We all have a right to express our views. That includes me.

The fourth phase came to fruition in the final placement when students became committed to social work so they could offer a coherent account of social work and convincing arguments around the social model when faced with multi-professional audiences (cf. Tew, 2005; Oliver and Sapey, 2006).

7.3 Agency Accountability

Students have inductions to orient them to the role and remit of their own agency and they visit other agencies to prepare for multi-agency working. It is advisable to do some homework before your initial placement by reading around the subject matter of organisations and their management (e.g. Hafford-Letchfield, 2009).

7.3.1 Being Accountable in Our Own Agencies

Social work in statutory settings has been dubbed 'bureau-professionalism' (Harris, 1998) since practitioners need to be efficient bureaucrats abiding by agency protocols as well as effective professionals with discretion in how they discharge their duties in the community. This bureau-professionalism applies across the public sector as result of the new managerialism in health, education and criminal justice (Clarke et al., 2000), and also affects the independent sector where charities and businesses are increasingly under the scrutiny of regulatory bodies. The result is that students in all settings will have to demonstrate their accountability in similar ways.

How can you demonstrate your accountability? Four themes were common to all placements. First, you have to attend all scheduled meetings with supervisors and service users as well as team events and duty sessions, and if you are unable to attend you must provide an apology and an explanation. Second, you must operate in accordance with health and safety measures prescribed by your agency for the purpose of safeguarding yourself, your colleagues and your clients. This includes making sure that you inform other staff about your visits, your estimated return to the office and your contact details. Students who fail to do this cause anxiety to colleagues and place themselves in jeopardy since if their return to base is delayed and they are at risk in the community, it is difficult to locate or communicate with them. Third, you need to record all your visits to service users and contacts with other professionals on the system used by your agency which is usually a computerised database. This constitutes the evidence for your casework which you will need to refer to in supervision, multi-professional meetings and court reports. There is a nationwide computer database in youth offending teams known as the Youth Offending Information System (YOIS) and students in these placements were told to memorise the motto 'If it's not on YOIS then it didn't happen'. Fourth, you are expected to adhere to agency policies in respect of all your casework. In the statutory sector, these are developed with reference to national legislation and then modified in the light of local decisions, so budgets will have been allocated for each area of service provision and eligibility criteria will have been established accordingly.

7.3.2 Contributing to Our Agencies

Unit 15 of the National Occupational Standards caused the most difficulties in the practice teaching community. It requires that students contribute to the management of resources and services, thus adding value to the agency, but a number of practice educators questioned whether this was appropriate for novices. Interestingly, many students on placements in voluntary agencies did make important contributions to the management of resources and services, whilst many of their counterparts in statutory agencies failed to do so. Why might this be the case, particularly when students in statutory agencies are usually on their final placement and exhibiting much greater competence? The answer is that voluntary agencies remain quite distinct from statutory agencies on a number of fronts. They are part of the independent sector which has more autonomy from local and central government, and they are smaller organisations where it is easier to engineer changes; so although they experience resource shortages just like statutory authorities, they are in a better position to respond to this with creative innovations (Harris and Rochester, 2001).

Students' portfolios showed that they could could add value to their agencies in various ways:

- Designing new referral, assessment and review forms for the agency when generic paperwork has to be updated on account of new law and policy, or when specialist supplements have to be created for the sake of service users with special needs.
- Developing resource directories on Excel spreadsheets so that staff and future students would have a database of relevant local and national agencies, helplines and websites.
- Obtaining funding from other organisations to pursue new projects. One student secured funding from a children's charity for a photography project for disadvantaged teenagers. This enabled her to hire the services of an expert to teach photography as well as equipment such as digital cameras, computers and printers, and the teenagers' work was subsequently displayed to the public.
- Acting as a consultant to the agency on matters where the student has greater expertise. One student was an IT expert and was astonished to find that his agency had an old-fashioned computer system and no Internet access which hampered the capacity of staff to access research, resources and multi-agency communication networks. He advised managers on the systems and software packages which were best suited to their purposes; then he researched funding options and submitted a successful funding application; and after the system was installed, he taught his colleagues how to use the software.
- Conducting evaluation research to enhance service provision (see Chapter 5: section 5.4).

7.3.3 Challenging Our Agencies

Students can become critical of their agency, but they typically lack confidence in their capacity to judge whether, when and how to challenge 'the way things are'. Critical reflection upon the agency in the context of the wider political economy was most evident among students in their final statutory placement. In child care teams, the recurrent complaint was that paperwork took precedence over people and that they spent far longer in the office than in the community, writing reports for courts and attending meetings (cf. CWDC, 2009a; SWTF, 2009). They also felt frustrated by the dearth of resources – the lack of money to assist struggling birth families and the lack of foster placements to accommodate children and teenagers who may consequently be left in a neglectful home or placed in a bed-and-breakfast. Whilst they reported a number of successful outcomes in terms of reunification with birth families, integration into substitute families and independent living for care leavers, they believed that the rate of successful outcomes could be dramatically increased if services were better resourced (see Sayer, 2008). Resource shortages were just as acute in statutory adult care (see Means et al., 2008). Budgets were typically in the red prior to the end of the financial year at the end of March, which meant that services which had been delivered during the months of April to December could suddenly be suspended in January, causing havoc to assessments, interventions and reviews.

What happens when students voice their concerns? One student was required to undertake a community care assessment by telephone – in relation to a woman with mental health and substance misuse problems who was in prison in another area but due to be released to her home town – since there was no money left in the travel budget to allow the student to visit her new client in prison. Although the student made strong representations to the team manager, arguing that a face-to-face meeting was crucial to undertaking a proper assessment and building trust with this vulnerable new client, it was to no avail. She was left with the impression that her professional duty was to acquiesce to all agency constraints as conveyed by managers, so that criticisms of such constraints were 'personal' views to be suppressed for the sake of professionalism. The problem with bureau-professionalism is that two conflicting meanings of professionalism are embedded within it, i.e. the professionalism of the modern bureaucrat consists of adhering to agency codes and constraints, whilst that of the reflective practitioner involves harnessing their knowledge and skills in the service of meeting people's needs for care, education and empowerment (Hugman, 1998). So it is almost inevitable that reflective practitioners will challenge agency codes and constraints when these militate against best practice.

But why don't social work teams mount a collective challenge to such constraints? Any attempt to answer this question would have to take account of the complexity of local government financing (Wilson and Game, 2006) and the culture of powerlessness or the culture of 'making do' in many social work teams (Bar-On, 2002). These factors are highlighted in the following dialogue:

> S: I'd say social workers are good at talking about challenging things, but not
>   so good at actually doing it.
> CH: You would have to challenge the council for its allocation of resources or
>   decision making around budgets ...
> S: I'm not sure that social workers feel they have enough power to do that
>   to be honest. They feel — I think — 'Well, this is our lot. We're just social
>   workers. We just have to do our best'.

Nevertheless, some students did mount successful challenges to their agency (see Chapter 10).

7.3.4 Being Accountable in Multi-agency Contexts

Complex cases are subject to multi-agency discussions and decision making. Intensive care packages to support disabled children or adults to remain in the community will require specialist assessments and interventions by different professionals as well as pledges to commit resources from different agencies. When people are at risk of neglect or abuse, plans to safeguard their welfare will be made in multi-agency child or adult protection conferences, and when people are deemed to pose significant risks to others on account of their history of criminal behaviour, there will be multi-agency risk assessment conferences. Service users, carers and their advocates are invited to many but not all multi-agency meetings, but invitations do not always translate into attendance, particularly if people perceive the meeting as a threat to their own well-being. On the one hand, multi-agency working can promote democratic dialogues between all parties resulting in clear plans and commitments; on the other hand, it can be plagued by disputes and stalemates (see Weinstein et al., 2003; Barrett et al., 2005; Morris, 2008).

You need to read the case studies in Exercises 7C and 7D carefully in order to make sense of the complex dynamics in multi-agency meetings and to prepare for the impacts these may have on you. During initial placements, you may simply be attending such meetings in an observational role, but during final placements you are more likely to be carrying case responsibility for a service user on behalf of your agency, although your practice teacher or manager will usually accompany you.

Exercise 7C   Dilemmas in Multi-agency Working with Adults

A student in a statutory placement was working with an elderly woman who was shunted from institution to institution. Initially, she only had a physical illness which required temporary hospital treatment; but the treatment was detrimental to her mental health and she was diagnosed as having a drug-induced psychosis; this resulted in a dramatic personality change with aggressive outbursts and her family refused to have her home.

The client was then moved between hospitals, nursing homes and residential care homes, with each set of managers forcing her to move out on the grounds that she did not fit their criteria. For example, the hospital only dealt with physical diseases and she was now physically well; a residential care home was geared towards younger adults so she was deemed 'too old'; and a nursing home specialised in older people but did not offer psychiatric care. Eventually, a multi-agency meeting was convened, but the client was too poor to fund her own care and none of the agencies were willing to pay for her care:

> S: Everybody's got their own agenda, everybody's got their own budgets ... I felt social services had their own agenda because they didn't have the resources to fund a residential placement ... The health service certainly had their own agenda, they wanted the hospital bed basically ... and I think they saw an opportunity to get some money back by charging for the delayed discharges ... Her family definitely had their own agenda because they didn't want her living at home ... There were queries about whether [the client] had mental health problems at all, or whether it was just basic distress from everything around her ... I mean, *this poor lady felt nobody wanted her – and they didn't!*

Ponder on the root causes of these problems and what kinds of measures might resolve the interagency disputes before turning to the end of the chapter for further guidance.

Exercise 7D   Dilemmas in Multi-agency Working with Young People

A student in a statutory placement was allocated the case of a teenage boy who was experiencing strong homosexual feelings and starting to act them out at home and at school by making sexual advances towards his brother and other male pupils. He was bullied at school on account of his sexual orientation and he retaliated by fighting back. The school referred him to a child psychologist who diagnosed Attention Deficit Hyperactivity Disorder (ADHD) and prescribed the drug Ritalin. This cured the aggression but the boy complained that he lost his sense of identity and refused to take any more.

(Continued)

(Continued)

Interagency meetings were convened where it was agreed by managers in health, social services and education that the boy should be pressurised into taking the Ritalin. Both the student and the boy's mother were unhappy with this course of action. The student argued with her practice teacher and manager but to no avail. She experienced inner conflicts:

S: He was competent and he didn't want to take his meds [medicine, i.e. Ritalin]. But his behaviour was out of control and nobody knew what to do. They couldn't force him to take his meds ... but I was presented with it as 'Well, you've got to tell him he's got to take them'. I was like '*No!*' because personally I agreed with [the young person]. But in my professional head I had to put aside my own personal view, I couldn't let it affect my practice ... He stopped taking his meds because he didn't feel himself on them, and I thought 'Oh I really agree with you!' But that was my little demon inside, and I was fighting it, it was so critical of what they were doing to this lad. But I thought 'I must put on my professional head' ... because I was part of the statutory agency, so I was a servant to them really, so I'd got to be professional on behalf of my agency and be accountable to them ...

CH: I wonder whether your inner voice, your little demon, didn't have a virtuous side to it?

S: No.

CH: There are social workers who would feel and believe just like that ...

S: I think I would if I was qualified and that's the difference ... I didn't feel I could argue my corner as much because I was still a student ... All the other professionals – teachers, special needs coordinators, psychologists – they were just forcing me into it. They were 'Meds, meds, meds! He needs his meds!' I was like 'No, no, no! He doesn't need his meds, he needs support' ... He was struggling with his sexuality ... He refused to take [his meds] because he said 'I just feel awful on them, I feel like a zombie, I don't like them, I don't feel like me, I can't be me' ... His mum supported him and I wanted to support them both ... but my manager said 'Well, we can't'.

CH: Why did your manager say that?

S: So it didn't come back and bite them on the bum I think, do you know?

CH: Just in case he got worse and then Social Services got blamed ... ?

S: Yeah.

Ponder on these questions before turning to the end of the chapter for guidance.

What is problematic about the multi-agency decision making in this case?

What is hampering the student's efforts to advocate on behalf of her client and his carer?

Points to Remember and Questions to Ponder

- The Key Role around assessments was covered in section 7.1. Why do some assessments require more than one visit, or more than one worker?

Remember that everyone needs time to reflect upon options (and that includes you) so don't rush from an assessment to an intervention or a care plan.

- The Key Role around working in partnerships was the subject of section 7.2. When and why are relationships the key to successful practice? Remember that there are different forms of advocacy, so you always need to pose the question: 'Which form of advocacy is best suited to this service user or carer – and why?'
- The Key Role around agency accountability was addressed in section 7.3. There are minimal requirements of any employee, but trainee professionals should also be asking: 'How can I contribute creatively to my agency?' and 'Do I have reason to reflect critically upon my agency or the wider political economy?' If you believe that you have a professional duty to challenge your agency on a serious matter, then try to access advice for yourself before taking action.
- Interprofessional and interagency working were also considered. You need to play an active role in multi-agency meetings, but if you are struggling to voice your opinions, it is helpful to ponder on the root causes. For example, does it reflect a lack of confidence, skills or knowledge on your part, or the way in which the meeting is being conducted? This will enable you to address the specific difficulty with your practice teacher – and to empathise with service users and carers who also struggle in such meetings.

Exercise 7C   Further Guidance

There are a number of root causes of the problem:

- Ironically, medical intervention triggered the psychotic condition in the first place. This phenomenon whereby medicine can have reverse effects is known as 'clinical iatrogenesis' (Tummey and Tummey, 2008). But doctors have no medicine to cure the psychosis and hospitals have no surplus or long-stay beds.
- The client has no effective advocates. Her capacity for self-advocacy has been impaired; her relatives have virtually disowned her; and her social worker is compromised by her agency which has a budgetary deficit and cannot afford a residential placement.
- Interagency conflicts are so strong that they eclipse the needs of this vulnerable old woman. Indeed, they have been exacerbated by the Community Care (Delayed Discharges etc.) Act 2003 whereby the NHS charges social services for any delays in discharging patients from hospital after the hospital has declared that they are fit to move back into the community (Brammer, 2010: Chapter 14).

Possible solutions to interagency disputes include:

- Multi-professional meetings should have an independent chair – someone who is in an authoritative position but independent of the agencies involved.
- Social workers can check whether independent advocacy services are available.
- Any professional who is concerned about the health and safety of a vulnerable service user can consult their professional regulatory bodies under the

(Continued)

(Continued)

Public Interest Disclosure Act 1998 ('the whistle-blowing Act'). If this seems too draconian, the charity Public Concern at Work offers off-the-record advice via its website and helpline.

But a more radical solution would be to change the laws, organisational splits and funding mechanisms which have contributed significantly to interagency conflicts. In Northern Ireland, social and health care are merged into a single organisation so there is a less scope for interagency disputes and more scope for serving vulnerable people (Heenan and Birral, 2006).

Exercise 7D   Further Guidance

This case of multi-agency decision making is problematic on a number of fronts:

- A consensus has been reached by senior managers across all agencies but it has been reached by overriding the wishes and views of the young person, his parent and his student social worker.
- The decision to pressurise the teenager into taking Ritalin is contrary to the Gillick competency ruling 1985 and the Children Act 1989 in England (and their equivalents elsewhere). A young person has the right to receive or refuse medical treatment when they are capable of understanding what that treatment entails (Brammer, 2010: Chapter 7).
- There is evidence of the hegemony of the medical model in determining diagnoses and interventions when the teenager's difficulties were arguably social and cultural. Social services managers did not promote an alternative social model because they were afraid that if the boy did not take the medicine then he might commit sexual offences against other children for which they could be blamed. This is known as being 'risk-averse' and it contributes to 'defensive practice' (Cree and Wallace, 2009).
- The evidence base around the use of Ritalin to treat ADHD has been disregarded. It does curb behavioural patterns in the short term, but it can have serious side-effects and it cannot resolve underlying issues in people's lives. It is rarely used in Europe where the social pedagogy approach means that education takes precedence over medicine (Coppock, 2002).

The student had a strong sense that the social work ethos along with human rights and social justice had been violated. But she was not supported by senior managers and came to doubt her own developing practice wisdom. She came to see her resistance as a 'personal' matter, even as an 'inner demon', which had to be separated out from her 'professional' duty to support her agency at all times. This resulted in an inner turmoil which hampered her advocacy on behalf of her client and his chief carer.

But there was a happy ending. The boy refused to take the Ritalin, a decision which was endorsed by his mother (explicitly) and his student social worker (implicitly). They continued to address the underlying issues of social and sexual development, and when the student left the placement, he was on track for becoming a happy homosexual.

Further Reading and Resources

Students are reminded that they need to consult law texts relevant to their own country, as well as policy and practice guidance within their own agency during placements.

A comprehensive introduction to law, policy and practice for all service user and carer groups is:

Wilson, K., Ruch, G., Lymbery, M. and Cooper, A. (2008) *Social Work: An Introduction to Contemporary Practice*. Harlow: Pearson Education. (This has a companion website.)

Other introductory texts on specific service user groups and settings include:
Archambeault, J. (2009) *Social Work and Mental Health*. Exeter: Learning Matters.
Barber, J. (2002) *Social Work with Addictions*. London: Macmillan.
Dugmore, P. and Pickford, J. with Angus, S. (2006) *Youth Justice and Social Work*. Exeter: Learning Matters.
Kirton, D. (2009) *Child Social Work: Policy and Practice*. London: Sage.
MacDonald, A. (2006) *Understanding Community Care: A Guide for Social Workers*. Basingstoke: Palgrave-Macmillan.
Ward, A. (2006) *Working in Group Care: Social Work and Social Care in Residential and Day Care Settings*. Bristol: Policy Press.
Weinstein, J. (2007) *Working with Loss, Death and Bereavement: A Guide for Social Workers*. London: Sage.

Books dealing with advocacy, agency accountability and multi-professional partnerships include:
Adams, R. (2008) *Empowerment, Participation and Social Work*. Basingstoke: Palgrave-Macmillan.
Barrett, G., Sellman, D. and Thomas, J. (eds) (2005) *Interprofessional Working in Health and Social Care: Professional Perspectives*. Basingstoke: Palgrave-Macmillan.
Hafford-Letchfield, P. (2009) *Management and Organisations in Social Work*. Exeter: Learning Matters.
Morris, K. (ed.) (2008) *Social Work and Multi-Agency Working: Making a Difference*. Bristol: Policy Press.
Weinstein, J., Whittington, C. and Leiba, T. (eds) (2003) *Collaboration in Social Work Practice*. London: Jessica Kingsley. (This collection also covers collaboration with service users and carers.)
You can also take a look at the *Journal of Interprofessional Care*.

Internet sites are available so that you can check out the rights of service users and carers, professional advocacy services and movements which promote self-advocacy:
A guide to citizens' rights in the UK – www.yourrights.org.uk
The National Youth Advocacy Service – www.nyas.net
Self-advocacy services for learning disabled people – www.in-control.org.uk
Self-advocacy services for mental health service users – www.u-kan.co.uk
A website for carers – www.direct.gov.uk/carers

8

Mastering Key Roles on Final Placements

Introduction

This chapter dissects the Key Roles of interventions, risk management and professional competence contained in the National Occupational Standards for Social Work (see Chapter 1: Table 1B). Although the formal assessment of these Key Roles is reserved for final placements, it is important to note that students will be undertaking interventions, assessing risks and evaluating their practice in initial placements, which is indeed the foundation upon which they build in final placements. Consequently, this chapter includes material from students on initial as well as final placements.

8.1 Interventions

The term interventions covers the entire gamut of social work activities – advice and advocacy; educational and therapeutic work with families and groups; networking and consciousness-raising in communities; and legal interventions with people who may be voluntary or involuntary clients in the spheres of child protection, adult protection, domestic violence, mental health and youth justice.

8.1.1 Working with Individuals

In the statutory sector, most work with individuals takes place within the framework of a plan. Some plans are drawn up between a student and a service user and agreed by an agency supervisor, but most plans are developed in multi-agency meetings, and some have been sanctioned by courts or tribunals. In child care settings, there are children in need plans, child protection plans, care plans and pathway plans for care leavers. In adult care settings, there are community care plans, respite care plans, residential care plans and intermediate care plans (see Wilson et al., 2008: Part 3).

The plan provides the basic framework which will structure tasks and timescales, but within this you should always try to work democratically, therapeutically and systemically. What does this mean? First, a democratic approach means that you draw up plans *with* people wherever possible. Even if service users are learning disabled, it is still important to draw up plans with them, explaining things to them, consulting with them and offering choices. Even if you are removing a child from home on a court order, you still need to involve the child and parents in future plans in order to take into account their wishes and views and to explore options around contact or even reunification.

Second, a therapeutic approach should be incorporated into casework in all settings. As a general rule, the more skilful you become in deploying therapeutic techniques in your initial placements with voluntary service users, the more successful your work with involuntary clients will be later on. Since these cases are more complex, you may need to combine techniques from different traditions, and such versatility is one of the hallmarks of practice wisdom. For example, a student in a Youth Offending Team working with a teenage girl who was subject to a court order in the aftermath of assaulting her stepfather had to combine traditions and techniques. Cognitive techniques included educating the girl about the physiology and psychology of aggression and explaining methods of defusing anger before it erupts by reframing events in our 'self-talk' (e.g. 'He isn't really trying to wind me up – he's just having a bad day. Let's try not to make it worse!'). This was reinforced by role plays of difficult situations – a behavioural technique. But the girl's aggression also reflected and reinforced difficult family dynamics, so the student borrowed from psychodynamic and systemic traditions. She encouraged the girl to discuss her relationships with family members, including her birth father, and arranged access to services including respite care for the girl and parenting guidance for the mother.

This brings us to the third point, i.e. that working with individuals should also be systemic. This is because no human being is an island, and our relationships to other people in the past, present and future are constitutive of our humanity. So although you may conduct sessions with individuals, you are never simply working with an individual. For example, one student spent a half-day per week of her placement undertaking life story work with a learning disabled man who had been moved from an institutional to a community setting. He remained a recluse and no one knew anything about his life, other than the fact that he had been committed to an institution in his adolescence. Most sessions were conducted on a one-to-one basis since the student had to access the inner world of a closed-up human being, but they were still governed by a systemic approach. After she had established a trusting rapport with the man, they visited the local library to inspect the records of births, marriages and deaths and drew up his family tree. The student wrote to family members who were still alive on behalf of the service user, and reunions were arranged with people who were able to provide vital missing pieces of the jigsaw, to shed tears with a long-lost relative and to pledge ongoing contact. When the student left the placement, the man was socialising far more in the community since he had recovered his sense of self and his sense of connectedness to others.

8.1.2 Working with Families

Table 8A provides an overview of basic techniques used in family therapy – for further details, students should consult the work of Rudi Dallos and Ros Draper (2000). Family therapy is a systemic approach insofar as a family

TABLE 8A   *Techniques from Family Therapy and Systemic Traditions*

A systemic approach is required when working with families since there are subsystems nested within the whole family system. Effective assessments and interventions require that we understand the whole and each of its parts and how these intersect.

- Genogram – this is a representation of family relationships (see Figure 8A).
- Chronologies – social workers draw up timelines when undertaking life story work to show the major events in the lives of service users. Family therapists take this a stage further by drawing up timelines with family members and exploring how these intersect. This is used to open up dialogues about relationships. It can then reveal how problematic patterns of attachments in partnerships or parenting have evolved, where they have been replayed and with what effects, whether there have been positive relationships or role models in people's lives etc.
- Circular questioning – this is a technique designed to bypass defences and elicit maximum information about family dynamics. It involves asking one member about the relationship between two other members, i.e. A is asked about the relationship between B and C; then B is asked about the relationship between A and C; then C is asked about the relationship between A and B. This diverts people from the blaming game, i.e. if A and B believe that 'C is the problem' then asking each person for their views will produce a stalemate since A and B will simply blame C who will probably clam up in self-defence.
- Hypothesising about problems – it is helpful for professionals to share their hypotheses and to check out the hypotheses of family members. You won't get far if everyone is committed to different hypotheses! But hypothesising allows flexibility and family therapists may suggest hypotheses which are designed to be therapeutic even if not proven to be true, e.g. 'Perhaps your son's delinquency is his way of saying that he needs both of you to spend more time with him'. This invites parents to reframe a problem so that they can help their son, instead of labelling him as 'being bad' and 'beyond help'.
- Imagining positive outcomes – this encourages family members to envisage a more positive future whilst also checking out whether their visions are compatible. A child's 'ideal future' might be that his stepfather moves out of the household, but this could be incompatible with the 'ideal future' envisaged by the adults. If you get stuck, you can conjure up a positive authority figure who is not actually present in the session, such as an overseas relative, a deceased ancestor, God or Confucius, i.e. anyone who commands the respect of all family members, e.g. 'What if your grandfather were here now? What advice would he give you?'
- Homework – this is vital as people must rehearse new ways of relating to one another in everyday life, and report back on their successes and setbacks.

can be viewed as a system containing a variety of subsystems – these subsystems refer to units within the family such as the couple, the siblings and parent–child relationships. But the basic techniques used by family therapists can be applied by social workers during visits to individuals as well as families. And some of these techniques are essential to social work practice, notably genograms. These are family trees drawn up in accordance with standard symbols, and they are routinely included in case files, life story books and court reports. Figure 8A shows how genograms display important information to guide assessments and interventions.

There are three reasons why working with families is more complex than working with individuals. First, the emotions expressed by any given member of the family can trigger reactions from all other members of the

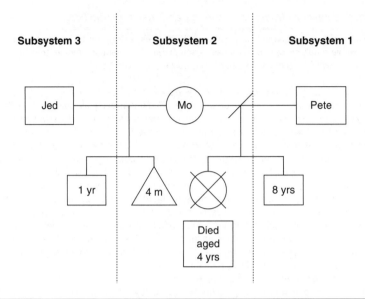

The genogram shows that there are three subsystems within this family: Mo was in a relationship with Pete which produced two children. But their daughter died and Mo became very depressed. She was desperate to have another daughter but Pete had had a vasectomy. So she started an affair with Jed, and moved in with him after she became pregnant. She gave birth to a son and soon became pregnant again, but since discovering that her unborn baby is another boy, she has been describing it as 'an alien inside me'.

Mo's grieving for her daughter and longing for a replacement means that she is isolated from the rest of her family and neglecting her duties of care towards the living. Pete looks after their eight-year-old son, and Jed does most of the child care for their one-year-old son. So there are three subsystems.

A genogram can show family members what is going on in their family, and can shape intervention strategies. In this case, Mo needs bereavement counselling.

The full set of genogram symbols is available at www.genopro.com

FIGURE 8A   *A Genogram*

family, and the more powerful this chain reaction, the more powerless a professional can feel when faced with it. This is known in family therapy circles as a 'dramatic enactment' of family dynamics (Dallos and Draper, 2000). One antidote to a sense of powerlessness is to 'bracket' the professional tendency to want to control situations – the chain reaction may be beyond your control, so unless serious harm is on the horizon you can let the drama play itself out, and work with family members afterwards. See Exercise 8A for a case example.

Exercise 8A   Family Dramas

Families experiencing conflict or crisis often engage in a spontaneous enactment of their family drama in front of us, and this 'dramatic enactment' conveys a lot of information about the 'scripts' internalised by family members and how they converge or clash, e.g. 'I'm a good mother/You're a bad daughter' and 'You're a bad mother/I'm a good daughter' represent a clash of scripts between a mother and daughter.

Family therapists work in pairs in a specialist suite with access to video equipment so that when such dramatic enactments unfold, one worker remains in a neutral observer role and the other engages more directly with the family if required. After the drama has played itself out, they show family members the video which encourages them to become reflective observers of their own family dynamics, which is often the catalyst for change.

Most social workers do not have access to specialist suites, and they need even more sensitivity and skilfulness since family dramas tend to be more dramatic in their natural settings. One student dealt admirably with a family drama during her initial visit, although the visit took three hours instead of the scheduled one hour:

- In the first hour, she undertook a family history from the mother whilst the children played elsewhere. The mother had been through a divorce and was complaining bitterly about her ex-husband. The teenage daughter arrived home and engaged in some eavesdropping. Eventually, she stormed in, screaming that her father had been good to her and that her mother didn't care about her.
- The student spent a second hour counselling the teenager on a one-to-one basis, and then invited mother and daughter to a reconciliation, which ended in a hug. The younger children arrived on the scene, witnessed the hug and demanded their own hugs. This triggered another crisis for the teenager who stormed out, complaining that her mother cared more about her younger siblings.
- The student spent a third hour calming down the teenager before re-engaging with the mother. It transpired that the mother devoted most of her attention to the younger children on the assumption that her teenage daughter had enjoyed her exclusive attention for several years before the others were born and could now look after herself. The mother was willing to review this assumption, and her 'homework' included spending quality time with her teenager daughter.

What is the main purpose of an initial visit? How far do you think this purpose was facilitated or frustrated by such a dramatic enactment?

What does this family drama tell us about the scripts of the mother and teenager? Can you detect the themes of attachment, separation and loss in their scripts?

What skills does the student demonstrate as part of her maturing practice wisdom?

Second, social workers in child care settings work with a diversity of family forms, and two or three families may be involved in providing care for any given child or sibling group. There are reconstituted families where step-parents have an equal share in parenting; kinship care arrangements where grandparents may be the primary carers; and substitute care arrangements involving foster families (Bell and Wilson, 2003; Farmer et al., 2008). Co-working is the most common strategy for dealing with such complexity. For example, there may be a social worker from a family support team working with birth parents, a social worker from a fostering team working with foster carers, and a social worker from a looked after children team working with the child.

Third, working with families can involve legal interventions when a child has suffered, is suffering or is likely to suffer significant harm, and the spectre of court work and enforced removals of children from birth families is anxiety-provoking for students. But some students on final placements reported positive experiences of child protection where negotiation skills helped to bring about a resolution with the agreement of all parties. For example, one student was on duty when a school's child protection liaison officer contacted social services to explain that a child had disclosed to a teacher that her mother had been beating her, and that a medical examination by the school nurse revealed extensive bruising. A social worker went to visit the mother who admitted injuring the child; it transpired that this was her eldest child, the product of a previous relationship, and the mother said that she simply did not want this child in her new family. Possibilities for kinship care were explored by the student and another social worker. At the end of the school day, a social worker, the student and a grandmother arrived to collect the child:

> S: It was done in a dignified manner ... Even though they had to do it in an emergency, they don't go barging in and tearing the children apart from the mother's arms and stuff like that which you hear about [in the media] ... It's done in a nice manner so it's not traumatic for the children, that's what I've witnessed ... [This child] was real close to her Nana and we explained that because of what she'd told [the teacher and nurse] we couldn't let her return home. We tell it in the most child-centred manner. She understood and she was frightened of her mum anyway. She was happy with her Nana, and we took them both back to Nana's house, and that's the nicest part.

Of course, legal measures may still be necessary in the aftermath of such interventions. For example, if the long-term plan is for the child to remain with her grandmother, then it would be advisable for the grandmother to apply for a residence order through the courts (Brammer, 2010: Chapter 8).

There is a question you should always ask yourself when working with families: where are the men? Social workers have all too often neglected men in families, but men can occupy a vital role – they may be a chief carer or an abuser in relation to a child; they may support or undermine the mother; either way, we should be including them in our work with families (Featherstone et al., 2007).

8.1.3 Working with Carers

Social workers encounter informal carers on a regular basis, and people who provide a substantial amount of care for relatives or friends with special needs are entitled to services in their own right, although research shows that only a tiny minority of informal carers receive services (Wilson et al., 2008: Chapter 14). So next time you visit a service user who is disabled and dependent on others in everyday life, you should check out whether the primary carer needs or wants assistance.

Formal carers who have been recruited to look after children or vulnerable adults who are strangers to them will have their own social worker. The role of the social worker is to assess their suitability for caring for children or vulnerable adults, then to assist in the process of 'matching' carers with a specific person needing a placement, and finally to support the carers during the placement (cf. Newton, 2006; Wheal, 2006). Students enjoy this area of work immensely. But formal carers occupy a strange liminal space in social work insofar as they are neither professionals nor clients in any traditional sense, and this can create tensions in partnership working. On the one hand, the majority of carers have a high level of expertise in looking after service users with specific kinds of disabilities or disturbances so students learn a lot from them, and a few carers have made significant and student-friendly contributions to social work theory and research (e.g. Archer, 1999a, 1999b). On the other hand, a tiny minority of carers have perpetrated physical and sexual abuse upon vulnerable people taken into their homes, and on occasion this has resulted in the death of a child (e.g. Leslie, 2001). You should remember that the remit of safeguarding children and vulnerable adults is paramount in all areas of social work.

8.1.4 Working with Groups

The techniques you acquire when working with individuals can be transposed into group work settings. Techniques from cognitive and behavioural traditions have been effective with groups of young offenders (Rose, 1998). Play and art therapy techniques can easily be adapted for groups of children and adolescents (Dwivedi, 1993). Other psychodynamic techniques have informed group work with adults suffering mental health problems (Yalom, 2005). Service users can run their own self-help groups which combine therapeutic healing with political empowerment (see Ernst and Goodison, 1981).

Concerns have been expressed about the 'demethoding' and depoliticisation of contemporary group work insofar as the majority of social care professionals will run groups at some point in their careers but only a minority of them exhibit the requisite skills, knowledge and values to utilise the group itself as a medium of therapy, education or empowerment (Ward, 2009). There is some truth in this, and most students ran groups on initial placements when their practice wisdom was still embryonic. For example, one student was working in a day centre for adults with mental health problems during her first placement, and she was charged with the task of setting up a group for women who constituted a silent and subordinate minority in the establishment. She arranged a series of sessions in the day centre so that the women could develop new skills in cookery and crafts, along with a series of outings in the community. The service users enjoyed this group work, but it is doubtful whether it contributed to their empowerment within the establishment, since the student did not address questions of gender or dynamics in the day centre. How should we evaluate this? Should we simply accept that service users expressed high levels of satisfaction or should we ask more critical questions about their empowerment in everyday life?

Running a group involves a great deal of preparation and it is always a good idea to co-work a group and to have access to a consultant (Preston-Shoot, 2007). It is easier to run groups when we have relevant life experience. Young students were well-equipped to run 'growing up' groups for adolescent girls, but they could be out of their depth in 'parenting' groups when they had no first-hand experience of parenting. Nevertheless, one of the features of group work is that it transports us beyond our existing horizons. One young student ran a reminiscence group for older people and had to undertake a lot of research into local history so that she could understand the social context of their lives during the twentieth century, including their experiences of two World Wars. Another student was asked to undertake group work with learning disabled adults with a view to teaching them new skills including art and drama. The student invited specialists to provide relevant training to the group (including herself), and then helped group members to write a play, design the scenery, rehearse and then perform the play in public. There was a glowing report in the local press, but the student had no previous experience of art or drama, and she had transcended her own stage fright in order to support her service users.

8.1.5 Working in Communities

Community work has also changed over the years so that social workers and students are more likely to work 'in' communities rather than 'with' communities (Mayo, 2009). A community may be rooted in geography (e.g. a neighbourhood), identity (e.g. Asian women) or life situation (e.g. carers). Students working in domestic violence projects would regularly offer sessions in the community as part of consciousness-raising – they explained the prevalence of the problem and services available to survivors by going into schools to talk with pupils and by convening public meetings.

Group work and community work can overlap insofar as both seek to promote supportive networks. An interesting example of this emerged in one agency across three cohorts of students. The agency specialised in recruiting carers for learning disabled adults who needed a family placement. The first student discovered that the carers were socially isolated and applied for funding to resource a carers' support group. The second student organised the group work. He arranged specialist sessions so that experts could provide information on practical, financial, legal and medical matters. The carers themselves set up a befriending service so that they could act as mentors to new carers, as well as a sitting service so that they could look after the learning disabled adult placed with another carer if that other carer needed a break. But the second student discovered that the learning disabled service users were also socially isolated in the community, and recommended that a parallel group be set up for them. The baton passed to the third student to set up a group for the service users. New groups spawned new networks and ultimately a new community of citizens.

8.2 Risk Management

This Key Role requires students to assess, manage and minimise risks to their service users and carers as well as themselves and their colleagues. All agencies in the statutory and independent sector alike will have tools to assess risks, policies to manage risks and procedures to minimise risks.

8.2.1 What Do We Mean by 'Risks'?

The term 'risk' typically refers to risks of harm in respect of health, safety and well-being. Making sense of risks is a complex business because risks are multi-dimensional in nature, multi-directional in respect of space, uni-directional in respect of time and multi-perspectival in respect of the human beings involved in the situation. Let us take a closer look at each of these factors.

Risks are multi-dimensional in nature so that the risk to health can refer to physical or mental health. There may be multiple causes as well. The risks in question may result from self-neglect or neglect by others; self-harm as a result of self-injury or substance misuse or harm from carers or strangers who have perpetrated physical or sexual abuse; or a variety of other forms of maltreatment, such as emotional maltreatment, financial exploitation or discrimination motivated by racism, sexism, disablism, ageism or homophobia (cf. Beckett, 2007; Pritchard, 2008). We have to understand the sources of risk, and to disentangle different types of harm, before we can intervene effectively.

Risks are multi-directional in respect of space insofar as service users may pose risks to themselves, others in their household, specific individuals or groups in the community, or professionals who intervene in their lives. Professionals may also pose risks to service users, as is clear from reports into neglect and abuse in institutional settings (Stanley et al., 1999). This makes for complexity in our assessments around 'who poses the most risk to whom?', but unfortunately it also contributes to a culture of suspicion (McLaughlin, 2007).

Risks are uni-directional in respect of time insofar as the concept of risk is future-oriented. Although we assess risks in the present and take into account actual harm in the past, decision making is governed by futuristic questions, i.e. 'are these risks likely to continue?' and, if so, 'is someone likely to suffer harm?', and, if so, 'how can we prevent this?' The problem here is that the future is by definition unknowable and unpredictable, so although professionals seek to provide evidence for their views from their casework, the client's history and current life situation, and wider research studies on a given client group, there will always be a margin of error. A 'false positive' is when we predict that harm will occur and it does not occur; a 'false negative' is when we predict that no harm will occur and it does occur (Munro, 2008).

Furthermore, risks are multi-perspectival in respect of human beings. This means that there may be differences of opinion about risks among service users, carers and professionals. A parent may not believe that using corporal punishment on children, or leaving children at home alone, constitutes any risk to the children, but child care professionals are likely to disagree. People who are regular users of legal and illegal drugs may be convinced that the benefits outweigh the risks. Women who have suffered domestic violence frequently return to their partners in the hope that things will change, regardless of the lack of objective evidence that anything has changed. Professionals need to be mindful of the distinction between 'objective risks' and 'subjective perception of risks'.

Finally, although the predominant discourse about risk in social work and society is steeped in negativity – i.e. risks are 'risks of harm' and therefore things to be avoided – risk is a socially constructed concept and there are alternative constructions (Webb, 2006). Young people need to take some risks in life if they are to grow up into robust and resilient adults, and adults have rights to self-determination which can include choosing lifestyles or life situations which may be deemed risky by others (O'Sullivan, 2009). Professional interventions are governed by legislation designed to protect children and vulnerable adults from significant harm caused by their own lack of capacity for self-care, or by neglectful or abusive carers, or by criminal offenders (Brammer, 2010: Chapters 9 and 17). But we cannot eliminate all negative risks, and we should not seek to eliminate positive risks.

8.2.2 When Should We Assess Risks – and How?

Agencies have policies to determine when risk assessments should be carried out which are conveyed to students during their induction, along with standard checklists of factors to consider in different types of risk assessments. It was clear from reading portfolios that students can gain just as much experience of risk assessments in initial as in final placements since they are now ubiquitous in social care (see Parsloe, 1999).

Risk assessments are undertaken whenever service users are in transition between institutional and community settings:

- Students based in day centres did a risk assessment whenever they arranged for a group of service users to have an outing in the community. They had to address questions such as: Is the mode of transportation safe? Is the museum or restaurant accessible to disabled people? Which service users are most vulnerable in terms of mental health or memory impairments which might result in them wandering off alone? Who among the staff escorting the group is trained in first aid?
- Students based in hostels for homeless people did a risk assessment whenever anyone asked for shelter. A person could be refused admission if they were deemed to pose too many risks to others on account of a history of violent offences or dependency upon illegal drugs.
- Students based in fieldwork settings were expected to incorporate risk assessments into routine child care and community care assessments. For example, if an elderly person is being discharged from hospital and returned to their own home, students have to address questions around risks relating to the person (e.g. is he or she capable of self-care or liable to self-neglect?), risks relating to the person–household interface (e.g. accidental falls due to mobility problems, or accidental fires due to memory impairments) and risks relating to the person–community interface (e.g. if the local shops are not accessible, then how is the service user going to replenish their food supplies?). All these factors have to be taken into account when developing a community care package.

Risk assessments are most highly developed in statutory teams dealing with child protection, adult protection, mental health and criminal justice. There is an important distinction between qualitative and quantitative methods of risk assessment (see Cree and Wallace, 2009):

- Qualitative methods of risk assessment are called professional or clinical methods. Here, the social worker's claim to have made an accurate and adequate assessment of risks is based upon their professional expertise in dealing with specific kinds of service users or situations, an expertise which they have brought to bear upon interviewing and observing the service user, reflecting upon the case history and the current situation etc.
- Quantitative methods of risk assessment are called statistical or actuarial methods. Here, the agency has a standard risk assessment schedule with a list of risk factors; the social worker allocates a numerical score to every item and adds them up; the total score is taken to be the measure of risk. The risk factors have been developed from research evidence in respect of relevant issues (e.g. perpetrator and victim profiles in domestic violence cases).

These methods should be combined in practice. However experienced we are as practitioners, we may still harbour subjective biases, and we should update ourselves on research evidence. However sophisticated risk assessment schedules may be, it still takes professional expertise to administer them and analyse the results. Table 8B show how these methods are combined in youth justice; further information is available in Dugmore et al. (2006) and Stephenson et al. (2007). In youth justice settings, students regularly undertake solo risk assessments, unlike in child protection, adult protection or mental health where they are typically co-working 'risky cases'.

8.2.3 Risk Management in Agencies

Initial placements are often in day care or residential establishments, and when these establishments cater for groups of people with challenging behaviour – notably adolescents and learning disabled adults – staff, students and other service users can be subject to verbal abuse as well as physical and occasionally sexual assaults (Brown et al., 1986; Oser, 2000; Kendrick, 2008).

Students in these settings were surprised to find themselves trapped in lone working situations, given that there are always other staff on duty. For example, a service user at a day centre made an innocuous request to make a private phone call in the staff office, but as soon as he was alone in the office with the student, he exploited the situation to vent his anger at the student about injustices in his life situation, and it transpired that there was

TABLE 8B *Risk Assessments in Youth Justice*

Youth Offending Teams use Asset to estimate the risk of reoffending and this informs their reports to the Youth Court. An Asset risk assessment involves interviewing young offenders and their relatives in order to gather information on 12 items:

1 The household (including housing itself)
2 Relationships in the family (which can include the extended family)
3 Education (and employment in the case of over-16s)
4 Neighbourhood
5 Lifestyle
6 Substance use
7 Physical health
8 Mental health
9 Perceptions of self and others
10 Patterns of thought and behaviour
11 Attitudes towards the offence
12 Motivations to change

Each item is given a score between 0 and 4 where 0 = no risk and 4 = high risk of reoffending. The higher the score, the higher the probability of reoffending, and magistrates impose more severe disposals on young offenders with high scores.

Asset is based upon statistical or actuarial methods of risk assessment insofar as most items have been derived from wider population studies which demonstrate that there is a positive correlation between poor housing/health/education, etc. and crime. But correlations are not causal relations and many of these factors are prevalent in the wider population of non-offenders so their predictive capacity is limited (Webster et al., 2006).

So the professional or clinical methods incorporated within it offer an important counterbalance, i.e. the items pertaining to the psychology of an individual offender. By combining methods, Asset has achieved a good success rate of around 75 per cent but this still means that in 25 per cent of cases the prediction is wrong (Whyte, 2004).

Youth justice workers had access to an additional checklist developed by experts in the field who treat the following factors as 'alarm bells', i.e. their co-existence in an individual indicates a very high risk of reoffending, likely to result in very serious harm to others:

- indifference to victims
- denial of the offence
- obsessive fantasies about hurting people or creatures
- compulsive quality of violent behaviours
- planned and premeditated attacks
- pathological hostility towards certain kinds of people
- regular use and misuse of legal and illegal substances.

no phone call to be made. Students are more susceptible to such situations than staff since their commitment to befriending service users outweighs their appreciation of other factors – such as the underlying volatility of service users' moods, the dynamics of transference and their own vulnerability as novices to boundary-breaking incidents.

It is precisely in establishments where there is continuous close proximity between staff and service users that boundaries need to be maintained.

Recommendations made by some of the earliest researchers and trainers in this area remain valid to this day (see Brown et al., 1986):

- Boundaries – you need a strong sense of yourself, and your role and responsibilities in safeguarding everyone including yourself. Maintaining some physical distance between yourself and service users will strengthen your boundaries and heighten your mindfulness of dynamics in the wider territory, so that if a threatening incident looms you are more likely to anticipate it, and your scope for reflection and action have not been compromised. But it is not always possible or even desirable to refrain from physical contact with service users. Practice wisdom is a balancing act between being able to engage in physical contact if required without losing our mindfulness of self–other boundaries and wider group dynamics.
- Understanding – alongside a general understanding of states of arousal – which can often be decoded before they spill over into aggression – you need to understand the triggers for each service user and the dynamics in the wider group of staff and service users.
- Early intervention skills – many critical incidents can be prevented by early intervention. Heightened states of arousal can be dealt with directly (e.g. counselling a distressed person), defused (e.g. using humour to dissolve tensions) or diverted (e.g. channelling the energy of arousal into other physical activities).
- Crisis intervention strategies – crises can be de-escalated by engineering timeout for the service users involved, or dealt with more directly by issuing a firm warning to an aggressive individual or calling upon others for assistance. Physical restraint is the last resort and only used to prevent people from harming themselves or others.

Our capacity to deal with crises also depends upon our relationships with service users. This is clear from a student's account of a critical incident between two young people in a residential home:

> P: I found [him] threatening his victim with a knife … [I was] truly frightened … I explained the seriousness of his actions and [said] that he should just lower the knife onto the counter and we would discuss the issues but until then I would be unable to help him further. I also explained that if he did not it would very much be put out of my hands and the issue would go to the police. After this he put the knife onto the counter and walked away … [It is so important] to be aware of the histories of service users and to build relationships on honest foundations so in moments of crisis they believe and trust what I say.

Risk management is most highly developed in secure units for young people who have a history of self-harm, absconding or committing criminal offences. Students in these units had to undertake two types of risk assessment at the point of admission. The person-based risk assessment involved taking a case history, summarising all incidents where the young person had put themselves or othes at risk of harm, and drawing up an individual vulnerability, risk and protection plan. This plan was reviewed on a monthly basis. The property-based risk assessment involved removing all property items which could potentially harm self or others, i.e. a razor blade or penknife can cut, a tie or belt can strangulate, an aerosol can be used for self-intoxication. The bedrooms were inspected regularly to search for such items.

The premises inhabited by fieldwork teams are not associated with high levels of risk, but staff have access to alarms when interviewing service users on the premises which may be carried on their person or located under their table or chair. Exercise 8B provides an example of a risky situation facing a student on his final placement when he was on duty in the agency.

Exercise 8B   A Risky Situation – But Risky for Whom and Why?

The following incident took place in an agency where a mature male student was on duty.

A service user arrived at the agency under the influence of alcohol. He was in distress and complained of terrible pain in one of his legs, which was swollen to double the size of the other leg. He was also verbally aggressive, shouting and swearing and hurling racist insults at the student who was from a minority ethnic background. The student tried to persuade the service user to seek medical assistance, but the service user was more concerned with continuing his journey to the social security office.

All professional parties involved reacted differently:

- The manager intervened by threatening to have the service user evicted from the premises and calling out a security guard, but the service user became more agitated and aggressive and the security guard did nothing.
- The student responded by stating that it was more important to seek medical assistance and he proceeded to telephone the service user's doctor.
- The doctor refused to intervene at all on the grounds that the patient was always having crises which subsided of their own accord, adding that he was a chronic alcoholic who brought such troubles upon himself.
- The student called out an ambulance himself; the paramedics transported the service user to hospital; the service user thanked the student on his way out.

Our responses to risky situations are shaped by our knowledge, skills and values. The student was commended for his response when the agency later undertook a critical incident analysis. He had experience of working with this

(Continued)

(Continued)

service user group and correctly judged that the man could be suffering from a deep vein thrombosis in the leg which, if not treated, could result in permanent disability (if the leg had to be amputated) or death (if it travelled to the lungs). He knew that the pain was so acute that the man would not be able to translate his verbal aggression into physical aggression, and consequently he did not feel under physical threat. He rose above the racist insults – they were irrelevant to his main task to secure medical assistance for the service user, and he regarded them as a by-product of the service user's distress. He remained calm and took charge of the situation, and by the time the ambulance arrived, even the service user thanked him.

Professionals do not always respond in the best way to risky situations since 'gut reactions' can take over. Identify the gut reactions of other players in this situation. In what ways did they reveal inadequate or inappropriate knowledge, skills or values?

8.2.4 Risk Management in Communities

Social workers in statutory teams are more vulnerable when visiting clients in the community, particularly clients in the spheres of child protection, mental health and criminal justice. It is vital to adhere to agency policies around co-working and carrying a mobile phone (which may have a pre-programmed 'distress code' to alert office-based managers if serious troubles are on the horizon).

The dangers of failing to adhere to agency policies were vividly illustrated by a student in a child protection team who was undertaking a joint visit with a social worker from another local authority to a family which had moved into the area covered by the student's agency. The children were subject to child protection plans and the father had a history of aggression towards professionals and owned dogs from dangerous breeds. The social worker reassured the student that agency policies would be followed in order to ensure their safety; these policies included having a police escort whenever visiting a client known to be violent towards staff and notifying clients with aggressive animals that they had to be tied up in an outhouse before visits. On her arrival outside the household, the student discovered that these measures had not been taken. Why not? The social worker said that she had been too busy with other cases to write letters to the family or liaise with the police; she added that a police escort might further antagonise the father. So what happened? The father became angry and ripped up the report on child protection concerns, and the dogs became agitated, prowling and snarling around these unwelcome guests. So the social worker and student made a rapid exit, having compromised their own safety without having secured a positive outcome for the children.

But the risks to vulnerable service users in the community are far greater than the risks to staff. Whenever we feel at risk in a family, it is probable that the vulnerable members of this family are living with far greater risks on a day-to-day basis, as testified by inquiry reports (Reder et al., 1993; Manthorpe and Stanley, 2004). The most important characteristic of risks in respect of service users is that they are cumulative in the sense that they spiral upwards in the absence of significant change, and that they can continue to spiral upwards in spite of professional intervention if this is not accompanied by a level of skills and/or resources which is commensurate with the level of needs. A child who has been neglected or abused within their birth family is more vulnerable to abuse in the wider community. The risks to such a child increase in the absence of professional intervention, but they can also spiral in spite of professional intervention. Why is this? Family support work may not suffice to bring about secure attachments in birth families, and substitute care placements may break down so that trauma accumulates; these young people are then at a much higher risk of homelessness and mental ill health in adulthood (Broad, 1998). The motto is: whenever there is clear evidence of problems in the present, the earlier the intervention, the better the prospects for successful outcomes. This motto applies equally to adults suffering from domestic violence, substance dependency, abuse or neglect from carers, self-harm or self-neglect. Table 8C illustrates the spiral of risks which can occur in respect of substance-dependent adults.

The most high-risk cases involve people who have been convicted of criminal offences against children and vulnerable adults and who are being supervised in the community as an alternative to custody or in the aftermath of a custodial sentence. These are dealt with under Multi-Agency Public Protection Arrangements (MAPPA). There are also Multi-Agency Risk Assessment Conferences (MARACs) which are convened in high-risk domestic violence cases with the aim of safeguarding victims as well as monitoring offenders (Harne and Radford, 2008).

8.3 Professional Competence

The Key Role of professional competence underpins all the other Key Roles insofar as students are expected to demonstrate professional competence in all Key Roles in their final placements. Ethical and evidence-based

TABLE 8C   *Cumulative Risks and Losses in Substance-dependent Careers*

Students working in the field of drug and alcohol services provided case examples of the cumulative nature of risks in the lives of service users at different stages of their substance-dependent 'careers'. You should note that loss features strongly in these narratives and is also cumulative in nature.

Stage 1: Voluntary clients – some people start out as voluntary clients who approach drug and alcohol services with the support of a parent or partner who is concerned for their welfare. If the client is motivated to change, or can be counselled to enhance their motivation – which will include informing them of risks – then a programme of substance reduction can be commenced.

Stage 2: Involuntary clients – if a substance-dependent career continues, then the chances of becoming an involuntary client increase. Physical or mental ill health can result in hospitalisation and criminal convictions generate compulsory supervision or imprisonment, i.e. some drugs are illegal and a high intake of alcohol or drugs is expensive so income may be secured through illegal means. So there are spiralling risks to the client along with spiralling losses, such as the loss of health, job and home. There are also spiralling risks to significant others. Partners may be susceptible to the transmission of infections, particularly with intravenous drug use, and domestic violence against a partner or child is not uncommon. This can result in the break-up of the family unit, hence further loss. Multi-agency working is essential when children are at risk but students reported that referrals to child protection agencies could jeopardise their partnership working with the adults. So whose needs and problems should be prioritised by whom and why?

Stage 3: Vulnerable clients – ultimately, such clients can become extremely vulnerable. One student was working with a middle-aged man diagnosed with Korsakoff's psychosis which results from the excessive toxins and insufficient nutrients associated with prolonged alcohol dependency. He had long since been abandoned by his family and friends. He had a recurrent pattern of drinking until he suffered falls and head injuries, then being hospitalised, only to be discharged home and to repeat the pattern. His lifestyle posed risks to no one other than himself. Should he be allowed to continue to live his life as he chose? Or should he be classified as a vulnerable adult lacking the mental capacity for self-care and self-determination which could warrant intervention under the Mental Capacity Act 2005? (see Brammer, 2010: Chapter 16).

---

practice are the most essential features of this Key Role; they are the bedrock of both our own professional development and the development of our profession itself.

8.3.1 Evaluating Our Practice

Students are required to evaluate their practice and to involve their service users and carers in this. The university or agency will provide a standard feedback form for service users and carers to complete, and a sample of forms is submitted as part of a student's portfolio. But feedback from service users and carers can be influenced by psychology, politics and practical tools. Older adults give more positive feedback than younger adults who harbour higher expectations or adolescents who are in a rebellious life stage, whilst people who are disabled and dependent upon professionals are often reluctant to voice concerns in case this adversely affects their care (Wilson, 1995). The majority of students become critical of such practical tools:

P: The forms give extremely good feedback. This does not give an accurate reflection of my practice abilities ... The service users ... have learning disabilities and were unable to complete the form without my help ... [so] they would give me positive results as I was filling in the form for them!

Critical reflections could in turn generate creative alternatives. Several students designed their own feedback forms tailored to the ages and abilities of their service users. Others came to suspect that the most authentic feedback could not be captured by any feedback form. A student who had been facilitating a young mothers' group reserved the final session for an evaluation of the group work and handed it over to the group itself. The young mothers decided to create a collective collage representing the group – and they depicted the student as an angel and an eagle, i.e. as a positive protective force, someone to watch over them, and someone to watch out for them. Another student had been undertaking group work with elderly people with memory impairments, and she was ecstatic when they thanked her personally, using her name, in the final session. Hitherto no one had used her name, and she had not known whether anyone even remembered her from session to session, and for her this final gesture made the entire placement worthwhile.

In statutory settings, we may need to deploy different criteria to evaluate our practice. A student in a Youth Offending Team was perturbed by the high recidivism rates among young offenders and by the harsh regimes in the secure estate, and questioned her practice teacher about the value of the team's work in terms of outcomes for young people. His reply helped her to reframe the issues: 'What is success? For some, success is about returning to the community and becoming a positive member of society. For others, it's a question of not ending up dead'. Surviving and thriving in social work is about balancing optimism and realism in relation to our aspirations and achievements, and being able to capitalise upon small breakthroughs.

You might like to ponder on what criteria you would use to evaluate social work in hospice settings where death is the inevitable outcome for patients?

8.3.2 Becoming Independent Professionals

During the final placement, you should be developing a sense of yourself as an independent professional who is capable of contributing to decision making in complex cases in an ethical and evidence-based manner *and* defending your judgements if they are contrary to the views of service users, carers or other professionals.

A student in a mental health team provided examples of her professional competence in relation to clients who had been detained on a compulsory basis in a secure psychiatric unit and who had applied for early release to the Mental Health Review Tribunal. In one case, she supported the release of a woman whose mental health problems had subsided and disputed the views of clinicians who wanted the woman to remain in hospital to receive treatment for her medical conditions. The student argued that medical and mental health matters were quite separate and showed that she could put together a viable community care package to address social and health care needs, and the Tribunal released the woman. In another case, she argued against the release of a man diagnosed with paranoid schizophrenia since there was no evidence of positive change. He had suffered a major relapse after a previous early release and had committed crimes of violence whilst under the influence of alcohol and illegal drugs which resulted in re-incarceration. The student had to defend her views under cross-examination from the client's lawyer, and the Tribunal rejected the application for an early release. The student explained her reasoning as follows:

> P: I was able to recognise that professional duties override the more basic values upheld by social work practice [in this case] ... My professional obligations require me to make recommendations which are in the 'best interests' of the service user ... [including] making judgements which relate to safeguarding the public and doing what is for the 'greater good'.

These examples show that critical reflection around ethics and politics is embedded within professional competence – this is so important that the next two chapters are devoted to it.

Points to Remember and Questions to Ponder

- Section 8.1 covered the Key Role around interventions. Can you remember why we should try to make interventions democratic, therapeutic and systemic?
- Section 8.2 gave examples of risk assessment and risk management. If you are on placement, you should ask yourself the following questions: Do I know the agency's policies and procedures around safety and risk? Am I confident enough to challenge a colleague who breaches the rules? What kinds of risks predominate in this agency and the community it serves? Do I have the requisite knowledge and skills to deal with these risks?
- Professional competence revolves around ethical and evidence-based practice and should have been demonstrated in relation to all the Key Roles by the end of the final placement.

Further Reading and Resources

There is a comprehensive guide to interventions in diverse contexts:
Shulman, L. (2005) *The Skills of Helping Individuals, Families, Groups and Communities*. Florence, KY: Wadsworth. (This has a companion CD Rom.)

You are advised to familiarise yourself with the entire gamut of social work journals so that you can locate articles on theory, research, law, policy and practice which are directly relevant to a specific service user or carer group, or a specific setting or method of intervention.

There is a critical overview of how we have come to frame and respond to risks in late modernity:
Webb, S. (2006) *Social Work in a Risk Society: Social and Political Perspectives*. Basingstoke: Palgrave-Macmillan.

The most recent Guidance for Employers and Guidance for Individuals on combating violence at work can be found on the Skills for Care website: www.skillsforcare.org.uk

Specialist texts on dealing with risks in relation to different service user groups include:
Beckett, C. (2007) *Child Protection: An Introduction*. London: Sage.
Cleaver, H., Nicholson, D., Tarr, S. and Cleaver, D. (2007) *Child Protection, Domestic Violence and Parental Substance Misuse: Family Experiences and Effective Practice*. London: Jessica Kingsley.
Geldard, K. (ed.) (2009) *Practical Interventions for Young People at Risk*. London: Sage.
Harne, L. and Radford, J. (2008) *Tackling Domestic Violence: Theories, Policies and Practice*. Maidenhead: Open University Press.
Peterson, T. and McBride, A. (eds) (2002) *Working with Substance Misusers: A Guide to Theory and Practice*. London: Routledge.
Pritchard, C. (2006) *Mental Health Social Work: Evidence-Based Practice*. Abingdon: Routledge.
Pritchard, J. (ed.) (2008) *Good Practice in Safeguarding Adults: Working Effectively in Adult Protection*. London: Jessica Kingsley.
Stephenson, M., Giller, H. and Brown, S. (2007) *Effective Practice in Youth Justice*. Collompton, Devon: Willan Publishing.

9

Ethics and Emotions: Developing Socio-emotional Intelligence

Introduction

This chapter will enable you to reflect more deeply upon the personal–professional–political interfaces in respect of ethics and emotions. Section 9.1 covers official codes of ethics governing social work in the UK, displaying their historical roots and disentangling their different dimensions. Section 9.2

explains the sources of value confusion and value conflict in social work, with guidelines to help students to navigate their way through value dilemmas. The role of emotions is considered in section 9.3. On the one hand, emotions play a positive role in the development of ethics and empathy, motivating us to act out of genuine concern for others. On the other hand, emotions can play a destructive role if we become excessively entangled with or estranged from our service users. Harnessing our emotions to ethical ends is at the heart of what is known as socio-emotional intelligence, and this is explored in the final section with further examples from students' casework.

9.1 Professional Ethics

Subscribing to a code of ethics is one of the hallmarks of a modern profession, although adherence to such codes cannot resolve all the ethical conundrums of practice (see Banks, 2004). Critical reflection on official codes and casework dilemmas is vital to developing professional competence both pre- and post-qualification.

9.1.1 Official Codes in Social Work

Social work ethics are subject to the same processes of construction and reconstruction as social work itself, and social work practitioners, educators and researchers can play an active role in this. From the late nineteenth century, religion and radical politics were the twin forces shaping professional ethics. Christians prioritised care in the casework relationship – our capacity to 'love' the stranger – whilst political radicals prioritised change in the wider society – our capacity to 'fight' for justice (Lynn, 1999). By the late twentieth century, new forces entered into the fray – consumerism reconfigured clients as consumers with choices and rights; service user and carer movements also emerged; and managerialism repositioned practitioners as guardians of the public purse who had to prove to government regulators that they were delivering 'value-for-money'. The attempt to accommodate all these diverse influences has given rise to what Sarah Banks (2006) dubs 'the new professionalism' in social work. So contemporary codes of ethics have been (re)constructed at the intersection of radically different principles, and although each has its own value and validity, combining them in practice is a complex business.

Students are expected to adhere to three sets of official codes in any placement, i.e. those of their regulatory body, their professional organisation and the agency under whose auspices they are operating. The Code of Practice for Social Care Workers issued by regulatory bodies in the UK was summarised in Chapter 1 (see Table 1C). As a code of conduct, it applies to concrete situations where we are expected to promote the rights of citizens and protect them from harm (GSCC, 2002a). The Code of Ethics published by the British Association of Social Workers is a more abstract account of the philosophical orientation of social workers in terms of their commitments to personal integrity, service to humanity and social justice (BASW, 2002). Both codes champion a humanistic ethic revolving around the intrinsic worth of every human being, and concur that professional competence is the necessary prerequisite for ethical conduct. Beyond this, they diverge in their emphases. The regulatory code was drawn up in consultation with service users and carers, and our regulators are always mindful of media criticisms of social work failings, so it highlights the need to earn the trust of service users and carers and uphold public confidence in the profession. The professional code was developed by practitioners and educators and shaped by their vocational ideals, so it places greater emphasis upon anti-oppressive practice in the name of social justice.

The principles in these official codes were translated into a set of values and ethics requirements and inserted into the National Occupational Standards for Social Work (TOPSS, 2002). Table 9A summarises these requirements. Practice teachers use them as a checklist for teaching and assessment purposes, and final reports by all parties must include reference to them.

TABLE 9A   *Values and Ethics Requirements for Social Work Students*

1	Develop awareness of your own values and prejudices, and reflect upon ethical dilemmas and conflicts of interest and their implications.
2	Respect each person as an individual and promote their independence whilst protecting them from harm.
3	Facilitate each person's chosen form of communication.
4	Value the diversity of individuals, families and groups, and respect their expertise in relation to their own situation.
5	Maintain the trust of service users, carers and communities.
6	Understand and make use of strategies to challenge discrimination and injustice.

9.1.2 Personal–Professional–Political Interfaces

Social work ethics harbours three distinct dimensions – the personal, the professional and the political – and professional conduct is carried out 'in the name of' an organisation which supplies a fourth dimension of professional ethics. Let us take a closer look at each of these dimensions:

- The 'personal' in social work ethics is allied to the tradition in moral philosophy called virtue ethics (McBeath and Webb, 2002). Here, the extent to which we are already 'a good person' or 'a good citizen' will determine the extent to which we can become 'a good social worker'. Virtues developed from prior life experience which need to be applied in our professional lives include honesty, integrity, empathy and compassion.

- The 'professional' in social work ethics draws upon the tradition in moral philosophy known as deontology, a term which translates as 'abiding by the logic of duty'. In social work, we have duties to adhere to the law, to safeguard people from harm and to practise competently. Duties are written into all official codes, Key Roles and agency policies.

- The 'political' in social work ethics pertains to our awareness of discrimination and oppression. It gives rise to commitments to alleviating the symptoms of injustice which are experienced by individuals and groups, challenging the sources of injustice and contributing to social change. It is informed by political rather than moral philosophy, which in turn is allied to critical social sciences and critical social movements.

- The organisational context of practice endows us with legitimate authority in discharging our roles and supplies the resources to assist citizens in need or at risk. But our organisations operate under constraints, both economic (shortfalls in resources) and political (regulation). At this point, the tradition in moral philosophy known as utilitarianism enters the scene since managers have to undertake a cost–benefit analysis of different services to make sure that resources are distributed in accordance with principles of utility – and this can include suspending services which are not cost-effective or restricting eligibility criteria to target scarce resources on those who are in the greatest need or at the greatest risk.

Becoming a critically reflective practitioner entails an examination of the hyphens which separate and connect these personal–professional–political–organisational interfaces. We must cultivate personal virtues in a manner which enhances professional practice, but to rely primarily upon the personal can be detrimental to professional practice, as the realm of the personal is vulnerable to biases stemming from our emotions and our biographies. Indeed, our integrity at work requires a separation of our personal and professional lives, as financial and sexual transactions between service users and social workers represent serious transgressions of professional codes (BASW, 2002; GSCC, 2002a). Likewise, the 'political' element of social work ethics does not give us a licence to use our profession or organisation for political ends – our professional duties are paramount when we are acting 'in the name of' our profession and our organisation. The organisational context of social work simultaneously facilitates and frustrates our political ideals. In other words, the ethic of serving citizens in need contributes to their social inclusion, but the utilitarian calculus of the organisation involves saying 'no' to some people, thus curtailing our ability to practise in anti-oppressive ways.

9.2 Decoding Social Work Values

Students and educators tend to talk about 'values' rather than ethics, which is unfortunate insofar as discourses around values are more ambiguous and therefore less amenable to analysis. But the task of analysis cannot be abandoned; it is only analysis which can cut a pathway through value confusion and shine a light on value conflicts.

9.2.1 Why Is There Value Confusion in Social Work?

Social workers are usually convinced that they are clear about their values, but confusion arises from the ways in which we talk and think about values. What are values? This is an abstract term with no concrete referent – we never 'see' a value as such. This does not mean that talk about values is meaningless – our language is replete with abstract terms – but rather that talk about values involves 'shifting signifiers' so that different people mean different things when they talk about values so they may be talking at cross-purposes. Value talk can involve circular or tautological reasoning insofar as anything we value can count as a value. In practice, values have to be 'read off' from other phenomena such as lifestyles (e.g. travelling families value freedom), beliefs (e.g. religious people value sacred scriptures and places of worship) or norms (i.e. rules or customs governing conduct – when we follow agency procedures around risk management, we show that we value things like safety and accountability). The result is that when social workers talk about 'values', they may be talking about lifestyles, beliefs or norms as well as (or even instead of) the values embedded within any given lifestyle, belief system or set of norms. They may also mean a variety of other things – bereavement counsellors will tell you that they value counselling skills, and staff working with women survivors of domestic violence will tell you that they value feminist theory. It is not surprising that commentators such as Chris Clarke (2000) have been critical of value talk in social work. But is it just a linguistic or conceptual confusion? Or does it spring from – or give rise to – a more substantive value confusion?

Practice educators were adamant that students' values were at the heart of practice wisdom. But what did they mean by students' values? Different practice teachers meant different things:

- The most common meaning was conveyed by the phrase 'the student's heart should be in the right place'. Here, the term 'values' pertains to personal virtues around compassion.
- For some practice teachers, the commitment to anti-oppressive practice was proof of having the right values. Here, the term 'values' is synonymous with the political element of ethics.

- For others, the capacity to become evidence-based practitioners was most vital to values. Here, the term 'values' includes skills in analysing information to assist decision making.

Students understood social work values in terms of humanistic ethics and anti-oppressive practice, but their capacity to be critically reflective upon these matters could be compromised by their claims that professional ethics were simply an extension of their personal ethics in everyday life to which they had already pledged their allegiance long before they signed up to any official codes. The result was that students from a wide variety of personal and political backgrounds concurred upon the importance of the 'same' social work values without appreciating that their understanding of these values could actually be very different, since values are influenced by our biographies, our politics and our world views. All students championed humanistic ethics, whether they were atheists, Christians, Buddhists or pagans. But people of different religions and no religion can have a very different vision of humanity and its place in the wider cosmos. In a similar vein, students committed to anti-oppressive practice included socialists, liberals, eco-activists and apolitical students with no interest in politics at all. But these political and apolitical standpoints can give rise to different understandings of the nature of oppression and anti-oppressive practice.

The vagueness of social work values has a certain virtue insofar as it allows everyone to sign up to them in spite of very different backgrounds, biographies and beliefs (cf. Clarke, 2000; Banks, 2006). But this cannot entirely compensate for the vices – we are left with the question of how to define and analyse our values with greater precision in order to adjudicate between competing values? Exercise 9A provides some guidance on dealing with value dilemmas in practice.

Exercise 9A   Navigating Your Way Through Value Dilemmas

When facing conflicting values in practice, ask yourself the following questions:

1 Is this a genuine conflict between your professional values?

Several students came to realise that what initially appeared to be professional value conflicts were more accurately described as conflicts between professional values and personal or political beliefs. An anarchist was uncomfortable in court settings where he had to 'bow' to the symbol of the Crown as his political beliefs set him against the monarchy, but his professional role was to

(Continued)

(Continued)

give evidence in court which included following the customs of the court, and he did believe in law and democracy. Your professional role and the values embedded within it should 'trump' your personal and political beliefs.

2 If there is a genuine conflict, which values are most appropriate in this case or context?

Students based in the secure estate experienced conflicts between professional values which are paramount in other settings (e.g. privacy, choice) and professional norms which governed interactions between staff and inmates (e.g. searches of persons and property, lock-ups at night). Such rules stem from the professional role of safeguarding ourselves and others from harm, which is itself an important social work value. Different norms and values are prioritised in different settings, suggesting that norms and values are relative rather than absolute, and the value of safeguarding people from harm usually 'trumps' other professional values.

3 If there is conflict between the values of a service user and the values of a social worker, whose values should be accorded priority?

The values and views of service users and carers should be respected even if they conflict with our own values and views, *unless* there is a duty to protect people under the law. One student valued housing, viewing it as a gateway to independence, but a homeless man sabotaged three housing arrangements which she had set up for him. The student was in despair; she felt she could not carry on working with him. Her practice teacher asked her to ponder on the questions 'Does this man share your values?' and 'If not, do you value his values?' The student had a moment of enlightenment – she realised that she had been imposing her own values upon a person with different values. He did not want the responsibility of being a householder; he preferred camping out but valued having access to a drop-in centre for meals and showers; this was his chosen lifestyle and his way of being independent. Liberated from the constraints of her own value system, she was able to work successfully with the service user on his own terms by respecting his values.

9.2.2 Why Are There Value Conflicts in Social Work?

There is a perpetual possibility for value conflict in social work since, as Richard Hugman (1998) points out, the profession is positioned at the intersection of three distinct territories – those of social care, social control and social change – and the agendas and activities associated with these territories often appear to be in conflict.

First, social care is about the provision of support and services to people who are vulnerable. It always involves humanistic ethics insofar as every human being is regarded as worthy of such care. It often involves a communitarian ethic insofar as social workers also support the development of networks in communities. It can involve a paternalistic ethic in cases where service users lack the capacity to look after themselves, to manage their finances or property, or to make decisions about their welfare, and in cases where they are vulnerable to neglect, abuse or exploitation by others. When social workers take charge of a situation by applying for court orders on behalf of a service user and sometimes against the wishes of relatives, social care starts to shade off into social control.

Second, social control revolves around safeguarding people from themselves or others. Whilst most citizens positively appreciate social care input, many resent social control interventions. Or rather, social control interventions can involve intractable conflicts of interest. Adults who are hospitalised on a compulsory basis under mental health legislation often object to the deprivation of their liberty, although their informal carers may express relief. Young people committed to a secure unit by a criminal court also complain about incarceration, but their victims may be satisfied that justice has been done. Sometimes social workers advocate for a person to safeguard their liberty, but sometimes they agree that only the deprivation of liberty will safeguard a person or even the public. These interventions pose dilemmas for social work ethics and politics since many of the secure institutions where people are placed may not be particularly humanistic let alone therapeutic, and since many of the people who are placed in such institutions have a history of personal abuse (e.g. domestic violence) or social injustice (e.g. stemming from poverty, disability or ethnicity). In other words, the social control agenda is often at odds with the agendas for social care and social change.

Third, social change entails challenging the sources of injustice and contributing to the empowerment of individuals and groups who have suffered injustices. This is a never-ending struggle for social workers. It is not just that the dimensions of injustice are ever-spiralling and the roots of injustices run deep (see Chapter 10). It is also that operating effectively in social care and social control territories is the priority of social care organisations and absorbs most of the energies of grassroots social workers, so the social change agenda can easily suffer an eclipse.

How can we resolve these tensions? We need to be explicitly embedding social care within our social control interventions and embedding social change within our social care and social control functions. How can we do this? Social change can be embedded within social care and social control territories, both by individual practitioners and by their agencies. One of the distinctive roles of social workers is to provide advocacy for service users and carers, and this gives them the leverage to practise in an anti-oppressive manner even when their main task is to fulfil social care or social control functions (Adams, 2008). One of the distinctive features of social work agencies is their commitment to involving service users and carers in the development of policy and practice, and this allows for a social change agenda to grow from within the womb of organisations with a social care or social control remit (Dominelli, 2004). Table 9B illustrates a Charter of Rights developed by disabled service users for a statutory agency.

TABLE 9B   *A Charter of Rights*

A student based in a community care team which specialised in providing services to adults with physical disabilities was asked to adhere to the following Charter of Rights developed by service users:

✓ Freedom of lifestyle and self-expression
✓ Protection of our person and our property from harm
✓ Participation in assessments, reviews and the care planning process
✓ Respect for our individual choices and our community cultures
✓ Exercise of choice and control in our lives, even if this entails some risks
✓ Access to accommodation, education, employment, recreation and transport
✓ Availability of an independent advocate if we need to make a complaint
✓ Rights to say 'no' to services we don't want as well as 'yes' to those we do want

The local authority had invited service users to tell staff about their needs, views and values, and then incorporated the resulting Charter of Rights into agency policies, so that it had to be included in all staff induction and training. Staff took a positive pride in the fact that they had consulted service users, and in the robust response of service users, and in their own ability to meet the challenge issued by their service users. Their reward was that their reputation in the local community was enhanced. Partnership working with service users can spawn important socio-cultural changes in a win–win situation.

A vivid example of embedding social care within social control was provided by a student based in a child protection team. At the beginning of her placement, she was shocked by the prevalence of 'cold calling' – i.e. staff made unannounced visits to families rather than arranging appointments in advance – and she construed this as oppressive practice. During the first half of the placement, she came to appreciate that cold calling was often necessary in child protection cases in order to discover the truth about the child's welfare and the family's situation. From her own cases and conversations with colleagues, she realised that some parents decide not to be at home if they know when a social worker is visiting, and some put on a 'false front' for the duration of a pre-arranged visit. During the second half of the placement, she resolved the care–control dilemma by reframing the social control agenda in the light of her genuine care for all family members, and she infused the detective role with a befriending ethos. In one case where she had a high level of concern around child neglect, most of her visits were cold calls, but she converted them into 'warm calls'. One week, she would pop round saying that she was in the neighbourhood and decided to make a quick visit to see if everything was okay. The next week, she would visit laden with toys for the children which she had secured from a local charity. A fortnight later, she would turn up with review forms so that she could review the child protection plan with the chief carer. By the end of the placement, she had acquired the art of anti-oppressive child protection practice.

9.3 Emotions at Work

Increasing recognition has been accorded to the role of emotions in the caring professions, their organisations and the welfare state itself (Hoggett, 2000; Fineman, 2005). Unfortunately, there has been a paucity of research into the role of emotions in practice learning, resulting in a lack of guidance for social work students (Barlow and Hall, 2007; Reupert, 2009). Case examples from students will help to redress this lacuna, but first we need to understand how emotions work.

9.3.1 The Roots of Empathy

Practice teachers and students were acutely aware of the umbilical cord between ethics and emotions, along with the vital role of empathy in practice settings. But they believed that such things were beyond the reach of professional training programmes, a verdict also reached by some experts in this area (e.g. Davis, 2002). How can we explain this? Our ethical and emotional lives develop hand-in-hand during primary socialisation and are mediated by attachments to significant others (Howe, 1995; Goleman, 1996; Killen and Smetana, 2006; Bilson, 2007). Our sense of what is 'right' and 'wrong' is closely bound up with our psychology and physiology, i.e. when witnessing harm perpetrated upon others we feel distress, and when injustices are remedied our body–mind relaxes. This mirroring between self and others whereby we can experience the joys and sorrows of another is at the heart of empathy, but the development of empathy – along with emotions and ethics more generally – can be disturbed by adverse conditions in childhood such as neglect, abuse or loss of a primary care-giver. What happens under these conditions? Some children switch off their emotions and cease to experience empathy. Others become hyper-aware of their own and others' emotions but go into an emotional overdrive as they are unable to regulate and relax their body–mind in the absence of a safe and secure parent; their compassion runs deep but it is not matched by competence in staying calm or helping others. Occasionally, a reversal of empathy sets in – a child may gain gratification from hurting others if he or she comes to identify with an abusive adult.

Emotions are a double-edged sword since they move us into action within a split second – indeed, motion is built into the term 'emotion' itself. Emotions activate the limbic system of the brain, which stores memories of emotion-laden events in our biographies, and this in turn activates all the physiological responses required for action, including fight or flight in stressful situations. Emotions can be our best friend if they inform us accurately about signals in the environment, enabling us to protect ourselves or someone else in an emergency. They can be our worst enemy if they misinform us of signals in the environment and give rise to inappropriate overreactions, which is particularly common among those whose biographies include unresolved trauma. Unless there is a genuine emergency, we should harness our emotions to reason by consciously reflecting upon the internal state of our body–mind and analysing the information from the environment prior to taking action. In other words, ethical conduct develops when emotions are harnessed to reason, not when emotions overrule reason, nor when emotions are ruled out of play (see Goleman, 1996).

Professional education refines the raw socio-emotional materials which adult learners bring with them; it cannot supply those raw materials from scratch in a person devoid of empathy or ethics; it cannot eradicate traumas or overreactions in people with stress-laden biographies. Of course, adults can re-educate their own body–mind if they commit themselves to this endeavour under favourable conditions, but this is the responsibility of the student, and beyond the remit of higher education. Recruitment of social work students is designed to select those with ingrained empathy and ethics, and students do exhibit a high level of empathy in respect of disenfranchised citizens at the start of their training. But during placements, they may suffer an excess of empathy resulting in self–other entanglements or a depletion of empathy to the point of self–other estrangement, and this is where professional education comes into play, as they need guidance on how to equilibrate their emotions.

9.3.2 Self–Other Entanglements

Many students over-identify with their clients and their casework, particularly in initial placements, so that their professional lives overspill into their personal lives. Some described this as a 'roller coaster of emotion' as they would experience a sense of elation when a client made a major breakthrough (which was enhanced by personal pride if the student's intervention had been the catalyst for change) and a sense of despair when a client suffered a setback (which was compounded by personal guilt if the student had been on leave and therefore not available to deal with the client's crisis). But is this simply empathy at work? Paradoxically, an over-investment in our clients can be symptomatic of an over-investment in our own egos, and genuine empathy should transcend the ego (cf. Heron, 1992; Brazier, 1995).

Most students came to appreciate the necessity of separating out the personal from the professional. The following student was working in a day centre for elderly people:

> P: I find it heartbreaking to think that when I drop certain service users back home at the end of the day ... they will not be speaking to anybody else until the next time they go to the day centre ... When I am at home I have been wondering if they are coping okay and if they are safe and warm? ... I need to learn to leave work at work otherwise it will start to interfere with my personal life and it is important to keep my professional and personal life separate otherwise it would send me crazy!

There are two sets of circumstances under which an excess of empathy can be dangerous for professional practice. Under these circumstances, an unhealthy entanglement develops between the student and the service user, mediated by the processes of transference and counter-transference (Grant and Crowley, 2002). In the first set of circumstances, the student is deploying empathy in order to befriend a service user who is isolated or depressed, but the service user interprets these attitudes and actions in the light of their own hopes and needs for intimacy, and comes to regard the student as a personal friend, a surrogate parent or a potential partner. This is a classic case of transference whereby service users with attachment histories characterised by deprivation project their own feelings and needs onto a professional who demonstrates genuine empathy for them. Students in day centre settings were most vulnerable to this form of transference, and could be deeply shocked when a service user whom they had befriended turned up at the day centre offering them gifts, hugs and kisses, and even in one case a marriage proposal. When students refused such offerings and clarified the boundaries around the professional relationship, some service users turned against them by ignoring, complaining or gossiping about them. This left students feeling more confused, and sometimes quite vulnerable themselves. But these service users were simply trying to cope with their sense of rejection; switching off from the person who has spurned us is a classic defence against the pain of rejection. Wise practitioners are clear about boundaries at the outset and avoid relating to one person in a group at the expense of others.

The second set of circumstances is when students over-identify with the plight of a service user and plunge themselves with great zeal into the advocacy role without pondering on the whole situation in terms of the different parties or perspectives involved. Dynamics of counter-transference are at work here since students' own feelings or needs are playing an active role in shaping the course of events. Exercise 9B provides an example – it is a more atypical example but it has pedagogic merit. Timeout for critical reflection and consultation is essential to combat counter-transference. The question is whether we will appreciate the value of such timeout? It is not just that strong emotions may give rise to swift action before we have had time to reflect. It is also that strong emotions impact upon the processes of reflection, perception and evidence-gathering so that we may only 'see' those things which are in accordance with our feelings and beliefs. Sometimes it is precisely when we experience 'absolute' convictions that we are most in need of a practice-wise outsider.

Exercise 9B   Entanglement at Work

A student based in a community centre for women became very involved with a service user whose baby daughter had been removed by social services after suffering a subdural haemorrhage which left her permanently brain-damaged. The injury occurred in the middle of the night when the father had tried to stop the baby crying. He claimed that he tripped and fell whilst holding the baby, and his partner believed that it was an accident, although she acknowledged that he had suffered a 'personality change' subsequent to the birth of their daughter. Doctors, social workers and police officers suspected that this was a case of Shaken Baby Syndrome.

The student identified with the woman at the outset:

> P: I really felt for this woman ... She cried uncontrollably and my heart ached for her. I am a mother and I could not imagine what it would be like to have your baby ripped away from you. I wanted to sob for her ... That night I could not stop thinking of this woman ... I remembered her sobbing like a small child and I felt coiled up inside.

The student decided to support the woman in mounting a challenge to social services. She researched misdiagnoses of Shaken Baby Syndrome and supplied a report to the civil court. Some of the paragraphs of this report were written in the first person 'as if' the student were the service user, indicating points of total self–other identification. The student attended the court hearing and construed the evidence presented by other professionals as being oppressive to her client on the grounds that the mother was forced to hear evidence which conflicted with her beliefs and caused her more distress.

The outcome in this case was that the civil court granted a care order with a care plan of adoption, and the criminal court found the father guilty of causing non-accidental injury.

You should consider the following notes and queries:

What made the student and the mother so convinced of the innocence of the father?
How far was the student's advocacy strengthened or undermined by her emotions?
Evidence-based practice is vital in all casework and court work but it cannot resolve all disputes. Sometimes there is not enough evidence – in these cases, we tend to 'fill in the gaps' with our own beliefs or preferences. But even if there is plenty of evidence, our personal, professional and political standpoints can still dictate how far we listen to it.
Our standpoints are also affected by our role and the remit of our agency. The student was based in an agency supporting women. If she had been based in the local authority's child protection team, how would this have altered her attitudes and actions?

9.3.3 Self–Other Estrangement

Students could feel estranged from service users and carers who did not share their emotions, empathy or ethics. They made a distinction between people whose capacities were impaired on account of neurological disability (e.g. autism) or disease (e.g. dementia) and people who appeared to have chosen 'the bad life' of harming others (e.g. violent offenders). When dealing with the former, students' capacity for ethics and empathy flourished, but when dealing with the latter, their capacity for ethics and empathy floundered. The question is whether or to what extent this is a valid distinction? Some violent offenders do appear to have chosen 'the bad life', but others have suffered abuse which crushed their capacity for ethics and empathy at such an early age that whatever choices they made were severely constrained, and recent research demonstrates that such early experiences can reconfigure our neurological networks (Goleman, 2007).

Estrangement is the mirror image of entanglement since our emotions and reactions are reversed. One student described how she felt physically sick when interviewing a pregnant woman who was describing a high intake of drugs which would harm the foetus. Another student recoiled in horror when a white client justified his racially motivated attack on a black man. What can you do in these situations? You need to respect that your emotions are conveying important information, but then harness these emotions to ethical and evidence-based practice, since expressing them directly is likely to do more harm than good. The following is a classic example in statutory child care:

> S: I knew that my personal values and my professional values were going to come into conflict somewhere along the line … It was a very large family. Mum had had several boyfriends, there'd been lots of domestic violence, the children had witnessed it, but Mum wouldn't accept any responsibility for how it affected them … [My conflict] was about not being able to say 'Look, you silly sod, can't you see what you're doing to your children? … Why have so many children if you can't afford them? Why have you got three flipping big dogs and two cats and God knows what else when you can't even afford to buy your kids new shoes?!' Those were my personal values, things I really wanted to say but, you know, *couldn't*.

An extreme case of self–other estrangement occurred when students worked with prison inmates who had been convicted of the most serious crimes of violence, which is the subject of Exercise 9C.

Exercise 9C   Estrangement at Work

Students working in the community were asked to undertake group work with prisoners in pairs, in order to extend their own learning opportunities and to contribute to the prison programme of education and recreation. During their induction, prison officers warned them to avoid conversations about their own personal lives and about the inmates' offences since these were among the most 'dangerous' prisoners convicted of rape, murder and child abuse, and they could easily misuse such conversations.

Students were shocked at these warnings and struggled to reconcile this advice with their beliefs in honest communications and humanistic ethics. As a consequence, some were subject to distorted game-playing by the prisoners. One student found herself listening with empathy to a prisoner who claimed that he was innocent, until she believed him and wanted to release him. Another student responded honestly to a prisoner's questions about her family, only to find that he was a child sex offender with contacts in the paedophile world, after which she worried about the safety of her own offspring, and started to lie to protect her own family. During some group work with these prisoners, one pair of students had developed a game whereby each group had to create a story around certain items including a pair of socks and a watch:

> P: I went from one group to the next to see how they were getting on with their stories … One service user replied with 'Well, we thought we could use the pair of socks to strangle somebody and then use the watch to time how long it takes that person to die', then another service user … [said] 'Well, that's what some of us are in here for anyway'. I was

completely taken aback ... I didn't know how I could possibly respond to something like that ... I certainly didn't want to laugh and joke with them about it ... I walked away.

These students experienced an extreme form of estrangement at first hand, and you should ponder on the following notes and queries:

Is it accurate or appropriate to regard prisoners as service users?
What may have motivated the prisoners to respond in these ways to students?
Social work ethics should not be approached in an absolutist manner, as we may need to reconfigure our conduct as we move between settings and relate to different service user, carer and client groups. Do you agree with the advice issued by the prison officers in this context, or do you have reservations about it in the light of other values?

Social workers are likely to encounter at least one person during their career who appears to be lacking in some of the attributes we associate with positive humanity (see Hare, 1999). Sometimes the best we can do is to protect ourselves and others from being exploited by such a person. But we should not abandon our own humanity, or our efforts to redeem the humanity of the other which spring from our humanity. A student in a community care team was asked to develop a care plan for a man who was due to be released from prison after a life sentence. She objected strongly to this as she did not believe that he deserved social care services; the man had sexually abused his daughter throughout her childhood and, in the student's eyes, he had lost his right to be part of humanity. Her practice teacher took the risk of sending the student out to meet the prisoner in the hope that she might learn a valuable lesson. The student reported that she met a human being who was completely broken as a result of decades of incarceration. This was a man who had lost the skills to survive in the community: a man with no home, no job, no family, no friends, no money, no hobbies; someone who had lost any sense of himself as a member of the human species. The student set aside her prejudices and his past mis-demeanours and created a care package to give him another chance in life. She helped to restore his humanity and journeyed deeper into her own.

Finally, we should remember that although entanglement and estrange-ment are polar opposites, it is possible to shift from one to the other. A student befriended a mother when she declared that she would prioritise the welfare of her children over her partner who was a convicted child sex offender. He had been required to leave the household as part of a child protection plan which the student was monitoring. The student regarded her support as vital to the mother's survival as a single parent, as if she was filling in the gap left by the ex-partner. She was devastated to receive reports from the police and other sources to the effect that the ex-partner was returning to the household every weekend, and felt bitterly betrayed by the mother. Paradoxically, entanglement can set us up for estrangement.

9.4 Developing Socio-emotional Intelligence

Socio-emotional intelligence is at the heart of the social work relationship (Howe, 2008). Emotional intelligence revolves around *intra*personal capacities (i.e. how we are within ourselves), whilst social intelligence revolves around *inter*personal capacities (i.e. how we are with others), and empathy is the vital link between them. Figure 9A provides a map of social and emotional intelligence adapted from the work of Daniel Goleman (1996, 2007).

9.4.1 Cultivating Healthy Relationships

The art of developing healthy relationships hinges upon our capacity to understand and make use of the hyphen in self–other relations, i.e. the hyphen which connects and separates social workers and service users (Barnes et al., 1998; Reupert, 2009). If we have reflected upon our biographies, then we can use our life experiences to help service users without projecting our own baggage onto them, and if we can regulate our own emotions then we can help service users to deal with theirs. When we maintain a healthy connection and separation between self and others, we can make use of empathic attunement without assuming that the experiences of others are identical to our own, and we can cope more easily with the rupturing of empathy without feeling so estranged that our ethics are in jeopardy. Nevertheless, all of us harbour a 'shadow self' as a result of the store of subconscious experiences and emotions we have accumulated, which sets limits to self-awareness (Goleman, 1997; Egan, 2002). This is why supervision is so vital in the helping professions, i.e. it is only another person who can 'see' the parts of us that we have hidden even from ourselves.

Cultivating healthy relationships is more dilemmatic in social work than in other caring professions since social workers rely heavily upon relationship skills and usually work in open settings without artificial boundaries between staff and service users. This promotes the egalitarian ethos and empathic attunement which are highly valued by social workers and their

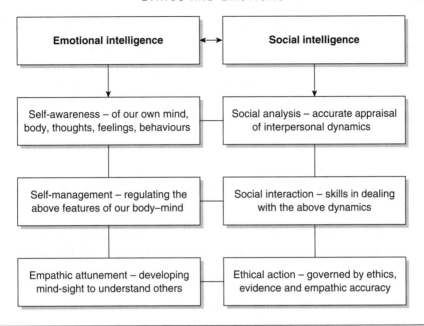

| Emotional intelligence | Social intelligence |

| Self-awareness – of our own mind, body, thoughts, feelings, behaviours | Social analysis – accurate appraisal of interpersonal dynamics |

| Self-management – regulating the above features of our body–mind | Social interaction – skills in dealing with the above dynamics |

| Empathic attunement – developing mind-sight to understand others | Ethical action – governed by ethics, evidence and empathic accuracy |

There are links between all aspects of emotional intelligence. The purpose of cultivating self-awareness is to enhance our self-management, and attuning to our own inner states should help us to attune to those of others.

There are links between all aspects of social intelligence. Accurate social analysis should translate into appropriate social interaction which includes ethical and evidence-based conduct.

There are links between emotional and social intelligence. Self-awareness can promote solitude and even selfishness in the absence of social awareness. Empathic attunement can be futile if it is not conjoined with social skills, and it can even be harmful if it is not harnessed to ethical ends.

FIGURE 9A   *A Map of Social and Emotional Intelligence*

service users, but it also lends itself to self–other entanglements. A counsellor has a consulting room which a client visits for a one-hour appointment; nurses and doctors in a hospital setting are clearly separated out from patients confined to beds; even community-based health visitors often wear uniforms and carry equipment acting as a symbol of their professional role. Social workers are indistinguishable from ordinary citizens; they take only themselves into the home territory of their community-based clients; and social care organisations such as day centres have few artificial props to separate staff and service users. Consequently there is a high risk of boundary blurring.

9.4.2 Constructing Safe Boundaries

One of the most important tasks facing students is to construct safe boundaries between themselves and their service users and carers in a manner which is appropriate to the setting. Some practice teachers asked their students to draw up a set of 'rules' to this end, and Exercise 9D will help you to ponder on these matters for yourself.

Exercise 9D   Constructing Your Own Personal–Professional Boundaries

A student based in a community care team working with disabled adults was asked by her practice teacher to draw up a set of 'rules' governing her relationships with service users. This is reproduced from her portfolio:

1 Reciprocation – I would expect service users to call me by my first name. I would not call them by their first name, unless they asked me to do so ... I would not allow a service user to come to my home ... I would never give my home address or phone number to a service user ...
2 Interview Culture – I would accept a cup of tea if it was offered ... I would never accept an alcoholic drink ... [or] a meal.
3 Self-disclosure – I would empathise with service users, but I would not make them aware of my personal feelings on their situation. I would only offer opinions and advice based on the organisation's policies and procedures ... I would not ... talk about my work with other service users ... due to issues of consent and confidentiality ... I would not divulge personal good news to service users ... [since they] may be in difficult circumstances and sharing good news might be seen as insensitive. I would not share bad news ... [since] this would take the focus from the service user's problems onto mine ...
4 Social Contact – I would not accept an invitation from a service user to go to an informal event. This is more an act of friendship and is not appropriate ... I want to keep my private life separate from my professional life ... I would never lend money to a service user.
5 Touch – I would be very inclined to touch a service user who was upset. However, I would be conscious that the contact was appropriate. I would touch them on the arm ... [but not] on the shoulders ... [or] the knees. I would never cuddle ... their children.

How might breaches of these rules adversely affect the student or her service users?

Are there circumstances in which a departure from any of these rules can be justified?

Which rules would have to be modified if the student moved to another setting (e.g. a residential care home) or worked with another service user group (e.g. children)?

You could draw up your own set of 'rules' – guidelines which you feel comfortable with – even if you have not yet started your placements. You can then adapt them over time as you move between placements and as your practice wisdom grows from within.

What factors influence the process of boundary construction? One set of factors stems from the student's own prior life and work experience. Mature students with prior social care careers were far more likely to enforce strong boundaries at the outset; the following extract is from a mature man who worked with groups of young people:

> S: I can't be a friend to all of them, and I try not to be a friend to any of them ... You can come up to the line but you must never cross it, *never*. I try not to be a father figure either ... Most of them have already got a father, or it might be a stepfather, but they've got one.

Another set of factors stems from your role in any given case which in turn is affected by the remit of the agency. Students in voluntary agencies were happy to disclose some of their own parenting lapses to parents who were struggling with child care in the service of promoting empathy, but those working in statutory child protection teams were wary of such self-disclosures in case this information was subsequently passed to the parents' solicitors and used against them in court.

Finally, students have to take account of the personal–professional interface which is unique to each student in relation to each setting. One student lived in the same community served by her agency and was acutely aware of the dilemmas this could pose for confidentiality if she met a service user or carer in everyday life and engaged in conversation in the presence of third parties, so she developed a rule to maintain boundaries which she explained to everyone at the outset:

> S: [On] an initial visit I say 'Look, if I see you out in public I will acknowledge you, I'll say hello, but that will be the end of it. That's because of confidentiality – if I'm with somebody, or you're with somebody, then I can't be talking about you to them'. That goes down quite well.

9.4.3 Dilemmas around Self-disclosures

The most common dilemma experienced by students is captured by the question: 'If I have relevant life experience here, will self-disclosure be helpful or harmful?' Unfortunately, self-disclosure is another double-edged sword in social work. On the one hand, a number of students found that significant breakthroughs occurred when they brought in aspects of their own life experience. For example, a student was working with an elderly couple who were in need of services as a result of chronic disabilities, but initially they rejected services as they were proud of their independence and could not countenance the idea of strangers coming into their home to help them with personal care or domestic chores. They only accepted a care package when the student disclosed that she had undergone a similar struggle to accept support in her own past and that the support she received had been the catalyst for positive change. On the other hand, self-disclosures can backfire on us. A young student told a child that she had suffered similar difficulties in her own childhood but that at the age of 19 she was confident that these had been overcome, thus demonstrating empathy with his plight and offering him hope for the future. But his mother was eavesdropping on this conversation and interjected with 'Are you only 19? How can you tell me how to parent my children?!' so the student felt that her credibility in the eyes of the parent had been undermined.

Social workers can draw upon life experience without making explicit self-disclosures to service users or carers, and it is possible to simply state that 'Yes, I do know about these things from my own life, but I'm not here to discuss my own life with you'. Nevertheless, there are situations where self-disclosures in relation to our biographies and emotions are entirely appropriate. For example, a hospice held a regular event where bereaved children gathered together to mourn the death of their parent. Staff and students were expected to participate in the rituals of the day which included discussing loved ones whom they had lost, along with praying, singing and lighting candles. Likewise, students who attend the funerals of clients have been moved to tears quite appropriately.

But self-disclosure starts long before we say or do anything at all. Our personal profiles around gender, age, disability and ethnicity have already conveyed information about us to service users and carers. There are ways of minimising the influence of personal profiles to ensure that they feature in the background rather than the foreground of our professional relationships. Practice teachers supervising young female students in the secure estate advised them to cultivate androgyny in their appearance in order to prevent unwanted sexual attention from male inmates. Students with invisible disabilities are in a similar position to lesbian and gay students insofar as they can usually stay in the safety of their respective closets – they disclosed their disability or sexuality to their supervisors, but not their service users. Black and overseas students cannot conceal ethnic markers of difference such as skin colour or foreign accent, and are compelled to make choices about how far to engage in self-disclosure when faced with explicit questioning about their country of origin by service users or carers (see Chapter 11: Exercise 11B). Likewise, a physically disabled student had no choice about disclosing her disability, and initially encountered discrimination from some service users and other professionals, but she increasingly integrated the fact of her disability into direct work with children (who were curious about her special equipment) and disabled adults (for whom she could represent a positive role model).

Points to Remember and Questions to Ponder

- Official codes were the subject of section 9.1. You should read these codes carefully – from the moment you step onto a social work programme, your personal as well as professional conduct can have implications for your progression. You should also ponder on your own personal–professional–political interfaces with the aim of identifying at least one potential 'trouble spot' which arises from your own biography or beliefs.
- Section 9.2 highlighted not only value dilemmas in social work, but also the dilemma caused by the ubiquity of value talk in social work. So the next time you read, hear, write or speak about 'values', you should ask: 'What is the meaning of this term in this context?'
- Section 9.3 warned against the twin dangers of entanglement and estrangement. How can you maintain emotional equilibrium so that you treat everyone in an equitable manner and keep an open mind which is so vital to evidence-based practice?
- The final section showed that the capacity to connect with others whilst also remaining separate from them is vital to the development of ethics and socio-emotional intelligence. Social workers have a responsibility to construct their own personal–professional boundaries in situations where there is a paucity of artificial boundaries. They also have to reflect upon their own profile around age, gender, disability and ethnicity, and consider how to minimise – or make use of – such aspects of selfhood in practice.

Further Reading and Resources

Your first port of call is to read the Code of Practice issued by your regulatory body as well as the Code of Ethics produced by the British Association of Social Workers (available on their websites). This will equip you to read critical and comparative accounts of professional ethics:

Banks, S. (2006) *Ethics and Values in Social Work*. Basingstoke: Palgrave-Macmillan.

Clarke, C. L. (2000) *Social Work Ethics: Politics, Principles and Practice*. Basingstoke: Palgrave-Macmillan.

You can also browse the journal *Ethics and Social Welfare*.

An excellent resource for pondering on the personal–professional interface is:

Barnes, E., Griffiths, P., Ord, J. and Wells, D. (1998) *Face to Face with Distress: The Professional Use of Self in Psychosocial Care*. Oxford: Butterworth-Heinemann.

The most accessible text on socio-emotional intelligence for students is by David Howe:

Howe, D. (2008) *The Emotionally Intelligent Social Worker*. Basingstoke: Palgrave-Macmillan.

10

Politics and Cultures: Developing Cross-cultural Sensitivity

Introduction

This chapter explores the social, political, economic and cultural contexts of social work. The first section sketches out the main types of inequality in terms of class, status and power; it is crucial that students understand these if they are to make sense of anti-oppressive practice. Section 10.2

examines the Personal–Cultural–Structural (PCS) model of anti-oppressive practice, showing that it has been subject to different interpretations within the social work community. Section 10.3 takes a closer look at the politics of social workers and their ambivalent relationship to power, and includes case studies of students challenging oppressive practice and mobilising power. Cross-cultural competence is now recognised as a necessary ingredient of anti-oppressive practice. Section 10.4 illustrates cross-cultural diversity in the UK and invites a re-orientation away from Anglocentric knowledge, skills and values. Section 10.5 indicates that ethnic diversity among students can be a valuable resource in this respect, although it can also pose dilemmas for pedagogy and practice.

10.1 The Nature of Inequality

Stratification in Britain and elsewhere is comprised of three types of inequality: class, status and power. These provide the material and cultural contexts in which service users and carers live their lives; they also furnish the background scenery for the entire welfare state apparatus (Powell, 2001).

First, class pertains to the economic aspects of inequality, notably disparities in income and wealth. Class-based inequalities are systematically generated and reproduced across generations and nations in the global capitalist economy. They revolve around exploitation since the majority of people work long hours for subsistence wages whilst lucrative profits accrue to a minority (Crompton, 2008). Wealth is concentrated within aristocratic and entrepreneurial elites and tied up in properties, businesses and investments; these families access private education and health care and their offspring inherit their capital. Income is more widely dispersed across a range of professional and occupational groups but the income ladder is so long that those on the higher rungs share in the privileges of the elite whilst those on the lower rungs are in relative poverty, currently defined in the UK in terms of income which is less than 60 per cent of the average household income (Palmer et al., 2008). Carers often suffer downward social mobility as a result of their caring role and its impact upon their employment prospects, and some will be plunged into poverty. There is also an underclass of people who are excluded from the economy, society or state altogether as a result of long-term unemployment, chronic disability or illegal migration (Morris, 1994). Poverty often places basic needs around health and housing in jeopardy and has a detrimental effect upon other life chances in education and employment, and it tends to be self-perpetuating in spite of measures to promote equal opportunity and social mobility (Alcock, 2006). Why is this? Relative poverty is rooted in the economic inequalities wrought by capitalism, and therefore will not be eradicated without its demise; but capitalism has been akin to a perverted human version of Lord Krishna's Juggernaut insofar as nothing appears to be able to overturn it (Giddens, 1990).

Second, status is concerned with the cultural aspects of inequality. Status differences are rooted in historical characterisations of different peoples who have been classified in accordance with their age, gender, skin colour, nationality, sexuality, disability and religion. Since they are not inevitable by-products of a capitalist economy, they are more amenable to social change in principle and they require different strategies to counteract them in practice (Humphrey, 2002). Status takes biological and cultural variations in the human species and superimposes value judgements upon them so that some differences are positively valued whilst others are negatively valued (Guillaumin, 1995). Under these conditions, diversity gives rise to discrimination, which includes discrimination in the economy, so that people who belong to a negatively valued status group are more likely to be confined to the lower classes (Alcock, 2006). Upward mobility in class terms may offset cultural subordination for some individuals but it cannot eliminate it, and upward mobility of the entire group can generate moral panics and persecution. For example, during the twentieth century, anti-semitism in Europe was fuelled by the educational and economic successes of the Jewish people who faced allegations that they were seeking to 'rule the world' prior to the Holocaust (Bauman, 1989).

Table 10A summarises the main dimensions of status-based discriminations. It may be helpful to conceptualise status-based discrimination as existing along a continuum of cultural oppression ranging from subordination to stigmatisation and ultimately persecution. All negatively valued status groups experience subordination but not all of them are subject to stigma where a sense of shame is attached to a social identity (Goffman, 1963). Women and children are subordinated across the globe but rarely stigmatised, presumably because both are essential to the survival of the species. Minority groups which deviate in some way from biological or cultural norms are stigmatised and this can give rise to outright persecution. Persecution also takes many forms – social ostracism, physical attacks, discriminatory legislation which results in incarceration or deportation, and even attempts to eliminate the group via eugenics policies. Such treatment is justified on the grounds that the minorities in question are 'unnatural', 'immoral', 'diseased' or 'undesirable'. Black people, Jews, disabled people and gay men are all acquainted with such treatment (cf. Bauman, 1989; Smith, 1994; Barton, 2001).

TABLE 10A   *Status-based Discriminations*

Disability	Disablism is the discrimination facing disabled people in housing, education, employment, transport, recreation and relationships. Disabled people have been subordinated, stigmatised and sometimes persecuted. They have often been shunned or institutionalised, and occasionally subject to eugenics policies in an attempt to 'purify' a nation of its 'defective citizens'. In the contemporary UK, they are more likely to be on the receiving end of pity and charity, but this can also contribute to their disempowerment (Barton, 2001).
Gender	Almost everyone is born into the male or female sex (other than hermaphrodites). Almost every culture has instituted gender inequalities beyond biological differences so that women occupy subordinate roles. Both sexes are necessary to the survival of the species and heterosexual men need/desire women, so that heterosexual women are not stigmatised as such (except during menstruation in some cultures). But transvestites and transgendered people who cross over the sex/gender divide are subject to stigma for their 'deviant choices' (Stryker and Whittle, 2007).
Sexuality	Heterosexuality is the statistical norm across the globe, and this is treated as synonymous with a moral norm by many states and religions, so that lesbian, gay and bisexual people are stigmatised even in 'liberal' countries and persecuted elsewhere (Lee Badgett and Frank, 2007). Heterosexism occurs when we see the world through heterosexual eyes and assume the normality or superiority of heterosexuality. Homophobia and lesbophobia refer to outright fear and loathing of gay men and lesbians respectively, and this can result in violent attacks.
Age	Age discrimination stems from 'adultism' – a term which means that power resides with adults – and results in the subordination of children and elderly people, even though they may be well looked after by relatives. Childhood and old age are natural phases of the life cycle, so that a subordinate status does not usually entail stigma. Indeed, children are highly valued for their youth in modern cultures, whilst elders are revered for their wisdom in many traditional cultures (Timonen, 2008). As a general rule, the more a culture values youth, the less it values old age and vice versa.
Ethnicity	Ethnic groups are distinctive on account of their culture. This usually entails a shared language, lifestyle and religion which derives from a shared history and country of origin and it often co-exists with biological markers such as skin colour. Racism revolves around a belief that people of 'other races' are biologically or culturally inferior to the indigenous people, but the entire concept of 'race' upon which it rests has been discredited (Laird, 2008). Ethnocentrism occurs when we take for granted the normality or superiority of our own cultural norms and values; Anglocentrism is a specific variant of this. Xenophobia refers to the fear and loathing of 'foreigners' in general; anti-Semitism is a specifically anti-Jewish ideology; and Islamophobia is a specifically anti-Muslim ideology.

Third, power is the political aspect of inequality. As a general rule, power accrues to the upper classes and positively valued status groups insofar as they can define the rules of the game in the state, economy and social institutions. Power is not as visible as class or status, and is therefore measured by its effects. At the macro-level of society, the question is: how far does the status quo serve the interests of a specific class or status group? At the micro-level of interpersonal relations, the question is: how far can an individual impose their will upon others so that they change their behaviours or beliefs in order to conform to the will of that individual? (Harrison and Dye, 2008). Institutional power takes the form of legitimate authority and is exercised by the government, the courts, the security forces, universities, workplaces and welfare agencies. Individual power is open to all – however powerless an adult may be in the political economy, he or she may wield considerable power over a partner, child or elderly parent. Power becomes 'hegemonic' when inequalities and the ideologies legitimating them are taken for granted as part of the natural order of things, so that we cease to challenge them (Roger, 1991). Class inequality, heterosexism and Anglocentrism are often naturalised in this way.

10.2 Anti-oppressive and Anti-discriminatory Practice

Anti-oppressive and anti-discriminatory practice are central to the political dimension of social work ethics. These terms are often used interchangeably, although it could be argued that anti-oppressive practice has more radical implications than anti-discriminatory practice given that liberal societies and states have already signed up to anti-discriminatory laws and policies. Social workers understand anti-oppressive practice in terms of the Personal–Cultural–Structural (PCS) model pioneered by Neil Thompson (1998) which depicts these three spheres as concentric circles. In the inner circle of the Personal sphere, we should be inspecting our own prejudices and counteracting discriminatory attitudes and actions in everyday life. In the outer circle of the Structural sphere, we need an understanding of the causes and consequences of economic exploitation and political oppression. The Cultural sphere is the link between them. This foregrounds status-based inequalities which are rooted in history and social psychology, but which often bring class and power inequalities in their wake, and which manifest themselves in grassroots communities and organisations. There are stronger and weaker versions of anti-oppressive practice, depending upon which sphere of oppression is foregrounded.

10.2.1 The Strong Version of Anti-oppressive Practice

The strong version of anti-oppressive practice has been championed by social work academics, notably Lena Dominelli whose writings on class, feminism and anti-racism are greatly respected (Dominelli, 1997, 2002, 2004). It prioritises the Structural and Cultural spheres of the PCS model. It is grounded in critical social science with its appreciation of the roots of social inequalities, and allied to critical social movements which seek to transform the structures and cultures which generate exploitation and oppression. The intellectual rigour and political robustness of this approach is attractive to academics, but it may be too strong to be sustained within everyday practice.

The political dilemma is twofold. On the one hand, social work does not enjoy a good track record of undermining inequalities in the wider society so we are vulnerable to charges of hypocrisy from socialists (Jordan, 2004). Some research shows that social workers avoid poverty-related problems and welfare benefits work which they regard as beyond their remit (Dowling, 1998). On the other hand, social work academics have not always articulated their vision of anti-oppressive practice in conjunction with service users or carers so we are vulnerable to charges of hypocrisy from our own service users (Wilson and Beresford, 2000).

The practical dilemma is that strong versions of feminism and anti-racism are not sufficiently flexible to accommodate to the diversity of practice scenarios confronting social workers. Radical political ideologies have tended to reproduce the dichotomies of men/women and white/black people in an inverted form in order to highlight the sufferings and virtues of the subordinated group. But practitioners in domestic violence projects encounter men who have been ill-treated by female partners, and practitioners in multi-ethnic communities work with white victims of ethnocentrism, so they need more flexible frameworks for practice. Some social work academics have been promoting cultural competence to this end (O'Hagan, 2001; Laird, 2008).

The pedagogic dilemma is that students have objected to what they regard as political correctness in the classroom when they are expected to assimilate professional–political world views around class, gender, sexuality and ethnicity (e.g. Chand et al., 2002). Social work education could be in danger of self-contradiction if it enjoins novices to become critically reflective practitioners but at the same time makes detailed prescriptions as to the outcomes of their critical reflection (Fook, 2002). (For further critical commentary on the roots of our allegiance to anti-oppressive practice, see Millar, 2008.)

10.2.2 The Weak Version of Anti-oppressive Practice

The weak version of anti-oppressive practice prioritises the Personal and Cultural spheres of the PCS model and is popular among students, practice teachers and service users. Many practice educators reported that students could be so overwhelmed by the strong version of anti-oppressive practice, believing that changing wider structures and cultures was beyond their comprehension and capacity, that a diluted version was essential to enable students to meet the final clause of their value requirements (see Chapter 9: Table 9A). Some agreed that their students could substitute the term 'enabling' for 'empowering' on the grounds that enabling a service user to manage their everyday affairs was a more realistic aim than empowering a service user to change their life or challenge disadvantage.

Some agencies invite service users to contribute to students' induction and training. These sessions are invaluable in highlighting service users' life worlds and their experiences of professionals as they explore 'a day in the life of ...' a disabled adult or a child in care. Service users' understanding of anti-oppressive practice is rooted in the Personal sphere insofar as they prioritise the empathy of an individual practitioner for an individual service user, although it links to the Cultural sphere insofar as they represent distinct communities seeking to advance their own education and empowerment. One student reported that a group of looked after young people engineered a role reversal to teach him about their experiences of being in care and having regular looked after children (LAC) reviews:

> P: I was asked to leave the room ... When I returned there was a chair in the middle of the room [for me] with other chairs around it in a semicircle. I was asked to sit down by the young people. They all began to fire questions at me ... 'How do you think you are doing at University? Do you think you will pass your course? Have you got any friends? What do you like doing in your spare time?' etc. I felt that these questions were very personal and I felt uncomfortable answering them ... [Then] they began to talk to each other about me; they did not include me in the conversation. Then I was asked to leave the room again ... I thought this was an excellent way of portraying their thoughts and feelings and making workers more aware of how they felt during LAC reviews.

So it is not surprising that the majority of students subscribe to a weak version of anti-oppressive practice during their placements. Some abandoned this term in favour of 'anti-discriminatory practice'. Two main versions of anti-discriminatory practice could be discerned. In the first version, a non-judgemental standpoint is allied to an ethical and evidence-based approach:

> CH: So what does it mean to you?
> S: Anti-discriminatory practice? It's just ... to go in with an open mind, no prejudices, being able to evaluate the case on the evidence that you've got, no predetermined judgements, and treating people fairly as you'd want to be treated yourself.

In the second version, the principle of equality is mobilised in response to a recognition of the diversity of service users and carers:

> P: Anti-discriminatory practice is a key contribution to my profession. It is paramount that I treat each individual with the same respect and dignity, no matter of age, gender, disability, religion or ethnicity.

These may be sound starting points for novices, but they cannot become the end goals. They could be dubbed 'non-discriminatory' rather than 'anti-disciminatory' insofar as they do not include the active challenges to discrimination implicit in the term '*anti*-discriminatory'. Furthermore, there is no recognition of the ways in which class inequalities compound status discriminations. This is not strong enough to sustain the PCS model of anti-oppressive practice. It does not venture further than the New Labour orthodoxy whereby everyone is to be accorded equal worth, equal rights, equal opportunities and equal responsibilities (Blair, 1998) or the existing panoply of anti-discriminatory laws and policies which are binding upon all public service providers (Brammer, 2010: Chapters 5 and 6). The structures and cultures which generate exploitation and oppression have not been dismantled by New Labour or new laws (cf. Freeden, 1999; Jordan, 2004). If students overlook these structures and cultures, it is not only symptomatic of their status as novices focusing upon concrete casework, but also testimony to the hegemony of institutionalised inequalities.

10.2.3 Revisiting the Personal–Cultural–Structural Model

If anti-oppressive practice means different things to different people, this may reflect the diversity of our roles within social work organisations as well as differences in our personal–political biographies. So we should not expect anti-oppressive practice to assume a single monolithic form, and Neil Thompson's (1998) PCS model can easily accommodate this diversity:

- The personal sphere – social workers spend most of their time with disadvantaged individuals and families so it is appropriate to foreground this sphere in our practice. But anti-oppressive practice should go beyond the ethics of equal respect for all, regardless of differences, since it is about celebrating diversity and challenging discrimination.
- The cultural sphere – group work with victims or perpetrators of domestic violence and community work in multi-ethnic neighbourhoods brings us directly into this cultural sphere. Organisations should be aligning their policies to the pro-diversity and anti-discriminatory agenda, and service user and carer movements make challenging contributions here.

- The structural sphere – changes to the wider political economy are made by collectivities rather than individuals – i.e. trade unions, professional associations, local authorities and national charities. But social work academics may undertake critical research into this sphere, and practitioners and students should always be mindful of the structural contexts of life worlds.

Exercise 10A provides a case example of a student who felt compelled to challenge a multi-agency panel in the name of anti-oppressive practice. Although this example is atypical, we could ask ourselves why many students and social workers would not even countenance such a challenge?

Exercise 10A   Challenging Oppressive Practice

A student placed in a community care team for adults with disabilities challenged the multi-agency panel which made resource decisions in his very first case. A middle-aged woman had multiple sclerosis, was unable to look after herself and had no family to assist her – she could not even get to the bathroom or make herself a drink – and she had plunged into a deep depression as a result. The student assessed her as needing residential care, but the panel refused this on the grounds of budgetary constraints and added that since it was the student's first assessment he may have exaggerated her needs. He was infuriated by this dismissive treatment of his client and his own capability.

S: It was 'Should this decision be purely based on a student's assessment?' ... But I got there in the end, and I got a pat on the back from my supervisor because I stood my ground, I gave the facts, I didn't back down, I fought for this case ... My adrenalin just went. I thought *'No, this is rubbish! You're sat there behind these money goggles, you're not hearing me, you're not seeing this person who needs help'*. So I stood up all six foot of me and I walked around the room, pacing ... When I stood up they started hearing me, you know. I don't want to say that I was physically intimidating them, and I should have been able to do it sat down, you know, but I couldn't, and when I stood up I felt I claimed my personal power back ... All through university we've had anti-oppressive practice drilled into us, but this was so oppressive, I couldn't believe what was happening, you know, this was really awful, this was really oppressive social work ... [To the panel] this person was another thing that drains the money that they haven't got. *But she wasn't!* This was a person who needed help, this was a person who'd worked most of her life, who'd paid taxes ... She'd given so much to society through her life, now she needed the system to give her something back and there was a brick wall in the way ... I wasn't going to let that brick wall be there, so I got my hammer and I smashed that wall down ... I just felt that I *was* that other

(Continued)

(Continued)

> person, *I was her in that panel,* I was the only person that was representing that service user and I felt that I was her voice. *I couldn't fail her!* You know, I couldn't go back to that person and say 'I'm sorry I didn't get your funding' ... I saw what state she was in ... Our help was the only thing that she was clinging onto and for me to go back and say 'You haven't got it' – [silence]. *It would have killed her.*

Ponder on the following questions before turning to my own reflections at the end of the chapter.

What factors enabled this student to successfully challenge the multi-agency panel?

How far are the tactics he adopted in this meeting useful or usable more generally?

10.3 Politics and Power in Social Work

Social workers cannot escape politics or power in their professional lives. Social work is not only a state-sponsored profession with powers to intervene in the lives of people who are often on the 'wrong side' of class, status and power divisions; it is also committed to critical reflection on the contexts of practice and the ideals of social justice which are inherently 'political' (Powell, 2001).

10.3.1 Where Do You Stand on the Political Spectrum?

Mainstream politics in modern nation states comes in three major guises. There are party politics between the main political parties seeking election in local and central government; there are class politics between trade unions and corporations negotiating over income and employment issues; and there are identity politics involving campaigns by civil rights activists and service user groups in relation to status-based discriminations (Giddens, 1990). Social workers are at liberty to participate in politics (or not) like any other citizen, but there are some political activities which conflict with anti-oppressive practice, such as becoming a member of the British National Party or protesting against lesbian and gay rights.

Nevertheless, the political spectrum in the social work community is very broad. Practice teachers and managers polarised into two camps, i.e. the political and the apolitical. Those in the political camp often had personal experience of one or more forms of oppression, which became the lens through which they perceived other forms of oppression, so that anti-oppressive practice became central to their understanding of social work ethics:

CH: Where does your ethics come from? What are you trying to teach
     students [here]?

T: I think mainly, for me, it's *class*. That's my starting point. I always considered
     myself as working class and now being in a middle-class profession, and a
     potentially *oppressive* profession … Through that you filter out other things
     as well. For instance, the single woman with a child – the working-class
     woman is a lot worse off than the middle-class woman with a child. So
     that's the feminist side. Also there's the race issues – a lot of them can come
     under the umbrella of *class*.

Some practitioners and managers self-defined as apolitical on the grounds
that politics itself could be oppressive insofar as it pigeonholed people in
accordance with identity and ideology labels (see Appiah, 2005). In their
view, the professional remit of social work was to rise above politics and
prejudices alike and to cater to the needs of service users and carers regardless of class, status or party positions. Nevertheless, we are not entirely free
to choose whether to be political or apolitical in a profession with a high
media profile. A manager of an advocacy project explained that their
partnership working with homeless teenagers had been vilified as an
example of 'loony left' politics in the local press, reminding us that we may
need to defend ourselves in political forums.

Most students also polarised into two camps which will be dubbed
the pre- and post-political camps. Many young students were pre-political
in the sense that they had not yet been acquainted with party politics
(e.g. some had never voted and did not know anything about the policies
of different parties) and only had a vague sense of class politics (e.g. some
had heard contradictory claims that 'we live in a class-divided society' and
that 'class is dead' but this left them confused as they did not know how to
decide which claim was true). Many mature students were post-political in
the sense that they had already travelled along the path of political activism,
but had become disillusioned with politics (see Fay, 1987). Some had chosen social work as an alternative to a political career, and some identified
with a spiritual rather than a political world view. Although their ideals of
social justice were intact, their priorities were to work with and for people
at the local level in the hope of sowing the seeds for social change without
worrying about the bigger picture:

CH: So do you think it's social work's job to try and change wider society?

S: No. I think social workers are there to help the people do it themselves, to
     give them the tools … You can't do it unless they want it … But you only
     need to get one that wants to change. Confucius say that the hardest part of
     the journey is the first step … Then the rest will come, it will snowball.

10.3.2 Why Are We So Ambivalent about Power?

Social workers need to access all the power available to them if they are to be effective change agents. What are the sources of our power? Personal power is about releasing the energy within ourselves and harnessing it to our work; those with a strong sense of personal efficacy, professional commitment and political conviction tend to have far more energy at their disposal and to channel it in more effective ways. Professional power stems from acquiring relevant knowledge along with skills in applying it. Institutional power includes the resources at our disposal for assisting citizens in need and the laws which endow us with legitimate authority to instigate a variety of interventions.

Arnon Bar-On (2002) has highlighted the ways in which social workers' anxiety and ambivalence about power can undermine their power in practice. Where does this anxiety and ambivalence come from? Ironically, they may be rooted in our own ethics and politics. Empathy is a central virtue in social work ethics, but if we regard ourselves as being 'with' the oppressed and if we experience their suffering directly or vicariously, then we can end up feeling powerless and demoralised ourselves. Anti-oppressive practice is central to social work politics, but if we regard ourselves as belonging to a potentially oppressive state-sponsored profession, we may be reluctant to make use of legal powers to intervene in people's lives on the grounds that we must never do anything which could be (construed as) 'oppressive'. Resource cutbacks and adverse publicity also add to the sense of powerlessness among social workers.

Some students interpret anti-oppressive practice as meaning that they are obliged to 'empower' everyone they encounter, but this fails to take account of the imbalances of power in any given situation or the differences between positive and destructive uses of power, and students rarely take into account their own power. How are you going to empower anyone if you don't have any power yourself or if you don't know how to access and apply it? Mapping out power relations within a family, including the power relations between family members and professionals, is a very useful exercise. Who holds power in this family and are they using it wisely for the benefit of others or destructively? Who needs to be empowered or disempowered in this situation and why? How is the social worker going to bring about changes in power relations? What might be the side-effects of changing these power relations? Abusers rarely give up power without a struggle, and families can disintegrate when women victims of domestic violence recover their voices and rediscover their power (Hanmer, 2000; Harne and Radford, 2008).

Anyone who wants to facilitate cultural or structural change within a neighbourhood or even a nation state will benefit from mapping out the power relations between groups and organisations. The most effective and enduring change is from *within* an individual, group or community, and consequently we need to ally ourselves with positive forces for change and to support self-help groups and self-organised movements among service users, carers and citizens. But the status quo always generates resistances to change not only from those who benefit from 'the way things are', but sometimes also from those who would benefit from change, and it takes courage to challenge oppression which is so taken for granted that it is not even recognised *as* oppression. Exercise 10B shows how one student took on such a challenge in a residential care home for elderly people.

Exercise 10B   Mobilising Power

This case study involves a student who challenged the culture of traditional institutionalisation in a residential home for elderly people with learning disabilities (Humphrey, 2009a). Identify the different sources of power at work – both those which the student mobilised to bring about change, and those which resisted her efforts.

Scenario: residents had no voice or choice in the present, little understanding of their family history or care history, and had not been informed that the residential home was due for demolition so that they had to be moved into community-based housing.

Challenges: the student challenged the care staff to no avail, and then took her concerns to a senior manager who was more sympathetic but wary of 'upsetting the apple cart'. So the student consulted with an academic who was happy to support her, researched the relevant literature, then took a plan of action to the senior manager. This involved a three-stage group work project in relation to a group of residents who were likely to be the first to be moved into the community. The plan was accepted.

Stage 1: 'The Past' – the student undertook reminiscence exercises with residents which was followed by life story work. In the process, they learned to do some artwork, take photographs, express themselves and connect with each other.

Stage 2: 'The Present' – the student encouraged the residents to discuss what they liked and disliked about life in the home, and to exercise more voice and choice in everyday life. This challenged care staff who had to adjust their own behaviours and attitudes.

(Continued)

(Continued)

Stage 3: 'The Future' – the student explained the forthcoming move to the residents and arranged an outing to a DIY store so that they could get involved in designing the decor for their new homes. Then they created a group collage portraying their ideal home.

Resistance: education and empowerment can be a tumultuous experience.

> S: One lady in particular ... pushed me off the chair. She was saying *'Don't you talk about that, don't you talk about that! This is where I live, I'm not moving!'* ... The staff would say 'Oh, here comes [student] ... so they'll all be upset by teatime!' I would say 'At least you know I've been!' [Laughter]

Sustenance: this student drew upon her Christian faith as well as her commitment to anti-oppressive practice to sustain herself and her project. She prayed to God every day, remained resolutely cheerful and reminded herself of the big picture – that these residents needed to be equipped for the challenge of community-based living.

Outcome: at the end of the placement, the staff and residents arranged a party for this student and asked for her ongoing input into the change process. She continued to undertake voluntary work at the establishment after the placement ended.

10.4 Developing Sensitivity to Cross-cultural Diversity

Sensitivity to cross-cultural diversity is an integral component of anti-oppressive practice. Official guidance on assessments in community care and child care requires that culture, 'race' and religion are taken into account (DH, 1991, 2000a). Pioneering work in cross-cultural competence in British social work by Kieran O'Hagan (2001) and Siobhan Laird (2008) demonstrates that it has significant implications for our values, knowledge base and skills repertoire.

10.4.1 Reflecting upon Our Values

Critical reflection is required in relation to the norms, values and beliefs embedded in British social work as well as those we have acquired during primary socialisation in families and communities. Siobhan Laird (2008) highlights the Anglocentrism which governs social work in many parts of the UK and which predisposes us to cross-cultural incompetence. 'Anglocentrism' simply means that our world view is steeped in an English heritage which is

taken for granted. The Anglocentric values around individuality and independence are at odds with the family- and community-based solidarity which
prevails among many minority ethnic groups. Intimate one-to-one dialogues
are a routine feature of our casework, but people from minority ethnic groups
can be uncomfortable with discussing the intimacy of their personal lives
with strangers, and often prefer other family members to be present when
dealing with officials. A secular world view underpins our welfare state, but
many minority ethnic groups adhere to a religious or spiritual world view.

How can we escape Anglocentrism? Students who had been brought up
within dual-heritage families and multi-ethnic communities were far less
afflicted by Anglocentric assumptions. Others had a steep learning curve during cross-cultural casework which could disturb their sense of identity. A student working with a gypsy-traveller family drew up a long list of items she
wanted to purchase for them as part of her needs assessment, only to find out
that the family did not want to clutter up their caravan with these modern
conveniences which they had managed without for generations. The student
was shocked as she had believed that she was prejudice-free, but it is precisely
when we take things for granted that we can make prejudiced assumptions
about their universality. A white student working with an elderly black man
who had suffered a vicious racist assault came to appreciate her membership
of the dominant ethnic group during their encounter, to the point that she felt
ashamed to be white. She had to revisit her colour-blind and culture-blind
approach to anti-oppressive practice. She had assumed that she could simply
treat everyone as 'equal' in the sense of 'the same' *regardless* of differences in
colour or culture, but equality at the level of humanity must go hand in hand
with an appreciation of diversity and discrimination at the level of ethnicity.

10.4.2 Reconstructing Our Knowledge Base

Critical reflection is also necessary in respect of received knowledge. How
many schools give a prominent place to the transatlantic slave trade in their
representation of English history? How many media reports are sympathetic to the plight of refugees and asylum seekers? How many social work
programmes incorporate religion and spirituality into the curriculum?
There is a formidable task in developing our knowledge base to redress
such distortions and omissions.

Exercises 10C to 10E have been developed from the work of Margaret
Crompton (1998), Cecil Helman (2001), Dewi Rees (2001) and Siobhan
Laird (2008). They are designed to provide basic information about cultural diversity and to invite critical reflection upon your own cultural
heritage. They should be read with two caveats in mind. On the one hand,

it is impossible for any of us to develop a detailed knowledge base in respect of all cultures; the best advice is to focus upon acquiring a practical understanding of the ethnic groups in your area which should be served by your agency (Graham et al., 2009). On the other hand, it is unwise to make assumptions about specific individuals or families on the basis of generic knowledge about their culture or country of origin since there will be differences within any given ethnic group, and these are often exaggerated by the process of migration itself (Laird, 2008).

Exercise 10C   Symbolic Markers of Cultural Difference

Language – some people from overseas arrive in the UK with no English language at all, whilst others are already bilingual or multilingual. Older people tend to have more difficulty acquiring a new language than younger people, and written and spoken English presents more difficulties for people whose native language is very different from English, so that Chinese people are likely to struggle more than Europeans on this front. Black people in the Caribbean developed hybrid languages (known as Creole) mixing their native African language with the English and European languages of the colonial powers. But the use of 'Black English' in British schools often gives rise to discrimination.

Questions: How would you communicate with a service user who has little or no English? What are the advantages and disadvantages of using family members or professional linguists as interpreters? Should teachers and social workers support Black English?

Embodiment – cultural norms can be inscribed upon our bodies and often reflect religious beliefs. Orthodox Jews do not cut or shave the hair on their head or body. Rastafarians have dreadlocks and it is a taboo for a non-Rastafarian to touch these dreadlocks. Muslim women wear long tunics to cover up their bodies and a veil to cover up their hair (and sometimes most of their face). Sikh men contain their uncut hair within a turban and carry a small knife along with other religious symbols. Such norms may be modified over time as a result of accommodating to British cultures and institutions.

Questions: How does your own embodiment reflect your cultural heritage? In what ways are white British people likely to misunderstand the cultural appearances and accoutrements of Sikh men and Muslim women respectively?

Diet – vegetarianism is the norm among Hindus, Buddhists, Sikhs and Rastafarians, although Western people of no religion may also become vegetarian. Jews and Muslims can only eat certain kinds of meat and only when the animal has been slaughtered in the prescribed manner, and they must ensure that all other foods are free from prohibited products. Alcohol and tobacco are forbidden in several religions, although cannabis has served an important social and spiritual function among Rastafarians. But, again, all these norms may be relaxed over time.

Questions: Why do you think that diet plays a major role in many religions? How far do services in domiciliary, day and residential care cater to diverse dietary requirements? Would you regard UK drug legislation as discriminating against Rastafarians?

Exercise 10D Ethnic Diversity in Social Relationships

Families – families in India, Pakistan and Bangladesh are patrilineal and multi-generational so that women live with their husband's family after marriage. When people from these countries come to live in the UK, they may adapt these arrangements so that each nuclear family inhabits its own household, but if they have houses along the same street, they may share meals on a daily basis. Caribbean families tend to be matrilineal so that mothers and grand-mothers undertake child care, and fathers are more likely to maintain a visiting relationship to the household.

Questions: Is there any objective reason why one form of family life is 'better' or 'worse' than any other form? What prejudices might white British people harbour in relation to traditional Asian and Caribbean living arrangements respectively?

Gender relations – gender segregation is most pronounced among Muslims. According to Islamic law, women and children should obey the male head of household who in turn has obligations to look after them. Muslim children undertake education, sports and social activities within same-sex groups, and there are restrictions on how far Muslim women can participate in public life and socialise with men. Homosexuality is prohibited by Judaism and Islam and associated with controversy within Christianity.

Questions: How can educational, recreational, health and social services cater for the cultural needs of Muslim children? In what ways are young people who identify as lesbian or gay 'at risk' within a family with a religious belief in the abnormality and immorality of homosexuality?

Generational relations – elderly people are respected and even revered in many cultures where men incur duties to support their elders financially, whilst women provide day-to-day care, although Muslim women may not be allowed to provide hands-on care for men outside of their immediate family. The cul-tural importance accorded to family solidarity means that a number of minority ethnic children provide regular care for disabled relatives or work in family businesses.

Questions: How might people from other cultures view the treatment of elderly people in the UK? What are the dangers of assuming that people from ethnic minorities will 'look after their own'? Should social workers be concerned about the welfare of child carers or child workers in minority ethnic families?

Exercise 10E   Spiritual Contexts of Life and Death

Religious practices – religion plays a key role in the life of many people from minority ethnic communities. Christians from Africa and the Caribbean established their own black churches in the UK as a result of discrimination from white Christian churches. Muslims have set up mosques although women may have to pray at home unless they can access a large mosque with a women-only section. Black churches and mosques tend to provide a wide range of practical, social and educational services to members. Hindus and Buddhists are more likely to maintain a shrine within their own homes in the absence of dedicated public space for their religious practices. Every religion has its own holy days, festivals and rituals for birth, marriage and death.

Questions: What are the dilemmas in placing a looked after child in a family whose religion is very different from that of the child's family of origin? In what ways can residential care homes for older people support diverse religious practices?

Health and illness – traditional medicine in many parts of the world is holistic, i.e. the healer works with the body–mind–spirit of the person who is suffering, and often with their family as well. Chinese practices such as acupuncture and herbal remedies are well-established in the UK. Disability and disease may be subject to spiritual interpretations and interventions. Hindus and Buddhists may view these as the karmic effects of past misdeeds, while Jews, Christians and Muslims may believe that the wrath of God is at work. Certain kinds of disease or disability, notably HIV/AIDS and mental illness, are so stigmatised that they can incur ostracism and even exorcism.

Questions: How far are spiritual readings of and responses to illness likely to be helpful or unhelpful? What are the merits and limitations of conventional and complementary approaches to medicine respectively?

Death and bereavement – there are enormous variations in our beliefs about and responses to death. Jews have a seven-day mourning period, whilst Rastafarians may not mourn at all or even attend a funeral since they believe that a Rastafarian never really dies. The belief in a cycle of existence involving some kind of reincarnation or karmic action across different lifetimes is found in Hinduism and Buddhism, whilst the belief in supranatural realms known as Heaven and Hell is found in Christianity and Islam. Folk religions in many parts of Africa and the Far East maintain that ancestors watch over us from afar, and ancestor worship is designed to ensure that they will intervene in our lives in positive ways.

Questions: What are your beliefs about death and what might lie beyond it? How could you support dying and bereaved people whose beliefs are very different to your own?

Students need to acquire basic knowledge about the history of migration, the ethnic composition of the UK population and research studies into social work practice with minority ethnic groups. The first anti-immigration legislation passed at the turn of the twentieth century targeted Jews and Irish people who were deemed to threaten the purity of the nation (Anthias and Yuval-Davis, 1992). Black and Asian people from Commonwealth countries were encouraged to emigrate to Britain after the Second World War in order to combat the labour shortage, only to be subject to racist discrimination which fuelled another raft of anti-immigration legislation. Xenophobia has now shifted to asylum seekers, and those from some European and Middle Eastern countries have been subject to a vitriolic Islamophobia (Hayes and Humphries, 2004). Gypsies and travellers have also suffered prejudice to the point of persecution, even though some were indigenous minorities and others had been in Britain for centuries (Cemlyn, 2008).

According to the most recent 2001 Census, minority ethnic people make up 8 per cent of the UK population with 50 per cent identifying as Asian, 25 per cent as black, 15 per cent as dual-heritage and 5 per cent as Chinese (Laird, 2008: 3). These minority ethnic groups tend to be concentrated in urban areas, unlike asylum seekers who have been relocated across the country as a result of a policy of dispersal. Black people from African states and Caribbean islands are predominantly Christian, although some are Muslim or Rastafarian. People from India are most likely to be Hindu or Sikh, whilst those from Pakistan and Bangladesh are predominantly Muslim. Chinese people have been more influenced by Buddhism (Laird, 2008: 25). Folk religions involving reverence towards ancestors or other deities, or beliefs in the powers of animals or evil spirits, may co-exist with mainstream religions. The indigenous British population tends to identify as Christian (nominally if not substantively) and there is a folk religion in the shape of paganism which is rooted in Celtic traditions and which reveres mother earth (Harvey, 1997).

Research in health, social care and criminal justice reveals significant differences in outcomes across minority ethnic groups (Chahal, 2004). Black and dual-heritage children and young people are overrepresented in all child care and youth justice systems, whilst Asians are underrepresented in comparison with their white British counterparts (Thoburn et al., 2005). African and Caribbean men are overrepresented in the mental health and criminal justice systems, and they are more likely to be subject to compulsory hospitalisation as well as high levels of restraint and medication by mental health providers (DH, 2005). These differences suggest discriminatory treatment by professionals who may neglect the needs of some ethnic groups and respond punitively to the problems of others. Discrimination can occur as a result of a subconscious mono-culturalism – there is no need for any conscious intention to discriminate on the part of any individual practitioner. Mono-culturalism literally means that we see the world through the eyes of one culture, and if this is the mainstream culture then it will be shared by most of our colleagues and clients so we rarely encounter challenges to our world view. It can lead us down the path of non-intervention if we are afraid of working across cultures or if we assume that Asian families are self-sufficient and in less need of services. It can also lead us down the path of over-zealous intervention if we misinterpret the cultural norms of Afro-Caribbean people and dispense medications or court orders to silence their expressive or challenging communications (Parrott, 2009).

10.4.3 Refining Our Skills

Partnership working with minority ethnic communities entails a dialogic process conducted between agencies and relevant local communities, a process which has to be repeated by each social worker in relation to each individual or family (cf. Graham et al., 2009; Parrott, 2009). Culturagrams are an important assessment tool which address cultural matters around language, religion and lifestyle, although they were designed for social workers in the USA and may need to be adapted for the UK (Congress, 1994). Students on placement should explore culturally specific resources for minority ethnic groups in their midst. Is there a black church or a mosque within travelling distance? Are there any organisations dedicated to the needs of Jews, Asian women or gay men? If not, what national helplines or Internet websites offer specialist advice or social support?

There is often a tightrope to be walked between respecting and challenging cultural diversity, and there can be confusion and uncertainty about who is in danger of being oppressed by whom, which accounts for the persistent tendency among social workers to avoid dealing with cultural issues (O'Hagan, 2001; Laird, 2008). Teams working with asylum seekers have developed practice wisdom in walking the tightrope. One team had a staff and student group which was culturally diverse but predominantly female, whilst most service users were men from countries with a strong gender segregation linked to women's subordination. The team accommodated to gender segregation by ensuring that male and female service users had separate social and sports facilities, whilst refusing to accept the subordination of women by informing men who refused to work with women social workers that agency policy was that service users had to work with whomever was allocated to them.

Muslim families presented the most dilemmas for students (cf. Graham et al., 2009). Two female students who were helping teenage girls from Pakistan with their English language skills and social integration reported that they had to rethink their intervention plan when the parents insisted that their daughters should not have any contact with boys or any conversations about puberty or sexuality. They also had to adjust their rules around personal–professional boundaries when the family provided a lavish feast for them at the end of their placement as a gesture of gratitude, as it would have been disrespectful to have refused such a gift. A student based in a secure unit was allocated an Asian boy who had been convicted of criminal offences and whose father insisted that he should learn Arabic and the Qur'an. His son was extremely reluctant to do this and the imam at the local mosque failed to respond to several communications on the matter. The student's questions were: should she support the father in spite of the son's expressed wishes on the grounds that learning about his cultural heritage was of overriding importance? Was the imam reluctant to work with a member of the Muslim community who had incurred stigma as a result of criminal behaviour, or reluctant to work with non-Muslim professionals in case they were carriers of anti-Muslim prejudices?

Sensitivity to cultural diversity does not mean that anything which is practised in the name of culture is acceptable. It is dangerous to succumb to a pure cultural relativism with its motto that 'all the beliefs and practices of all cultures are equally OK'. The bottom line for social workers is that they must safeguard vulnerable people from harm, so beliefs and practices which cause harm warrant critical challenges or compulsory interventions. Figure 10A illustrates the acceptable and unacceptable faces of cultural diversity.

This bottom line also applies to situations involving white British citizens. For example, a student based in a community mental health team worked with a woman who had suffered a psychotic breakdown. It emerged that her devoutly Catholic mother had been worried about her daughter's deteriorating health and had persuaded a priest to perform an exorcism on her daughter, which triggered the final breakdown. In such cases, we have to tread a tightrope between rejecting specific beliefs and practices which have proved harmful without rejecting the entire culture or religion itself, and we must do this in a manner which enables service users to rethink their own relationship to their culture or religion, recognising both its virtues and its vices.

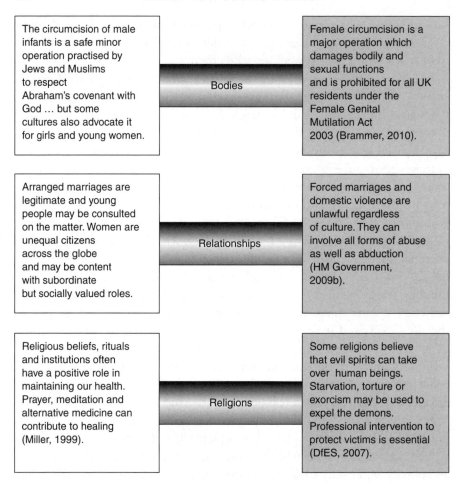

FIGURE 10A   *Cultural Relativity and Its Limits*

10.5 Dilemmas in Practice Education

Practice educators reported two main dilemmas when dealing with cultural diversity among service users and students. The first dilemma pertained to the question of 'ethnic matching' where they found a conflict between the preferences of many service users from minority ethnic backgrounds who responded more positively to students from similar backgrounds and the pedagogic needs of students, particularly those from the white majority who had to learn to work across cultures (cf. Laird, 2008). The second dilemma emerged in relation to the assessment of students from minority ethnic communities where they experienced a

conflict between assessing students' competence in relation to standardised norms of practice and respecting students' cultural heritage. For
example, an overseas student claimed that it was contrary to his class and
cultural background to undertake the fundraising task allocated to him
by his practice teacher; he had been brought up to believe that his duty
was to 'bestow' gifts upon others and he was horrified by the idea of
'begging' for charity.

Other dilemmas surfaced for students themselves. Some students from
minority ethnic backgrounds experienced discrimination from service
users and carers. On occasions, there was overt abuse in the form of racist
name-calling, but most forms of discrimination were more covert. For
example, a black student would arrange to visit a white family in need,
only to be refused entry to the household for no apparent reason beyond
the colour difference, or a student with a foreign accent would return a
telephone call to a person in crisis only to be told that they would prefer
not to have a visit from the student, although the crisis remained unresolved (cf. Razack, 2001). If such episodes were repeated, then students'
learning opportunities could be compromised and their confidence
undermined. Nevertheless, other black and minority ethnic students from
the UK and overseas claimed that they had not faced any discrimination,
and had been given a warm welcome by all their clients.

Confusion and controversy reigned over spirituality and religion.
Spirituality tends to refer to the processes of meaning construction which
take place within our own psyche when we ponder on things which reside
outside of the realm of scientific knowledge, such as the reasons for our
existence and the nature of our relationship to the cosmos or to a Creator.
Religions are born when a specific set of spiritual beliefs and practices
becomes institutionalised in the form of organisations with prescribed
scriptures, orthodox rituals and social hierarchies. There can be a disjuncture
between these – some people may attend religious institutions without
experiencing an inner spirituality, whilst others may be committed to a
spiritual world view or spiritual healing practices without identifying with
any mainstream religion (Moss, 2005). Whatever our own position on
these matters, it will have implications for practice. Students who identified
as agnostic or atheist were perplexed by questions around 'spiritual need'
in community care paperwork and sometimes disregarded these issues,
even when they were salient to service users. Students who adopted a
fundamentalist reading of their religious scriptures struggled to accept the
legitimacy of lesbian and gay families so their personal standpoints placed
them at odds with policy statements in the arena of fostering and adoption
(Humphrey, 2009b).

But cultural diversity among students can be a positive resource for education and practice. An overseas student gave a presentation to hospice staff in connection with beliefs about death and rituals around mourning in her culture of origin to promote cross-cultural education. A pagan student developed exercises in meditation and relaxation for young people based upon his own spiritual practices which proved to be effective stress-management techniques (cf. Humphrey, 2009b; Ng and Chan, 2009). The challenge facing educators is to integrate such insights and innovations within the mainstream curriculum and practicum.

Points to Remember and Questions to Ponder

- Three types of inequality were outlined in section 10.1. Can you name them and explain the differences between them?
- The next two sections were devoted to anti-discriminatory/anti-oppressive practice and the conundrums around politics/power in social work. Do you subscribe to a strong or weak version of anti-oppressive practice? Can you think of an occasion when you successfully mobilised your own power to challenge discrimination? If you are on placement and dealing with difficult dynamics in a family, community or agency, you may find it beneficial to map out the power relations between the main players and share it with your practice teacher.
- The final two sections explored cross-cultural diversity. Do you understand the distinct dangers posed by mono-culturalism and cultural relativism respectively? If you are allocated service users or carers from minority ethnic backgrounds, you should do some homework around their culture of origin, the use of culturagrams and relevant community resources. If you are from a minority ethnic background, can you convert this into a positive resource for education and practice?

Exercise 10A   Further Reflections

Several factors came together to make this a successful challenge:

- The student knew his case well as he had undertaken a thorough assessment as the basis of his recommended care plan and request for funding.
- He was committed to anti-oppressive practice and advocacy for service users.
- The panel's dismissive response to his assessment and his service user's plight triggered a 'fight' response. He was emotionally and physically aroused to defend his recommendation and his empathic identification with his client meant that he experienced it as a matter of life and death, as she did.

- The student had the intellectual capacity to articulate this to authority figures.
- This 'fight' response took the panel by surprise and they had no counter-defences to a strong challenge which was so unusual and unexpected.
- The student's supervisor offered tacit support in the meeting.

But the specific tactics used here may not be useful or usable more generally:

- The student made his presence and power palpable by physically pacing around the panel with his six-foot frame. Would a petite female have the same impact?
- If the student returned to the panel in future, panel members would be prepared for such a challenge and could have counter-measures in place.
- Supervisors do not always support the use of unconventional tactics.

So the best advice is to stay grounded in the evidence base of your client's situation and the ethics of your profession, and to stay calm and in control of your body, mind and speech, even and especially when you are mounting a challenge to 'the powers that be'.

Further Reading and Resources

For a critical account of the social, economic and political contexts of practice, see:
Powell, F. (2001) *The Politics of Social Work*. London: Sage.

Accessible works on anti-oppressive practice and cross-cultural diversity include:
Laird, S. (2008) *Anti-Oppressive Social Work: A Guide for Developing Cultural Competence*. London: Sage.
Thompson, N. (2006) *Anti-Discriminatory Practice*. Basingstoke: Palgrave-Macmillan.

The UK poverty website maintained by the Joseph Rowntree Foundation – www.poverty. org.uk
The website of the Equality and Human Rights Commission – www.equalityhumanrights.com

For case examples of cross-cultural assessments with families – www.priory.com/ SEBULIBA.htm

For guidance on organisational policies and practices, you need to consult the following text:
Hill, H. and Kenyan, R. (2007) *Promoting Equality and Diversity: A Practitioner's Guide*. Oxford: Oxford University Press.

Part 3

Becoming a Qualified Practitioner

11

Navigating Your Way Through Assessments

Introduction

Assessment tends to be anxiety-provoking even for the most competent students, so this chapter will include advice on how to manage your anxiety as well as guidance on the criteria used by assessors to judge your products and performances. Sections 11.1 and 11.2 sketch out assessment criteria in relation to academic assignments and practice competence respectively. Section 11.3 provides an overview of discrimination facing students from minority groups and duties to promote a level playing field in higher education. The final section outlines options available to students who may have fallen at an assessment hurdle and clarifies the meaning of 'fitness to practise'.

11.1 University-based Assessments

Universities are required to use diverse assessment strategies to maximise validity, reliability and equity in the assessment process (Wakeford, 1999; Crisp and Lister, 2002; QAA, 2008). Most university assignments are 'summative' assessments such as essays and exams, i.e. they test your knowledge at the end of a module and your marks will affect your progression and final degree classification. Table 11A provides a basic guide to the criteria against which essays are judged.

TABLE 11A   *Academic Criteria for Marking Essays*

- Are you the author of this essay? Is most of it written in your own words so that it represents your own understanding of the topic?
- Have you addressed the question? Is the material you have used clearly relevant to answering this question?
- Does your writing conform to standard norms around spelling and grammar? Remember that computerised checks of spelling and grammar have limitations. Spell-checks will not tell you whether or not you have used the correct word for the context, only whether or not the word is properly spelled.
- Is the essay well-structured so that themes or sections follow logically from one another, and so that the reader can see the links between them?
- Have you included your sources at all relevant points within the text, and have they been listed alphabetically by author in your reference list at the end? Failing to reference your sources may result in allegations of 'plagiarism' which is a disciplinary offence in higher education.
- Have the connections to social work practice been highlighted, including issues related to anti-oppressive practice?
- Is there evidence of critical reflection upon the topic? You should always try to think 'beyond' the material you have read to demonstrate such critical reflection.

Sometimes tutors include 'formative' assessments within the module so that you can get feedback on your performances for the purpose of enhancing your future learning, but these do not result in a 'pass' or 'fail' or percentage mark. For example, group projects which culminate in presentations to the rest of the class are usually designed to help you to develop team-working skills and public speaking skills. Ironically, students tend to worry far more about live presentations in front of an audience even if they are not officially marked. A student who had been a member of a group which gave an exemplary presentation to the rest of the class confessed that her anxiety about such public performances did not abate over time:

> S: For people who can't do that sort of thing it's just *torture*. It doesn't get better no matter how many presentations you do! I still don't sleep a week before I have to do it … And I don't benefit from being in a group – you can't hide away, you've still got to talk to the audience. That's why we gave handouts in our group – and the PowerPoint slides – to stop people from looking at us!

Like many students, she preferred written assignments which allow more control over the process of production. Exercise 11A will help you to manage your anxiety about live performances, and the advice here is equally applicable to presentations in placement settings.

Exercise 11A   Managing Performance Anxieties

If you are prone to anxiety when giving presentations to an audience, the following advice will be helpful. However, some of the most important techniques for managing anxiety work best when we practise them regularly in everyday life, i.e. not simply a day or two before the presentation. If you can take 10, 20 or 30 minutes of 'time out' every day to tune into your breathing, relax your body or promote a positive frame of mind through creative visualisation, you will find that your capacity to manage anxiety in all aspects of your life and work will improve.

Part 1: Preparation prior to the presentation

- Preparing the material – mastery of the topic gives confidence as well as competence.
- Preparing yourself – deep, regular breathing calms the body–mind; anxiety always shows up in shallow breathing, rapid breathing or even no breathing (holding your breath). You can develop a creative visualisation by imagining yourself performing at your best; this exercise can be just as effective as a concrete rehearsal of the performance.
- Preparing the environment – you may be able to visit the site, check out the seating arrangements and test out any audio-visual equipment in advance.

Part 2: Principles during the presentation

- Staying grounded – deep, regular breathing for a minute or two before you start talking will keep you grounded in your body; if at any point you start to panic, return to this deep, regular breathing. Sitting down on a chair or holding onto a table can also help to ground your body; if there is no chair or table available, then you can imagine roots connecting your body to the earth via your feet.

(Continued)

(Continued)

- Connecting to others – after you have grounded yourself, you can connect to the other people in the room as you will feel stronger within yourself. Try to smile as this will radiate positive energy, and this will be reciprocated by your audience since emotions are contagious (even if your smile has been feigned, it can still be effective!). If something goes wrong, try to convert it into a joke, since laughter always diffuses tension.
- Transcending your ego – anxiety is the by-product of an ego feeling under threat, so if you want to bracket anxiety you will need to bracket your ego. The more absorbed you are in the material and explaining it to others, the less you will worry about how others might be judging you. The more you believe that your topic is important to social work and service users, the more you will rise above your own anxiety.

11.2 Community-based Assessments

Placements involve a continuous assessment with contributions from different stakeholders who invoke different criteria to judge a student's competence as a result of their distinct positions and perspectives. But there is also more scope for students to contribute to their own assessment on placements by supplying sound evidence and writing reports on their own progress.

11.2.1 Evidence-based Criteria

All practice educators need to see tangible evidence of your competence in interactions with service users, carers and other professionals so they will observe a sample of these meetings and provide a report on their observations with space for you to contribute your own views. They will check your work records to verify that you are mastering paperwork, procedures and ICT systems. They also need to be convinced that you are acquiring the art of reflection, which they will ascertain from supervision sessions and reflective journals. At the end of the placement, all parties (the practice learning assessor, the agency-based supervisor, where appropriate, and the student) write reports demonstrating that the Key Roles for that placement have been met. All of this evidence is then presented in a file and submitted to the university – see Table 11B for a summary.

Practice teachers who identify strongly as practice learning assessors and who adopt an evidence-based assessment model of supervision (see Chapter 4) rely heavily upon objective documentary evidence, and believe

TABLE 11B   *Evidence of Practice Competence*

Students build up a portfolio of evidence of their practice competence during each placement. In some programmes, the portfolio may go by another name such as a record of practice competence. Its main elements will typically include:

- a learning agreement between the student, university and agency
- records of induction, supervision and training during the placement
- samples of work undertaken, e.g. a care plan; a court report; groupwork activities; a PowerPoint presentation; a research project
- reflective journals where students ponder on their theories, values and emotions and write up critical incident analyses
- feedback from a sample of service users and carers
- feedback from staff who have observed the student's practice
- reports on the student's progress in meeting Key Roles and adhering to Codes of Practice written by practice teaching staff
- a report from the student who takes an active role in assessing their own progress and identifying future learning needs.

All records and reports must be anonymised in respect of service users and carers to preserve confidentiality. Do not use real names in your journals, and erase all names and addresses in work records which appear in the portfolio. Failure to remove identifying information about service users and carers will be regarded as a breach of professional ethics.

that this provides a safeguard against subjective bias. Managers in statutory agencies as well as some long-arm practice teachers have embraced the PLA role in this manner. Long-arm PLAs are far more reliant upon objective evidence of work records, given that they do not work in the agencies, whilst managers in the statutory sector typically prioritise analytical skills embedded in work records over people skills enacted in everyday life. Why is this? From a managerial perspective, analytical skills can be more crucial to safeguarding service users and the reputation of the agency. However empathic you have been with service users, if your analysis of needs, risks and options is not clear, then your plans will be built upon shifting sands, and if your reports to conferences and courts are of a poor standard, then this reflects badly upon the agency.

The advantage for students is that these PLAs provide clear and critically constructive feedback at every point in the placement, and tick off each of the competencies as soon as the student supplies the evidence. The disadvantage is that these PLAs adhere to high professional standards and tend to treat everything as a summative assessment, a strategy which is more appropriate for students on final placements than those on initial placements. For example, if a student missed vital clues during an observed home visit (even if it is a first observation), then these PLAs could count this as a failure and arrange a repeat observation. Nevertheless, some students reported that they appreciated a robust approach to assessment insofar as it alerted them to their own shortcomings and ultimately made them stronger people and more skilful practitioners.

11.2.2 Pedagogic Criteria

Other practice educators, particularly those in the independent sector, took a different approach to student assessment. In essence, they tailored the assessment to each student. Their reasoning was that the diversity of starting points among students had to be respected, and a young student with limited experience of social care could not be expected to attain the same level of competence in the same time span as a mature student with a decade-long career in social care. Assessments are characterised by relativity insofar as the progress of the student is measured in relation to the learning curve of that student, and what mattered most to these practice educators was that the student should provide evidence of a sustained learning curve throughout the placement.

   Those who adopted a pedagogic approach to supervision (see Chapter 4) saw themselves as engaged primarily in formative assessments. They expected students to make mistakes on the learning journey; as long as a student recognised their mistakes, no penalties were incurred. If an observed home visit is problematic (even if it is a final observation), the student is not usually asked to repeat it, providing that the supervisor is satisfied that the student is now aware of what went wrong and how it should be rectified, so the student's learning is tested in the context of supervision rather than in the context of practice as such. Some practice teachers rejected the entire terminology around 'passing' and 'failing', insisting that their task was to provide a safe and supportive environment for personal–professional growth:

> T: I tell people at the beginning of the placement that we've never failed anybody … Life is not that straightforward – win/lose, fail/succeed. I think it's more about them finding a way through … and they will get support from the team … If there is a problem it will be identified and discussed … They can go to a worker at any time … Our ethos is that there is no such thing as a silly question … I've been doing this job for 15 years but I'm still learning, so that's the ethos we try to put across … It's the idea that life is a learning process, that we are all learning together.

This approach is more suitable for students on initial placements than those on final placements. Whilst it is easier for students to pass a placement under these conditions, it is not impossible for them to fail if they do not learn from their mistakes, or if their mistakes are so serious that they amount to misconduct. And a sustained learning curve should transport all students to the level of 'basic' competencies, whilst propelling some students towards much higher levels of expertise.

11.2.3 Person-centred Criteria

Person-centred criteria are paramount for those who value people skills above analytical skills. Practice teachers who adopt a person-centred approach to supervision tune into the person inside the professional; they want to know if a student's heart is 'in the right place' in terms of ethics and empathy; if they believe it is, then they will support a student to deal with any other shortcomings. This may sound easy enough, but some students find it more onerous than an evidence-based approach which can allow them to 'hide' behind work records.

Service users and carers also invoke person-centred criteria when assessing students and social workers, as illustrated in Table 11C. Students are expected to ask a sample of their service users and carers for feedback on their competence (see Chapter 8). Service users and carers are often in the best position to judge your people skills since they have immediate experience of your attitudes and communication styles and will sense whether or not you are congruent within yourself and comfortable with them. Ideally, practice teachers should include service user and carer feedback when they undertake a direct observation of students' practice during home visits. This allows for what is known as 'triangulation', i.e. the three perspectives of the practice teacher, student and service user or carer all

TABLE 11C   *Service Users' and Carers' Person-centred Criteria*

Service users and carers are most concerned about the humanity of social workers in everyday encounters, and their recognition of the humanity of others, but clearly this needs to be supplemented by the appropriate knowledge and skills to do the job. When service users and carers contribute to the assessment of students, they ask fundamental questions – ostensibly quite simple, but actually profound and challenging:

- Do they care about us, respect us and treat us as equal people?
- Do they listen to us and look us in the eye?
- Are they honest with us and with themselves?
- Are they frightening to us or are they frightened by us?
- Do they talk to us or to other people about us?
- Can they get the job done?
- Are they open to being challenged by us?
- Can they challenge others on our behalf?

Source: Advocacy in Action with University of Nottingham (2006)

contribute to the assessment of a student's performance (Shardlow and Doel, 1996). Unfortunately, there is a tendency for observed home visits to become single-party assessments by practice teachers who then share their report with students (Humphrey, 2007b).

Students feel under continuous scrutiny during placements, and internalise this in the form of a continuous self-monitoring, as illustrated in the following dialogue with two students:

> S1   You get more self-aware when you get feedback [from an observed visit] because you think to yourself:'Am I doing it right now? … Have I got good body language now? …Am I speaking clearly? Am I taking information in? Am I reassuring the client?'That's going though your mind *constantly* …
>
> CH: But are you thinking all those things on an ordinary visit or just when you're being observed?
>
> S1 and S2:   *All the time!*
>
> CH: *All of the time?*
>
> S2:   Every visit, every meeting.
>
> S1:   Even every phone call.

11.3 A Level Playing Field?

Equity is an important principle in assessment. It simply means that there should be a level playing field so that no group of students is systematically disadvantaged in the assessment process (Wakeford, 1999). But society is characterised by inequalities which are reflected in universities and communities, and which can adversely affect the progress of students from disadvantaged groups.

11.3.1 Discrimination and Equality Duties

Who is likely to be disadvantaged in the assessment process? In terms of essay-writing, the list would include dyslexic students (Riddell et al., 2005), mature students returning to higher education after a long absence (Archer et al., 2003) and overseas students for whom English is a second language (McNamara and Harris, 1997). In terms of practice learning, the list would include students with physical or sensory impairments, young students with limited work experience and students whose ethnicity marks them out as 'different' from the majority of staff and service users.

As a result of anti-discriminatory legislation, there are equality duties in higher education in relation to 'race' (Commission for Racial Equality, 2002), disability (Disability Rights Commission, 2006), sex and gender (Equal

Opportunities Commission, 2007). This means that universities are obliged to promote equality of opportunity when admitting and assessing students, to eliminate discrimination and harassment, and to institute positive measures for disadvantaged groups. Examples of positive measures for disabled students can be found in Table 11D. Equality of opportunity embraces *everyone* in respect of the relevant categories, i.e. 'sex' includes men who may be entitled to positive measures if they become a disadvantaged group, and 'gender' includes transgendered people.

Research has highlighted a paradox in social work education. On the one hand, social workers are committed to anti-discriminatory practice and practice teachers have reported a reluctance to fail students from disadvantaged backgrounds (cf. Lefevre, 1998; Collins, 2006). On the other

---

TABLE 11D   *Positive Measures for Disabled Students*

The Special Educational Needs and Disability Act (SENDA) 2001 provides for 'reasonable adjustments' to be made for disabled students to enable them to complete their programme of study on equal terms with non-disabled students.

Positive measures for students with specific learning difficulties include:

- receiving handouts in advance of lectures
- special tutoring or study skills classes
- using voice-activated computer software.

Positive measures for students with physical or sensory impairments include:

- loop systems in lecture theatres and meetings
- accessible premises for study and work
- placements which do not require home visiting.

Positive measures for students with mental health problems include:

- part-time routes through the programme
- student counselling services
- intercalation (taking time out) to recover from a crisis.

To access positive measures, students need to talk with a Disability Tutor or refer themselves to Student Disability Services. They may need to participate in diagnostic tests in respect of learning difficulties or discussions about their medical condition or mental health history. This results in a report with recommendations as to the reasonable adjustments which academic tutors and placement supervisors should put in place. Some measures are cost-free; but students who need special equipment receive a grant to finance this.

Positive measures are about reducing barriers which may prevent disabled students from becoming social workers; they do not confer any other 'special treatment' which makes disabled students more likely to pass the programme than non-disabled students; disabled students still have to complete all the assignments and placements, meet Key Roles and abide by Codes of Practice.

Disabled employees are also entitled to reasonable adjustments. If you are disabled, then getting a proper assessment plus adjustments during your degree will serve you in good stead for your later career.

hand, statistical analyses of progression rates of students on the DipSW and new degree programmes in England show that students who belong to a minority group (i.e. men as well as disabled and black students) are consistently less likely to pass their programmes on time compared with other students, and more likely to fail or withdraw from the programme (Hussein et al., 2006, 2009). How can we explain this paradox? There is likely to be a combination of factors at work, so that some students suffer disadvantages which outweigh whatever support measures staff have put in place. A study of black African students showed that they struggled to acculturate to the UK where they were subject to racism, and that they had more onerous life situations than other students in terms of health problems, informal caring roles and financial burdens (Bartoli et al., 2008). Let us consider some case examples from practice teachers who grappled with this paradox.

11.3.2 Dilemmas for Practice Educators

Practice educators reported three types of scenarios which could result in students taking longer to complete the programme, and which could occasionally result in a failure to complete it. The first scenario arises from discrimination from service users and carers who may not want to work with a student who is obviously 'different' on account of a visible disability, skin colour or foreign accent; repeated rejections from service users and carers will jeopardise learning opportunities (cf. Razack, 2001; Crawshaw, 2002). One agency decided to 'screen' all new referrals in order to create a level playing field. Staff conducted initial visits where they explained that the agency had staff and students from a variety of backgrounds and that it had policies prohibiting racism, disablism and other forms of discrimination. If service users or carers expressed prejudices against a particular minority group, then they would not be allocated to a student who came from this minority group.

The second scenario is when the student carries unresolved baggage from their own biography which compromises relationships in the workplace. These students can make life extremely difficult for their colleagues and supervisors, but they can also be gifted in relating to service users and carers, probably on account of their insider understanding of suffering which is the source of their commitment, insight, empathy and creativity. Case examples from practice teachers indicated that the ways these difficulties manifested themselves varied in accordance with the age of the student. A few young students with a history of childhood abuse or neglect treated their supervisors (and other colleagues) as surrogate counsellors, pouring out their troubled histories on a regular basis so that there was little scope to discuss casework. The most common solution here is to advise the student to take time out of the programme in order to undergo professional counselling. But mature students with a similar history could be antagonistic towards their supervisors (and other authority figures) whilst denying vehemently that they had any problems. One practice teacher asked a student to transfer to another agency to complete the placement; she felt that her capacity to assess the progress of a student who seemed to attack her at every point was compromised; but she also believed that the student was gifted in dealing with service users and carers with complex problems, and therefore wanted her to have a fresh start somewhere else. If such unresolved baggage gives rise to a mental health diagnosis, then additional assistance can be made available under the disability equality duty. Unfortunately, the stigma associated with mental health problems means that students may be reluctant to seek a diagnosis, and if they already have a diagnosis, they may be reluctant to disclose it just in case this results in discriminatory rather than anti-discriminatory treatment (cf. Manthorpe and Stanley, 1999; Collins, 2006).

The third scenario stems from a mismatch between the cultural profiles of a student and their service users or carers, which tends to manifest itself in relation to overseas students. An agency specialising in work with bereaved families received complaints from service users as a result of what they regarded as culturally inappropriate advice around mourning from an overseas student. In her native country, mourning was a prolonged, community-wide affair involving much weeping and wailing, but in the UK mourning is a more privatised, diluted and truncated affair (see Rees, 2001). A practice teacher in an agency working with older people reported that one of her students had returned completely bemused from a home visit as she did not know what a 'bucket' was and therefore could not work out what the problem was that she was supposed to address. An elderly woman was unable to access her upstairs bathroom and consequently was going to the toilet in a bucket and throwing the contents outside, much to the consternation of her neighbours. The student still did not understand the problem after looking up the word 'bucket' in a dictionary, so her supervisor had to bring a bucket into the office to show the student what was meant. This left the supervisor wondering what else this student may have misunderstood during home visits? Once again, these students may need a longer period of time to complete their Key Roles – but the dilemma for practice educators is that it can take years rather than months to become sufficiently acculturated to work in another country and in another language.

Exercise 11B provides an interesting case example of an overseas student who was confronted with discrimination from service users in spite of her linguistic capacities and cultural competence. It shows how students from minority groups may need to use their advocacy and assertiveness skills on their own behalf in order to ensure a level playing field in practice learning.

Exercise 11B   Challenging Discrimination in Practice Learning

A black African student was based in a day centre where all the staff and service users were white British. She faced two types of discrimination and mobilised different strategies to combat them.

The first type of discrimination pertained to intrusive questioning about her origins from service users who had never encountered a black person before. Here, she refused to answer questions since she did not want to be treated differently from any other student or member of staff. Eventually, service users respected her strong boundaries and even enforced them for her by telling new service users not to ask her anything about her native country, culture, language or religion.

The second type of discrimination pertained to erroneous assumptions about her understanding of issues and use of language. This was a multilingual student with a perfect grasp of the English language and a sound grasp of social problems in the UK. But when her practice teacher invited her to a review of a care plan, the service user objected to the student's presence on the grounds that 'mixed race' people might not understand what was going on and he would not understand their use of language. The student was proud of her black African heritage and rose to its defence, telling the service user that she was pure black African rather than mixed race, and inviting him to tell her exactly which parts of her use of language he was unable to understand? He acknowledged that he could understand her and consented to her attendance at the meeting. He spent the rest of the day apologising to her and went on to tell other service users what a good social worker she would be.

By the end of the placement, this student had earned the trust, respect and affection of everyone. The agency manager commended her for having broken through the barriers of 'race' in a way which would facilitate the integration of future students, staff members or service users from minority ethnic backgrounds. She was given gifts to remind her of the placement. Her own parting gift was to deliver a presentation on her country of origin to staff and service users which was extremely well received.

Ponder on the following notes and queries:

- Students facing discrimination may have to be assertive in undertaking self-advocacy. How can other students and staff assist them in challenging discriminatory treatment?
- Different kinds of discrimination may require different strategies. Why were the strategies mobilised by this student effective? What difference would it have made if her choice of strategies had been reversed, i.e. if she had opened up about her country of origin at the outset, or refused to speak out in the review meeting?
- Why did everyone come to the conclusion that she would make a good social worker?

11.4 The Final Hurdle

In academic terms, the final hurdle consists in passing the final set of assignments, or the dissertation in some programmes. What happens if you fail? As a general rule, you can resubmit the assignment(s), making sure that you seek advice from a tutor before you do so. In terms of practice, the final hurdle consists in being signed off as 'fit to practise' by your PLA in your final placement. What happens if you are not regarded as fit to practise? If you simply need additional time to meet all of the competencies, your placement may be extended; if there are more complex issues, then you may be given the opportunity to repeat the entire placement elsewhere.

Your programme of study will only be terminated in the event of repeated failures to pass modules or placements, or serious misconduct which casts grave doubt upon your professional suitability. Serious misconduct includes forming personal relationships with service users involving financial or sexual transactions; being dependent upon alcohol or drugs to the point that it compromises your capacity to fulfil work commitments; and receiving a criminal conviction for a serious offence (see Currer and Atherton, 2008). Universities are obliged to report serious misconduct to regulatory councils and, after investigating the case, they may invoke procedures for deregistration.

'Fitness to practise' is a term which has been subject to a great deal of debate (see Pithouse and Scourfield, 2002). Whilst all students need to demonstrate basic competence in each of the Units which make up the Key Roles, there may be considerable variability in their levels of competence in respect of some of these Units. This variability arises from the diversity of starting points among students, the diversity of placements and the sheer breadth of the territory – it is impossible to develop practical expertise in every aspect of social work and in relation to all service user groups within a degree programme. And remember that your competence is assessed in relation to the competence expected of a *beginning* social worker; no one is demanding that you operate at the level of qualified staff with many years in the field (Fook et al., 2000; ESWDET, 2008: Chapter 10).

Nevertheless, it is increasingly acknowledged within the caring professions that there can be a world of difference between meeting basic competencies and being a truly competent, caring professional (Phillips et al., 2000; Lafrance et al., 2004). Why is this? The majority of people can learn to do the majority of tasks across most professions given sufficient time, training and effort; but some of these people go on to do the job in a more superficial, mechanical or bureaucratic manner, whilst others who are committed to the vocation become caring, creative and critically reflective practitioners. It is only the latter people who make excellent social workers, i.e. they do additional training and reading to find out about new resources and interventions to help their clients; they support team members during stressful periods; they challenge agencies in the service of anti-oppressive practice; and they go on to lead projects and educate students. The most vexing issue for PLAs arises when they can tick off all the Units of the Key Roles but continue to have doubts about the suitability of the student (Furness and Gilligan, 2004). Exercise 11C explains what many practice educators and managers are looking for when signing someone off as fit to practise, or when interviewing candidates for a job, and invites you to assess your own profile against these more covert but all-important criteria.

Exercise 11C   Practice Educators' and Managers' Criteria for Fitness to Practise

Read the following accounts by practice educators, two of whom were also managers of their agencies with responsibilities for staff recruitment. You should ask yourself: do I meet these criteria for fitness to practise? You could discuss this question with your own practice teacher: do your answers to this question correspond?

1 The Safe Practitioner

CH: How would you describe what you need to see before you'd pass somebody off as fit to practise?

T: It's that *in all aspects of what they do they're a safe practitioner.* That's the bottom line for me. I have this nominal view of what a safe practitioner is: it's that *when there are risky situations they make the right decisions most of the time*. You don't make the right decisions all the time, but *most* of the time ... A safe practitioner is also *ethical* – someone who is trustworthy and honest, will regularly consult with people ... a supportive team member, but who can also be assertive.

2 The Insightful Practitioner

T: It's about being able to grasp *what the issues are* ... [and] presenting that to me in supervision ... I don't expect social workers to have all the answers. *How can you? You can't!* But you have to have a grasp of what the issues are in order to know the right *questions* to ask ... The classic thing would be doing an assessment [on prospective foster carers or adopters] ... where you uncover that one of the adults has suffered abuse as a child. It's not just about *describing* that. It's about *what that means*. What does it mean for that person who's wanting to become a carer? ... How has that person *resolved* those difficulties? ... What's the *impact* likely to be on any child who might be placed with them? I need a social worker to be able to *see* that those are the issues – but I'm not saying they've got to resolve them, or even to have the counselling skills to do that.

3 The Trustworthy Practitioner

CH: What are you looking for in a final placement student?
T: The bottom line is: *would you let this social worker into your house?*
CH: Into your own house?
T: Yes. If you had a problem, would you let this person in? If you feel comfortable with that, then it's a fair assumption that the student's going to be okay ...
CH: So what is it ... that makes a trustworthy social worker?
T: Well, it isn't about expertise because you don't expect them to be experts at that point. It's about trust and faith that I know this person is going to do the best they can do for me, and if they can't they will find somebody who can. It's that sort of trust.

Points to Remember and Questions to Ponder

- A good study guide will help you with the practicalities of completing academic assignments; acquiring the arts of relaxation and creative visualisation will help you to conquer anxieties in respect of live performances before an audience.
- Remember that many stakeholders will be assessing your progress on placement, and that you are one of them! If you take a more active role in self-assessment, you will contribute to your own education and empowerment.

(Continued)

(Continued)

- Are you a member of a disadvantaged group? Or do you believe that you are experiencing discrimination within the university or community? You may be entitled to extra assistance, although you should be prepared to advocate on your own behalf as well.
- Have you stumbled at an assessment hurdle? Don't despair. Arrange to meet with your personal supervisor to discuss the options available to you.

Further Reading and Resources

University handbooks provide guidance on the assessment apparatus, referencing your work, student welfare services and specialist services for disabled and overseas students, etc.

There are a number of books available for general study skills and essay-writing skills:
Cottrell, S. (2008) *The Study Skills Handbook*. Basingstoke: Palgrave-Macmillan.
Greetham, B. (2008) *How to Write Better Essays*. Basingstoke: Palgrave-Macmillan.

These study guides are equally relevant to literature-based dissertations. However, if your dissertation involves empirical research, you need to consult the following text:
Whittaker, A. (2009) *Research Skills for Social Work*. Exeter: Learning Matters.

If you want to learn skills in relaxation and creative visualisation, CDs are a better resource:
Gawain, S. (2002) *Creative Visualization Meditations*. Novato, CA: New World Library.
Levey, J. (2000) *The Fine Art of Relaxation: Self-Guided CD*. Seattle, WA: Earth View.

The equality duties in higher education can be accessed on the website of the Equality and Human Rights Commission – www.equalityhumanrights.com

12

Establishing a Career Pathway

Introduction

During placements, students are actively formulating and reformulating their career preferences, and most start to apply for jobs before the end of their programme. Section 12.1 examines employment prospects for newly qualified social workers (NQSWs) and offers guidance on job interviews, whilst section 12.2 explains the significance of continuing professional development (CPD). But if you are to survive and thrive in social work, you need to pay attention to occupational health and hazards, so section 12.3 outlines the sources of stress in social work and offers advice on preventing burnout. Finally, I shall highlight the role of faith in the caring professions.

12.1 Employment Prospects

Employment prospects for social workers are very good. The vast majority of graduates are employed within months of qualification, and the majority of them secure permanent posts, mostly in local authorities; the tiny minority who remain unemployed a year after qualification are typically those who are unsure of their vocation and exploring other options (Lyons and Manion, 2004).

The best advice is to construe your career preferences broadly when applying for posts – you may be passionate about adult mental health, but there are more jobs in community care which will provide a stepping stone towards your ideal post. If you have such a strong sense of your 'ideal post' that you are reluctant to compromise on the timescale for reaching this goal, then you may have to apply for relevant posts regardless of their location. Geographic mobility is not always feasible for mature students with families and mortgages, but other students may relish such opportunities, and some are keen to work abroad as well. If you have no clear plans, then you may prefer to sign up with employment agencies to do temporary work in different settings or with different service user groups. Final-year students will benefit from visiting the Careers Service in their university and attending Careers Fairs where social care employers are available to discuss job opportunities. Exercise 12A will help you to prepare for job interviews. It is important to treat a job interview as an opportunity for a two-way dialogue, and if you are not successful, to get feedback on your performance. But you also need to keep your fears in perspective so that they do not adversely affect your chances.

Exercise 12A   Preparing for Job Interviews

Four kinds of reflection should govern your preparation for interviews:

1 Reflecting upon your self-presentation on the day of the interview – you need to remain calm and centred in your own body–mind, whilst also being open to meeting new people and engaging in dialogue. Revisit Chapter 11: Exercise 11A
2 Reflecting back on your trajectory to date and forward to your career future – interview panels usually ask a few general questions at the beginning and end of proceedings, for example:

   • Why did you apply for this job in this agency with this service user group?
   • What relevant life or work experience would you bring to this job?
   • Tell us about a critical incident on placement and how you handled it.
   • Where do you see yourself in five years' time?

3 Reflecting upon the person specification and job description provided by the agency – you should be prepared for questions on relevant knowledge, skills and values, for example:

- Knowledge – jot down key themes around law, policy, theory and research so that you can demonstrate your knowledge. Employers like to see evidence of practical applications (e.g. How have you used attachment theory?) and critical reflection (e.g. What are your views on new policy proposals?)
- Skills – some interview panels ask for a case example from placement to satisfy themselves that you have acquired relevant skills; others provide a hypothetical case scenario and ask how you would deal with it.
- Values – you may be asked about what value dilemmas you would anticipate in this setting or with this service user group and how you would address them.

4 Reflecting upon your own needs and interests as an NQSW – you will be able to ask questions at the end of the interview, and you should formulate these in advance, for example:

- Do NQSWs receive protected caseloads or enhanced supervision?
- If you have a specialist interest in therapeutic interventions or evaluation research, then flag this up at the interview. This could represent an important way of adding value to the agency, and you need to know whether your specialist interests will be supported.

Students' worries can be summarised in the form of three questions:

- Do employers favour NQSWs with a higher-class degree or a distinction above others? Degree classification is only vitally important if you want to pursue an academic career. Employers are more concerned about the suitability of the person for the job than the specifics of their degree classification, and it is impossible to read off one from the other. High-flying academics can be ill-suited to practice – although if they are well-suited to practice, they make excellent practitioners and soon become managers. Likewise, a lower-class degree does not make you a lower-class practitioner – but if it reflects a limited engagement with the programme, then this does matter and it will show up in interviews.
- Are students disadvantaged in the labour market if they have not had a placement which is directly relevant to their preferred career specialism? Employers are aware that the degree in social work is a generic qualification which requires exposure to diverse service user groups and settings so no one is expecting to see a one-to-one correspondence between your placement profile and your career preference. The task for students is to capitalise upon transferable learning in respect of whatever skills and knowledges they have gained.
- How far do economic recessions cast a shadow over employment prospects? Some agencies freeze vacancies during a recession, although they may also hire temporary staff to deal with the volume of work; others continue to recruit as new

streams of funding are made available to deal with new social problems. A social work qualification is a versatile asset in the multi-professional world of welfare and you are not restricted to traditional social work posts.

New recruits to any job will have a six-month probationary period. All employers provide induction, supervision and in-house training to new staff, and some provide additional facilities for NQSWs such as one-to-one mentoring or peer group support (CWDC, 2009a; SWTF, 2009). In Northern Ireland, there is an Assessed Year in Employment (AYE) for all social work graduates so that the full qualification is dependent upon satisfactory completion of this AYE, and there are plans to develop a similar scheme in England (SWTF, 2009). Under these conditions, it is possible for people to obtain a social work degree without obtaining a social work qualification if they fail to complete their Assessed Year in Employment, in which case they might continue working in social care without occupying the role of a qualified social worker. But this should be unusual insofar as support and training for new recruits, along with protected caseloads, will go hand in hand with assessment.

12.2 Continuing Professional Development

There will always be a gap between the skills and knowledges acquired during a degree programme and the skills and knowledges required for any given social work post (cf. Marsh and Triseliotis, 1996; CWDC, 2009a). A social work degree is designed to provide education in theory, research and policy in a manner relevant to contemporary practice, rather than training for any specific job. Placements provide relatively sheltered work experience and should not require students to shoulder the same workload or casework complexity as their qualified counterparts. Furthermore, some roles are reserved for qualified social workers who have undertaken additional training, notably in mental health and child protection. You should note that ongoing training is one of the requirements for renewing your registration or licence to practise as a qualified social worker with regulatory councils, and that it may be allied to career progression (see SWTF, 2009: Chapter 3). Professionals across the public sector and elsewhere expect to have regular staff appraisals as part of their contract of employment as well as their own continuing professional development (CPD).

Three types of training are available to social workers. First, employers provide their own in-house training courses on matters which are pertinent to the everyday tasks of staff. This includes guidance on new legislation and working in courts or tribunals where appropriate; it may include managing budgets, dealing with aggressive clients or working in multi-ethnic communities; and some courses will be designed and delivered in multi-professional contexts. There is a growing appreciation of the need for CPD to be embedded in everyday working life, so that some employers encourage staff to experiment with action learning sets, group supervision and evaluation research (see Gould and Baldwin, 2004). This embedded approach to CPD has been strongly endorsed in Scotland (SSSC, 2008).

Second, there are specialist training programmes which are delivered by a consortium of educators and employers and which lead to post-qualification (PQ) awards. You need to complete your probationary period or AYE before you are eligible to apply for a PQ programme. You also need to be clear about your career pathway since these programmes are designed in accordance with specialist roles, i.e. there are PQ awards in child care, adult care, mental health, practice education and management (cf. CCW, 2005; GSCC, 2005; Department of Health, Social Services and Public Safety, 2006). The PQ framework is currently under review in England and Wales.

Finally, if you have a specific career plan which falls outside of the remit of CPD or PQ studies, then you can adopt a 'do-it-yourself' approach to career progression, although you may have to 'fund-it-yourself' as well if you cannot secure sponsorship from a university, employer or charity. If you are interested in therapeutic ways of working with a view to establishing your own independent practice, then you need specialist training in a relevant therapy (e.g. psychotherapy or family therapy). If you aspire to an academic career, then you can apply to undertake a PhD, and some universities offer sponsorships for professional doctorates designed especially for practitioners.

12.3 Occupational Health and Hazards

Occupational health comes under the umbrella of human resources and is regarded as a shared responsibility between employers and employees. Employers have a duty to provide the conditions under which people can operate safely and effectively which includes training and supervision; many large employers also subscribe to employee assistance schemes so that they can refer staff with work-related stress for counselling (cf. GSCC, 2002b; Lewis and Thornbory, 2006). Employees have a duty to take care of themselves so that they remain fit for work. But it is important to take care of yourself for your own sake – not simply for your employer or your service users.

12.3.1 Stress in Social Work

Stress follows an upside-down U curve. In the absence of stress, we stay on the ground and fail to grow. Positive stress – known as 'eustress' – acts as a stimulus to growth, keeping our body–mind alert. Peak performances often flow from challenging periods in our working lives when stress levels are high but we stretch ourselves to meet the challenge. But beyond this peak lies distress which is associated with deteriorating performance, i.e. the challenges outstrip our coping capacities. If this continues, it literally brings us back to the ground until we suffer the exhaustion and disillusionment associated with burnout (Shapiro and Clawson, 1988; Goleman, 1996).

Social work is a stressful occupation, but it is also a satisfying occupation where high levels of eustress contribute to a sustained learning and growing curve (Cree, 2003; Rose, 2003). This may be a double-edged sword, since when individuals are already operating at their peak, they are more vulnerable to a downhill slide when required to take on 'more'. Research findings over the past decade indicate that the following factors can be prevalent in social services and mutually reinforcing, so their co-existence is likely to tip some social workers over the edge from eustress into distress (Davies, 1998; Balloch et al., 1999; CWDC, 2009a; SWTF, 2009):

- The complexity of casework – particularly with involuntary clients and decision making in situations with multi-directional but not always readily calculable risks.
- The high level of vacancies, particularly in local authorities in urban areas – this has repercussions on caseloads, and if cases are stacked some of them will become crises; and it impacts upon support levels as managers may be less available for consultation.
- The rapid pace of organisational change – senior managers may decide to restructure the agency and redeploy staff in an effort to deal more effectively with incoming referrals; they may be forced to revise policies and procedures as a result of new legislation; major changes create an atmosphere of uncertainty and anxiety.

It is noteworthy that none of these factors is under the direct control of any individual. The sense of not having any control or choice in respect of the conditions of our life or work is positively correlated with distress and can contribute to dysfunctional patterns of coping if people internalise apathy ('learned helplessness') or if they externalise anger ('blaming others'). But it is essential to reclaim our power and to recognise that the experience of stress is always mediated by ourselves and our social networks, so that some individuals continue to thrive under pressure and some teams increase in solidarity during stressful periods (cf. Morrison, 2007; Collins, 2008).

12.3.2 Coping Strategies

If you have survived your social work programme, then it is fair to assume that you have already evolved some healthy coping strategies. Can you identify your own healthy coping strategies? But research shows that our coping strategies can break down if we are confronted by chronic and complex cases in situations where there is not enough space and time to process events and emotions and not enough support from colleagues and managers (Satyamurti, 1981; Davies, 1998). This provides an opening for unhealthy coping strategies to take over – most of us already have a few of these anyway, but we usually function effectively as long as our healthy strategies outweigh our unhealthy ones. You might like to pause to consider what unhealthy coping strategies you may have succumbed to in times of duress. When the balance shifts and unhealthy coping strategies predominate, it impairs our functioning.

Dysfunctional coping is associated with the mobilisation of defence mechanisms and may take various forms depending upon the defence deployed. Child protection cases provide ample evidence of which defences operate under which conditions and with what consequences (Reder et al., 1993; Brandon et al., 2008) although these defences can operate in any setting:

- Denial of the possibility of change resulting in disengagement – this is most common in cases of child neglect where parents seem unable or unwilling to learn new skills. Here, social workers start to mirror the negativity of the parents until they give up on the family. There is psychological disengagement so that visits become mechanical affairs, followed by physical disengagement in the form of case closure, even though nothing has changed for the child.
- Denial of problems resulting in false optimism – this is most common when parents are minimising their difficulties or actively concealing neglect or abuse. Here, social workers mirror the positivity of the parents, taking the adults' account of their situation at face value without checking out other evidence. It makes for a cosy relationship but there is collusion so that social workers lose their objectivity and fail to recognise harm to children, thereby placing their primary clients at greater risk.
- Projection of blame resulting in coercion – when social workers recognise high levels of risk but have been unable to remedy them through partnership working, they may resort to the blaming game where they project their own anger and anxiety onto clients and threaten them with court action. This invites a self-fulfilling prophecy – if a social worker abandons partnership working in high-risk situations, legal coercion may be the only avenue for achieving change.

It should be noted that how and why we do something often matters just as much as what we do. Sometimes closing a case may be the only thing we can do after months of futile attempts at assistance, but we should always check out whether other approaches or agencies would be more helpful. Sometimes legal intervention is necessary, but it should result from an objective appraisal of risks and benefits rather than dynamics of blame and shame, and we still need to work in partnership with people long after a court hearing. Unsatisfactory case closures and coercive measures can leave us with negativity about our profession, our own capability and certain clients, but we must guard against internalising this negativity to the point that it solidifies into negative stereotypes which we carry over to other cases.

The antidote to this negativity is socio-emotional intelligence. In other words, we need a healthy separation between self and others which allows us to preserve our own sense of worth even when things go wrong, as well as the space to process evidence and emotions without succumbing to entanglement or estrangement (see Chapter 9). But what can you do to promote this? On an individual level, you need to cultivate practices in your everyday life which release stress and relax your body–mind. These dissolve the defences associated with dysfunctional ways of coping since defences are erected in response to threats (i.e. perceived stressors) and a truly relaxed person has no need of them. Exercise 12B provides guidance on managing stress and preventing burnout.

Exercise 12B   Preventing Burnout

Maxim 1: Take care of yourself in everyday life (under all circumstances)

Remember that human beings need adequate nutrition, exercise and rest if they are to survive at all. Do not under any circumstances forgo your human needs for the sake of your job; you are worth more than any job. Many hobbies promote relaxation and stress release as well as helping us to preserve a healthy sense of our own personhood, for example:

- Swimming and jogging release muscular tension and build up stamina.
- Yoga and t'ai chi promote a calm, confident and coordinated body and mind.
- Meditation and prayer can help people to let go of everyday ego-based worries.
- Art and music provide opportunities for creativity as well as relaxation.

Maxim 2: Deal proactively with problems in your working life (when necessary)

Everyone experiences difficulties in their working life at some stage of their careers. If you are experiencing difficulties, do not resort to denial in the hope that they will disappear by themselves, and do not take refuge in a victim role.

Many of the difficulties reported by NQSWs could be prevented if all parties were clear about workloads and support levels at the outset. You must be prepared to negotiate on these matters at a job interview and during your induction period, and if you find that agreements are being breached then you need to express your concerns.

Beyond this, a positive attitude towards yourself and other people is crucial. You have chosen and been chosen for this job; you should assume that you are capable of doing it well with the right support, and that other people are willing to support you if you are struggling. But people may not know you are struggling unless you tell them!

Maxim 3: There are always alternatives (under extreme circumstances)

If your working life becomes unbearable, there are always alternatives. If your line manager is not supportive, you can consult with other managers or occupational health or professional associations. If your health is deteriorating, your GP should give you some time out to recover. If you believe that you are not well-suited to this setting or service user group, there are other settings and other service user groups.

Remember that as long as you recognise problems and seek to remedy them, you are not 'failing' but simply renegotiating your life–work pathway.

12.3.3 Organisational Cultures

Socio-emotional intelligence is not simply an individual matter since we inhabit organisations with cultures which can facilitate or hinder its development. The term 'cultures' refers to norms, values and beliefs which are embodied and embedded in everyday life; they can be decoded from informal relationships in the workplace as well as the formal apparatus around supervision and team working. When someone is upset after returning from a visit, does anyone notice this? If so, do they offer a listening ear? If this offer is accepted, do they provide sound advice and respect confidentiality (unless this is impossible)? NQSWs are more dependent upon the external environment to provide the safe container in which to process casework, unlike experienced practitioners who can work with a higher level of complexity for longer periods via self-supervision (Hawkins and Shohet, 1989).

Research shows that some social services organisations are characterised by dysfunctional cultures which predispose them to dealing with their own staff as well as service users in defensive ways (Menzies, 1970; Balloch et al., 1999). Local authorities can be vulnerable to defensive ways of operating precisely because they are large bureaucracies charged with statutory responsibilities for high-risk cases within the context of multi-agency working. Elongated hierarchies enable practitioners to project blame upwards and managers to project blame downwards when something goes wrong. Labyrinthine mazes of procedures, along with the associated record-keeping systems, can interfere with the face-to-face interactions with service users and other professionals which are so vital to socio-emotional intelligence. Multi-agency meetings can also be arenas for retreating behind protocols, securing a collusive consensus or projecting blame elsewhere.

The antidote to dysfunctional cultures is the learning organisation which values democratic debate (including dissent) in respect of its operations; here, managers take into account the experiences of staff and service users at the grassroots, and favour bottom-up changes over top-down engineering (Gould and Baldwin, 2004). It will also be an emotionally intelligent workplace which foregrounds the concrete humanity of staff and service users rather than abstract bureaucratic protocols; here, managers acknowledge the pivotal role of emotions and relationships in all human endeavours, since these can make or break our individual and collective spirits (Churniss and Goleman, 2001). Fortunately, our regulators and employers are waking up to the importance of organisational health and harmony. The Scottish framework for continuing professional development is based upon the literature on socio-emotional intelligence in individuals and organisations and its aim is to promote healthy workplace relationships (SSSC, 2008). In England, there are plans to implement a new national standard for employers to ensure that staff have access to high-quality supervision and other facilities, and that they are consulted about occupational and organisational health on a regular basis (SWTF, 2009: Chapter 2). So there is every reason to believe that the tide is turning.

12.4 Sustaining Faith

A long time ago, the sociologist Paul Halmos (1978) studied the works and writings of people in the caring professions and claimed that they were sustained by a faith in their vocation which transcended the official sets of theories and techniques associated with their profession. What is the nature of this faith? It is a faith which binds our sense of self to our vocation in serving others. It is a faith that social work is a worthwhile profession which can contribute to social care, social control and social change in positive ways. It is a faith in our own capacity to grow within the profession and to reach out and help others to grow as well. In itself, it is a secular faith in the humanity of ourselves, others and our profession, although it can co-exist with a spiritual or religious faith. How does this faith bear fruit? It keeps us weaving the tapestry of knowledge and skills beyond the requirements of official training programmes. It keeps alive our convictions in social work and social justice, even and especially when our efforts to help have backfired and when our profession is subject to adverse publicity. It prevents us from the descent into disillusionment and despair which are often precursors to burning out or dropping out altogether from social work. How is this faith nurtured? Ideally, students would be surrounded by positive role models – i.e. educators and practitioners who radiate the light of their own faith – and would witness the positive workings of social work for themselves in their dealings with service users and carers. Once nurtured, it can sustain us in the face of cynical colleagues or challenging clients.

Some students arrive on the programme with this kind of faith which they radiate out to others; many acquire it during their placements; but a small minority become cynical by the end of their degree, reporting that they have developed a dislike of bureaucracy, a distrust of certain client groups and a disdain for theories and textbooks[1]. Whatever the reasons which give rise to such reactions – and there will be reasons, perhaps good ones – the measure of our maturity as human beings will be found in the extent to which we take responsibility for our own development. There is always choice in whether to adopt a standpoint of conviction or cynicism and whether to take the path of growth or stagnation. A handful of students decided that they would apply to join other professions after their social work degree, but their faith in the value of social work could still remain intact. One student had just been accepted as a trainee police officer, but he was convinced that the fundamental changes to his character and outlook brought about by social work training would enable him to undertake the social control functions of a police officer in a far more critical and compassionate manner:

> S: You're trained into the care kind of life … Five years ago I'd walk past a tramp in a doorway or someone who's on drugs and drinking and I'd think 'Oh what a waste! What a leech on society!' But now when I walk past that person I think 'Now, what happened to them in their lives to cause this? And what help does this person need?' And that's what this social work degree has done for me.

A social work degree opens up a new world of opportunities, but whatever pathway you take has to be backed up by faith. If you lose faith, then you are likely to lose your way, and to lose others along the way. If you sustain faith, you will find that it sustains you in troubled times, and others too.

Points to Remember and Questions to Ponder

- Remember that continuing professional development is one of the requirements for ongoing registration or re-licensing with regulatory councils.
- Surviving and thriving in social work presupposes sound strategies of self-care and stress management, but the culture of a team or organisation is also important. Placements provide ideal opportunities for analysing workplace dynamics; by the time you apply for jobs, you will be better equipped to check out the health or otherwise of a team or organisation.
- What is the role of 'faith' in the caring professions?

Note

1   This finding is based upon a survey of BA students at the end of their programme.

Further Reading and Resources

Social work posts are advertised in *Community Care* – www.communitycare.co.uk

Compass holds Careers Fairs for social work graduates every year in London, Leeds, Birmingham and Manchester – www.compassjobsfair.com

Careerjet is an employment search engine where you can look for social care vacancies across the UK and overseas – www.careerjet.co.uk

A good guide for NQSWs with specialist chapters on different service user groups is:

Tovey, W. (ed.) (2007) *The Post-Qualifying Handbook for Social Workers*. London: Jessica Kingsley.

Neil Thompson hosts a 'well-being bookshop' on his website with books on stress management – www.avenueconsulting.co.uk/neil-thompson.html

Professional organisations assist our development and provide advice in times of duress:

British Association of Social Workers – www.basw.co.uk

UNISON: a trade union for employees in social care and local government – www.unison.org.uk

Appendix: The Study of Students and their Educators

Becoming a Social Worker: A Guide for Students is based upon original research with students and their educators which was conducted during the period 2004–08 in England. Ethical approval was granted by the relevant university and financial support was forthcoming from the Higher Education Funding Council for England. The focus was upon students undertaking a BA in Social Work programme, and the aim was to explore what is entailed in becoming a social worker in contemporary Britain in the hope that this would be helpful to future generations of student social workers and their educators. The students who volunteered their time and energy to participate in interviews and who volunteered their portfolios for the research expressly wanted their stories to become educational resources for future students.

My task as the author has been to select case examples from students and their educators which best fit the pedagogic purpose of this textbook, and to supply the contexts for these case examples so that readers can make sense of them. In the process, I have drawn upon my own practice wisdom acquired over several years as a social worker, practice teacher and academic tutor. But the case examples themselves are real-life stories of social work education and practice which have not been subject to reconstruction, although of course they have been anonymised in relation to individual participants and their practice agencies. 'Insiders' who participated in the project may discover their own case example in the pages of this textbook, and others who were directly involved in a case may also occupy an 'insider' position, but 'outsiders' will not be able to identify any individual or agency. Readers across the UK may find that several stories resonate with their own experiences – this is a by-product of the rootedness of this textbook in the everyday life worlds of students, practitioners and educators, and similarities (as well as differences) in our life worlds are to be expected.

Certain measures were built in to the project in order to minimise the chances of identifying individuals or agencies. Case material was supplied by students across four successive cohorts since pilot studies were conducted simultaneously with three student cohorts in Years 1, 2 and 3 of their programmes prior to the main study which followed students in a single cohort from the start to the end of their programme. Practice teachers provided additional case examples of student learning, some of which pertained to students from other cohorts and other programmes. Portfolios were selected from students based in 23 agencies and authorities, and interviews with students and practice teachers enabled access to material from additional agencies and authorities.

Methods of data collection were combined to maximise the validity and reliability of findings:

- A survey questionnaire was administered to 80 students during their first week of the BA in Social Work programme. This was used as the basis for developing the typology of service user, personal carer and citizen routes into social work examined in Chapter 2.
- Interviews were held with 30 students at different stages of the programme. Students had a choice in whether to be interviewed as individuals or in small groups, and almost all of them opted for individual interviews, although there was one dyadic interview. An open-ended interviewing style was adopted to encourage students to discuss their experiences on their own terms, although efforts were made to ensure that specific themes were addressed in each interview in order to promote consistency. All interviews were recorded and transcribed to preserve the accuracy of accounts.
- Six focus groups were convened for students on initial placements in agencies which had a Practice Learning and Teaching Unit taking a number of students. These took place towards the end of the placement when students had formed into a cohesive group; the dynamics and discussions emerging in each of these groups were therefore quite distinctive. Focus group discussions were also recorded and transcribed.
- Forty portfolios from placements were read – 15 from students on initial placements and 25 from students on final placements. Work records provided insights into the policies, paperwork and procedures of agencies and authorities and their impacts upon practice. Placement reports proved to be an excellent source for understanding how students met their Key Roles in different settings. Reflective journals showed how students grappled with emotional, ethical, political and cultural dilemmas, and how their capacity to reflect upon casework and its contexts developed over time.
- A survey questionnaire was administered to students at the end of their programme. Not all students were available for this session, but analysis of the 50 completed questionnaires was helpful in understanding students' evaluations of professional pedagogy as well as their career intentions.

Deploying multiple methods in a longitudinal project provides ample opportunities to refine, refute or corroborate hypotheses, interpretations and conclusions. Themes which emerged in the pilot studies and Year 1 survey were explored further during individual interviews and focus groups. The surveys in Year 1 and Year 3 were distributed to the same cohort of students and therefore allowed for some cross-referencing of data from both surveys. Some students volunteered to participate in the project at different stages and in different ways, so that the accounts they supplied during individual or group interviews could be cross-checked with their portfolios from initial or final placements. This also enabled me to witness at first hand some of the dramatic changes students could undergo over a three-year degree programme.

The project was designed to be student-centred and therefore required a participatory approach. At key intervals throughout the project – such as the start of the academic year or the end of a placement – I met with groups of students (and sometimes an entire cohort) in order to brief them on the project, providing information sheets with consent forms for those who wished to sign up for an interview or to volunteer their portfolio. After the first year, I was able to give feedback to students about general themes which had emerged from the research and how these had been presented in conferences or publications so that they could develop a clearer sense of how their stories could be used, which furnished an additional safeguard for informed consent.

It was important to seek the views of educators in order to produce a more rounded account of social work education which would respect the diversity of stakeholders and standpoints. Practice teachers from a wide area were invited to attend initial briefing sessions on the project, and informa-tion sheets were sent out to those who were unable to attend. Academic tutors, social services managers and voluntary agency supervisors were also informed about the project. In total, 30 educators volunteered for interview, most of whom were practice teachers in the community. They were inter-viewed as individuals, in pairs or in small groups and all interviews were recorded and transcribed. Educators' perspectives upon university-based teaching, community-based supervision, the role of theory in practice and the dilemmas around student assessment were particularly significant and occupy a prominent place in the relevant chapters.

Service users and carers are also significant stakeholders in social work education, but it was not possible to interview them directly during this project on account of constraints around my own time and energy as a solo researcher. Readers will realise that the predicaments and perspectives of service users and carers are actually at the heart of most of the case exam-ples supplied by students and educators. Without them, there is no social work practice or pedagogy.

References

Adams, R. (2008) *Empowerment, Participation and Social Work*, 4th edn. Basingstoke: Palgrave-Macmillan.

Adams, R., Dominelli, L. and Payne, M. (eds) (2009a) *Critical Practice in Social Work*, 2nd edn. Basingstoke: Palgrave-Macmillan.

Adams, R., Dominelli, L. and Payne, M. (eds) (2009b) *Practising Social Work in a Complex World*. Basingstoke: Palgrave-Macmillan.

Advocacy in Action and Sure Search Collective (eds) (2006) 'Service users and carers in social work education', *Social Work Education*, 25 (4) (special edition).

Advocacy in Action with University of Nottingham (2006) 'Making it our own ball game: learning and assessment in social work education', *Social Work Education*, 25 (4): 332–47.

Alcock, P. (2006) *Understanding Poverty*, 3rd edn. Basingstoke: Palgrave-Macmillan.

Aldridge, M. (1994) *Making Social Work News*. London: Routledge.

Anthias, F. and Yuval-Davis, N. (1992) *Racialised Boundaries: Race, Nation, Gender, Colour and Class and the Anti-Racist Struggle*. London: Routledge.

Appiah, K. A. (2005) *The Ethics of Identity*. Princeton, NJ: Princeton University Press.

Archambeault, J. (2009) *Social Work and Mental Health*. Exeter: Learning Matters.

Archer, C. (1999a) *First Steps in Parenting the Child Who Hurts: Tiddlers and Toddlers*. London: British Agencies of Adoption and Fostering.

Archer, C. (1999b) *Next Steps in Parenting the Child Who Hurts: Tykes and Teens*. London: British Agencies of Adoption and Fostering.

Archer, L., Hutchings, M. and Ross, A. (2003) *Higher Education and Social Class: Issues of Exclusion and Inclusion*. London: Routledge-Falmer.

Auchmuty, R. (1989) ' "By their friends we shall know them": the lives and networks of some women in North Lambeth 1880–1942', in Lesbian History Group (ed.) *Not a Passing Phase: Reclaiming Lesbians in History 1840–1985*. London: The Women's Press. pp. 77–98.

Audit Commission (1995) *Paying the Pipe … Calling the Tune: People, Pay and Performance in Local Government*. London: HMSO.

Balen, R. and White, S. (2007) 'Making critical minds: nurturing "not-knowing" in students of health and social care', *Social Work Education*, 26 (2): 200–6.

Balloch, S., McLean, J. and Fisher, M. (eds) (1999) *Social Services: Working under Pressure*. Bristol: Policy Press.

Banks, S. (2004) *Ethics, Accountability and the Social Professions*. Basingstoke: Palgrave-Macmillan.

Banks, S. (2006) *Ethics and Values in Social Work*, 3rd edn. Basingstoke: Palgrave-Macmillan.

Banks, S. and Barnes, D. (2009) 'Planning research and evaluation projects in social work', in R. Adams, L. Dominelli and M. Payne (eds) *Practising Social Work in a Complex World*. Basingstoke: Palgrave-Macmillan. pp. 257–70.

Barber, J. (2002) *Social Work with Addictions*, 2nd edn. London: Macmillan.

Barlow, C. and Hall, B. L. (2007) 'What about feelings? A study of emotion and tension in social work field education', *Social Work Education*, 26 (4): 399–413.

Barnes, E., Griffiths, P., Ord, J. and Wells, D. (1998) *Face to Face with Distress: The Professional Use of Self in Psychosocial Care*. Oxford: Butterworth-Heinemann.

Bar-On, A. (2002) 'Restoring power to social work practice', *British Journal of Social Work*, 32 (8): 997–1014.

Barrett, G., Sellman, D. and Thomas, J. (eds) (2005) *Interprofessional Working in Health and Social Care: Professional Perspectives*. Basingstoke: Palgrave-Macmillan.

Barretti, M. (2004) 'What do we know about the professional socialisation of our students?' *Journal of Social Work Education*, 40 (2): 255–83.

Barron, C. (2004) 'Fair play: creating a better learning climate for social work students in social care settings', *Social Work Education*, 23 (1): 25–37.

Barter, S. (1997) 'Social work students with personal experience of sexual abuse: implications for DipSW programme providers', *Social Work Education*, 16 (2): 113–32.

Bartoli, A., Kennedy, S. and Tedam, P. (2008) 'Practice learning: who is failing to adjust? Black African students' experience of practice learning in the social work setting', *Journal of Practice Teaching and Learning*, 8 (2): 75–90.

Barton, L. (ed.) (2001) *Disability, Politics and the Struggle for Change*. London: David Fulton.

Bauman, Z. (1989) *Modernity and the Holocaust*. Oxford: Polity Press.

Beckett, C. (2007) *Child Protection: An Introduction*. London: Sage.

Bell, M. and Wilson, K. (eds) (2003) *The Practitioner's Guide to Working with Families*. Basingstoke: Palgrave-Macmillan.

Beresford, P. (2000) 'Service-users' knowledges and social work theory: conflict or collaboration?', *British Journal of Social Work*, 30 (4): 489–503.

Beresford, P. (2007) *The Changing Roles and Tasks of Social Work from Service Users' Perspectives: A Literature Informed Discussion Paper*. Shaping Our Lives National User Network. Available at www.gscc.org.uk/NR/rdonlyres/072DD7D6-B915-4F41-B54B-79C62FDB9D95/0/SoLSUliteraturereviewreportMarch07.pdf (accessed 21 October 2009).

Beresford, P. and Campbell, J. (1994) 'Disabled people, service users, user involvement and representation', *Disability & Society*, 9 (3): 315–25.

Beresford, P., Croft, S. and Adshead, L. (2008) ' "We don't see her as a social worker": a service user case study of the importance of the social worker's relationship and humanity', *British Journal of Social Work*, 38 (7): 1388–407.

Bernard, M. and Scharf, T. (eds) (2007) *Critical Perspectives on Ageing Societies*. Bristol: Policy Press.

Beverley, A. and Worsley, A. (2007) *Learning and Teaching in Social Work Practice*. Basingstoke: Palgrave-Macmillan.

Biggs, J. (1999) *Teaching for Quality Learning at University*. Buckingham: Open University Press.

Bilson, A. (2007) 'Promoting compassionate concern in social work: reflections on ethics, biology and love', *British Journal of Social Work*, 37 (8): 1371–86.

Blair, T. (1998) *The Third Way: New Politics for a New Century*. London: The Fabian Society.

Blewett, J., Lewis, J. and Tunstill, J. (2007) *The Changing Roles and Tasks of Social Work: A Literature Informed Discussion Paper*. London: Synergy Research and Consulting.

Blytheway, B. and Johnson, J. (1998) 'The social construction of carers', in A. Symonds and A. Kelly (eds) *The Social Construction of Community Care*. Basingstoke: Macmillan. pp. 241–51.

Booth Davies, J. (1997) *The Myth of Addiction*. Amsterdam: Harwood.

Bowlby, J. (1969) *Attachment and Loss: Volume 1. Attachment*. London: Penguin.

Bowlby, J. (1973) *Attachment and Loss: Volume 2. Separation, Anxiety and Anger*. London: Penguin.

Bowlby, J. (1981) *Attachment and Loss: Volume 3. Loss, Sadness and Depression*. London: Penguin.

Brammer, A. (2010) *Social Work Law*, 3rd edn. Harlow: Pearson Education.

Brandon, M., Belderson, P., Warren, C., Howe, D., Gardner, R., Dodsworth, J. and Black, J. (2008) *Analysing Child Deaths and Serious Injury through Abuse and Neglect: What Can We Learn? A Biennial Analysis of Serious Case Reviews 2003–2005*. London: DCSF.

Brazier, D. (1995) *Zen Therapy: A Buddhist Approach to Psychotherapy*. London: Constable & Robinson.

Briggs, S. (2008) *Working with Adolescents and Young Adults: A Contemporary Psychodynamic Approach*. Basingstoke: Palgrave-Macmillan.

British Association of Social Workers (BASW) (2002) *The Code of Ethics for Social Workers*. London: BASW.

Broad, R. A. (1998) *Young People Leaving Care: Life after the Children Act 1989*. London: Jessica Kingsley.

Brown, R., Bute, S. and Ford, P. (1986) *Social Workers at Risk: The Prevention and Management of Violence*. Basingstoke: Macmillan.

Burns, T. and Sinfield, S. (2008) *Essential Study Skills: The Complete Guide to Success at University*. London: Sage.

Burr, V. (2003) *Social Constructionism*. London: Routledge.

Calder, M. and Hackett, S. (eds) (2003) *Assessment in Child Care: Using and Developing Frameworks for Practice*. Lyme Regis: Russell House.

Care Council for Wales (CCW) (2003a) *The National Occupational Standards for Social Work*. Cardiff: CCW.

Care Council for Wales (CCW) (2003b) *Code of Practice for Social Care Workers*. Cardiff: CCW.

Care Council for Wales (CCW) (2005) *Modular Framework for PQ Learning and Development in Social Work*. Cardiff: CCW.

Cemlyn, S. (2008) 'Human rights and Gypsies and Travellers: an exploration of the application of human rights perspective to social work with a minority community', *British Journal of Social Work*, 38 (1): 153–73.

Chahal, K. (2004) *Experiencing Ethnicity: Discrimination and Service Provision*. York: Joseph Rowntree Foundation.

Chand, A., Clare, J. and Dolton, R. (2002) 'Teaching anti-oppressive practice on a diploma in social work course: lecturers' experiences, students' responses and ways forward', *Social Work Education*, 21 (1): 7–22.

Children's Workforce Development Council (CWDC) (2009a) *New Qualified Social Workers: A Report on Consultations with Newly Qualified Social Workers, Employers and those in Higher Education*, Leeds: CWDC.

Children's Workforce Development Council (CWDC) (2009b) *The Common Assessment Framework for Children and Young People: A Guide for Practitioners*. Leeds: CWDC.

Christie, A. (ed.) (2001) *Men and Social Work: Theories and Practices*. Basingstoke: Palgrave-Macmillan.

Christie, A. (2006) 'Negotiating the uncomfortable intersection between gender and professional identities in social work', *Critical Social Policy*, 26 (2): 390–411.

Christie, A. and Kruk, E. (1998) 'Choosing to become a social worker: motives, incentives, concerns and disincentives', *Social Work Education*, 17 (1): 21–34.

Christie, A. and Weeks, J. (1998) 'Life experience: a neglected form of knowledge in social work education and practice', *Practice*, 10 (1): 55–68.

Churniss, C. and Goleman, D. (eds) (2001) *The Emotionally Intelligent Workplace*. San Francisco, CA: Jossey Bass.

Cigno, K. and Bourn, D. (eds) (1998) *Cognitive–Behavioural Social Work in Practice*. Aldershot: Ashgate.

Clarke, C. L. (2000) *Social Work Ethics: Politics, Principles and Practice*. Basingstoke: Palgrave-Macmillan.

Clarke, J. (1997) 'Capturing the customer: consumerism and social welfare', *Self, Agency and Society*, 1 (1): 55–73.

Clarke, J., Cochrane, A. and Smart, C. (1987) *Ideologies of Welfare: From Dreams to Disillusion*. London: Routledge.

Clarke, J., Gewirtz, S. and McLaughlin, E. (eds) (2000) *New Managerialism, New Welfare?* London: Sage.

Cleaver, H., Nicholson, D., Tarr, S. and Cleaver, D. (2007) *Child Protection, Domestic Violence and Parental Substance Misuse: Family Experiences and Effective Practice*. London: Jessica Kingsley.

Coles, C. (1998) 'How students learn', in B. Jolly and L. Rees (eds) *Medical Education in the Millenium*. Oxford: Oxford University Press. pp. 61–82.

Collett, P. (2003) *The Book of Tells*. London: Doubleday.

Collins, S. (2006) 'Mental health difficulties and the support needs of social work students: dilemmas, tensions and contradictions', *Social Work Education*, 25 (5): 446–60.

Collins, S. (2008) 'Statutory social workers: stress, job satisfaction, coping, social support and individual differences', *British Journal of Social Work*, 38 (6): 1173–93.

Commission for Racial Equality (2002) *Framework for Race Equality Policy for Higher Education Institutions*. London: CRE.

Congress, E. (1994) 'The use of culturagrams to assess and empower culturally diverse families', *Families in Society*, 75 (9): 531–40.

Coppock, V. (2002) 'Medicalising children's behaviour', in B. Franklin (ed.) *The New Handbook of Children's Rights: Comparative Policy and Practice*. London: Routledge. pp. 139–54.

Corby, B. (2005) *Child Abuse: Towards a Knowledge Base*, 3rd edn. Buckingham: Open University Press.

Cottrell, S. (2008) *The Study Skills Handbook*, 3rd edn. Basingstoke: Palgrave-Macmillan.

Crawshaw, M. (2002) 'Disabled people's access to social work education', *Social Work Education*, 21 (5): 504–14.

Cree, V. E. (ed.) (2003) *Becoming a Social Worker*. London: Routledge.

Cree, V. E. and Davis, A. (2007) *Social Work: Voices from the Inside*. London: Routledge.

Cree, V. E. and Macauley, C. (eds) (2000) *Transfer of Learning in Professional and Vocational Education*. London: Routledge.

Cree, V. E. and Wallace, S. (2009) 'Risk and protection', in R. Adams, L. Dominelli and M. Payne (eds) *Practising Socal Work in a Complex World*. Basingstoke: Palgrave-Macmillan. pp. 42–56.

Crisp, B. R. and Lister, P. G. (2002) 'Assessment methods in social work education: a review of the literature', *Social Work Education*, 21 (2): 259–69.

Crompton, M. (1998) *Children, Spirituality, Religion and Social Work*. Aldershot: Ashgate.

Crompton, R. (2008) *Class and Stratification*, 3rd edn. Bristol: Polity Press.

Csikszentmihalyi, M. (1990) *Flow: The Psychology of Optimal Experience*. New York: Harper and Row.

Currer, C. and Atherton, K. (2008) 'Suitable to remain a student social worker? Decision-making in relation to termination of training', *Social Work Education*, 27 (3): 279–92.

Dallos, R. and Draper, R. (2000) *An Introduction to Family Therapy: Systemic Theory and Practice*. Buckingham: Open University Press.

Davies, R. (ed.) (1998) *Stress in Social Work*. London: Jessica Kingsley.

Davis, M. (2002) *Profession, Code and Ethics*. Aldershot: Ashgate.

Department for Education and Skills (DfES) (2004) *Every Child Matters: Change for Children*. London: TSO.

Department for Education and Skills (DfES) (2007) *Safeguarding Children from Abuse Linked to a Belief in Spirit Possession*. London: TSO.

Department of Health (DH) (1991) *Care Management and Assessment Practice Guidance*. London: HMSO.

Department of Health (DH) (1998) *Modernising Social Services: Promoting Independence, Improving Protection, Raising Standards*. London: TSO (Cm 4169).

Department of Health (DH) (2000a) *Framework for the Assessment of Children in Need and their Families*. London: TSO.

Department of Health (DH) (2000b) *No Secrets: Guidance on Developing and Implementing Multi-Agency Policies and Procedures to Protect Vulnerable Adults*. London: TSO.

Department of Health (DH) (2001a) *The Children Act Now: Messages from Research*. London: TSO.

Department of Health (DH) (2001b) *A Practitioner's Guide to Carers' Assessments under the Carers and Disabled Children Act 2000*. London: TSO.

Department of Health (DH) (2002a) *Requirements for Social Work Training*. London: TSO.

Department of Health (DH) (2002b) *Fair Access to Care Services: Policy Guidance.* London: TSO.

Department of Health (DH) (2005) *Delivering Race Equality in Mental Health.* London: TSO.

Department of Health (DH) (2009) *Safeguarding Adults – Report on the Consultation on the Review of No Secrets.* Available at www.dh.gov.uk/prod_consum_dh/groups/ dh_digitalasstes/documents/digitalasset/dh102981.pdf (accessed 30 July 2009).

Department of Health, Social Services and Public Safety (2006) *Northern Ireland Post-Qualifying Education and Training Framework in Social Work.* Belfast: DHSSPS.

Dewey, J. (1910) *How We Think.* Boston, MA: D. C. Heath.

Disability Rights Commission (2006) *Further and Higher Education Institutions and the Disability Equality Duty: Guidance for Principals, Vice-Chancellors, Governing Boards and Senior Managers Working in Further and Higher Education Institutions in England, Scotland and Wales.* London: DRC.

Doel, M. and Shardlow, S. M. (2005) *Modern Social Work Practice: Teaching and Learning in Practice Settings.* Aldershot: Ashgate.

Doel, M., Deacon, L. and Sawdon, C. (2007) 'Curtain down on Act One: practice learning in the first year of the new social work award', *Social Work Education,* 26 (3): 217–32.

Dominelli, L. (1997) *Anti-Racist Social Work.* Basingstoke: Palgrave-Macmillan.

Dominelli, L. (2002) *Feminist Social Work: Theory and Practice.* Basingstoke: Palgrave-Macmillan.

Dominelli, L. (2004) *Social Work: Theory and Practice for a Changing Profession.* Cambridge: Polity Press.

Dominelli, L. (2009) 'Social work research: contested knowledge for practice', in R. Adams, L. Dominelli and M. Payne (eds) *Practising Social Work in a Complex World.* Basingstoke: Palgrave-Macmillan. pp. 241–56.

Dominelli, L. and Bernard, W. T. (eds) (2003) *Broadening Horizons: International Exchanges in Social Work.* Aldershot: Ashgate.

Dowling, M. (1998) 'An evaluation of social work practice in relation to poverty issues: do social workers' attitudes and actions correspond?', in J. Cheetham and M. Kazi (eds) *The Working of Social Work.* London: Jessica Kingsley. pp. 135–50.

Dowling, S., Manthorpe, J. and Cowley, S. (2006) *Person Centred Planning in Social Care: A Scoping Review.* York: Joseph Rowntree Foundation.

Dugmore, P. and Pickford, J. with Angus, S. (2006) *Youth Justice and Social Work.* Exeter: Learning Matters.

Dwivedi, K. (ed.) (1993) *Group Work with Children and Adolescents: A Handbook.* London: Jessica Kingsley.

Egan, G. (2002) *The Skilled Helper: A Problem-Management and Opportunity-Development Approach to Helping.* Pacific Grove, CA: Brooks/Cole.

Egeland, B., Bosquet, M. and Chung, A. L. (2002) 'Continuities and discontinuities in the intergenerational transmission of child maltreatment: implications for breaking the cycle of abuse', in K. Browne, H. Hanks, P. Stratton and C. Hamilton (eds) *Early Prediction and Prevention of Child Abuse: A Handbook.* Chichester: John Wiley & Sons. pp. 217–32.

Equal Opportunities Commission (2007) *The Gender Equality Duty and Higher Education Institutions: Guidance for Public Authorities in England.* London: EOC.

Equality Challenge Unit (2009) *The Experience of Lesbian, Gay, Bisexual and Trans Staff and Students in Higher Education: Research Report.* London: Equality and Human Rights Commission.

Ernst, S. and Goodison, L. (1981) *In Our Own Hands: A Women's Book of Self-Help Therapy.* London: The Women's Press.

Evaluation of Social Work Degree in England Team (ESWDET) (2008) *Evaluation of the New Social Work Degree Qualification in England. Volume 1: Findings.* London: Kings College and Social Care Workforce Research Unit. Available at www.dh.gov.uk/prod_consum_dh/groups/dh_digitalassets/@dh/@en/documents/digitalasset/dh_086077.pdf (accessed 3 October 2009).

Eyben, R. and Moncrieffe, J. (2007) *The Power of Labelling: How People are Categorised and Why it Matters.* London: Earthscan.

Farmer, E., Moyers, S. and Stein, M. (2008) *Kinship Care: Fostering Effective Family and Friends Placements.* London: Jessica Kingsley.

Fay, B. (1987) *Critical Social Science: Liberation and its Limits.* Oxford: Polity Press.

Featherstone, B., Rivett, M. and Scourfield, J. (2007) *Working with Men in Health and Social Care.* London: Sage.

Fineman, S. (2005) *Understanding Emotion at Work.* London: Sage.

Fish, D., Twinn, S. and Purr, B. (1991) *Promoting Reflection: The Supervision of Practice in Health Visiting and Initial Teacher Training.* London: West London Institute Press.

Fonagy, P. and Target, M. (2003) *Psychoanalytic Theories: Perspectives from Developmental Psychopathology.* London: Whurr.

Fook, J. (2002) *Social Work: Critical Theory and Practice.* London: Sage.

Fook, J. and Gardner, F. (2007) *Practising Critical Reflection: A Resource Handbook.* Maidenhead: Open University Press.

Fook, J., Ryan, M. and Hawkins, L. (2000) *Professional Expertise: Practice, Theory and Education for Working in Uncertainty.* London: Whiting and Birch.

Freeden, M. (1999) 'The ideology of New Labour', *The Political Quarterly*, 70 (1): 42–51.

Frost, N. (2009) 'Evaluating practice', in R. Adams, L. Dominelli and M. Payne (eds) *Practising Social Work in a Complex World.* Basingstoke: Palgrave-Macmillan. pp. 296–307.

Furness, S. and Gilligan, P. (2004) 'Fit for purpose: issues from practice placements, practice teaching and the assessment of students' practice', *Social Work Education*, 23 (4): 465–79.

Gardiner, D. (1989) *The Anatomy of Supervision: Developing Learning and Professional Competence for Social Work Students.* Buckingham: Open University Press.

Garrett, P. M. (2003) *Remaking Social Work with Children and Families: A Critical Discussion on the Modernisation of Social Care.* London: Routledge.

Gawain, S. (2002) *Creative Visualization Meditations.* Novato, CA: New World Library.

Geldard, K. (ed.) (2009) *Practical Interventions for Young People at Risk.* London: Sage.

General Social Care Council (GSCC) (2002a) *Code of Practice for Social Care Workers.* London: GSCC.

General Social Care Council (GSCC) (2002b) *Code of Practice for Social Care Employers.* London: GSCC.

General Social Care Council (GSCC) (2005) *Post-Qualifying Framework for Social Work Education and Training.* London: GSCC.

Giddens, A. (1990) *The Consequences of Modernity.* Cambridge: Polity Press.

Gilligan, P. (2007) 'Well motivated reformists or nascent radicals? How do applicants to the degree in social work see social problems, their origins and solutions?', *British Journal of Social Work*, 37 (4): 735–60.

Gilligan, P. and Akhtar, S. (2006) 'Cultural barriers to the disclosure of child sexual abuse in Asian communities: listening to what women say', *British Journal of Social Work*, 36 (8): 1361–77.

Glaser, D. and Prior, V. (2002) 'Predicting emotional abuse and neglect', in K. Browne, H. Hanks, P. Stratton and C. Hamilton (eds) *Early Prediction and Prevention of Child Abuse: A Handbook*. Chichester: John Wiley & Sons. pp. 57–70.

Goffman, E. (1961) *Asylums: Essays on the Social Situation of Mental Patients and Other Inmates*. New York: Anchor Books.

Goffman, E. (1963) *Stigma: Notes on the Management of a Spoiled Identity*. London: Penguin.

Goleman, D. (1996) *Emotional Intelligence: Why It Can Matter More Than IQ*. London: Bloomsbury.

Goleman, D. (1997) *Vital Lies, Simple Truths: The Psychology of Self-Deception*. London: Bloomsbury.

Goleman, D. (2007) *Social Intelligence: The New Science of Human Relationships*. London: Arrow.

Gould, N. and Baldwin, M. (eds) (2004) *Social Work, Critical Reflection and the Learning Organisation*. Aldershot: Ashgate.

Graham, J. R., Bradshaw, C. and Trew, J. L. (2009) 'Adapting social work in working with Muslim clients', *Social Work Education*, 28 (5): 544–61.

Grant, J. and Crowley, J. (2002) *Transference and Projection: Mirrors to the Self*. Buckingham: Open University Press.

Greetham, B. (2008) *How to Write Better Essays*, 2nd edn. Basingstoke: Palgrave-Macmillan.

Grimwood, C. and Popplestone, R. (1993) *Women, Management and Care*. London: BASW.

Guillaumin, C. (1995) *Racism, Sexism, Power and Ideology*. London: Routledge.

Hafford-Letchfield, P. (2009) *Management and Organisations in Social Work*. Exeter: Learning Matters.

Halmos, P. (1978) *The Faith of the Counsellors*. London: Constable & Co.

Hanmer, J. (ed.) (2000) *Home Truths about Domestic Violence: Feminist Influences upon Policy and Practice*. London: Routledge.

Hare, R. D. (1999) *Without Conscience: The Disturbing World of the Psychopaths Among Us*. New York: Guilford Press.

Harne, L. and Radford, J. (2008) *Tackling Domestic Violence: Theories, Policies and Practice*. Maidenhead: Open University Press.

Harris, J. (1998) 'Scientific management, bureau-professionalism, new managerialism: the labour process of state social work', *British Journal of Social Work*, 28 (6): 839–62.

Harris, M. and Rochester, C. (eds) (2001) *Voluntary Organisations and Social Policy in Britain: Perspectives on Change and Choice*. Basingstoke: Palgrave-Macmillan.

Harrison, B. C. and Dye, T. R. (2008) *Power and Society: An Introduction*. Florence, KY: Wadsworth.

Harvey, G. (1997) *Listening People, Speaking Earth: Contemporary Paganism*. London: Hurst & Co.

Harvey, J. (1998) *Total Relaxation: Healing Practices for Body, Mind and Spirit*. New York: Kodansha.

Hawkins, P. and Shohet, R. (1989) *Supervision in the Helping Professions*. Buckingham: Open University Press.

Hayes, D. and Humphries, B. (2004) *Social Work, Immigration and Asylum: Debates, Dilemmas and Ethical Issues for Social Work and Social Care Practice*. London: Jessica Kingsley.

Healy, L. (ed.) (2001) *International Social Work: Professional Action in an Interdependent World*. Oxford: Oxford University Press.

Heenan, D. and Birral, D. (2006) 'The integration of health and social care: the lessons from Northern Ireland', *Social Policy and Administration*, 40 (1): 47–66.

Helman, C. G. (2001) *Culture, Health and Illness*. London: Arnold.

Heron, C. (1998) *Working with Carers*. London: Jessica Kingsley.

Heron, J. (1992) *Feeling and Personhood: Psychology in Another Key*. London: Sage.

Higgs, J. and Titchen, A. (eds) (2001) *Practice Knowledge and Expertise in the Health Professions*. Oxford: Butterworth-Heinemann.

Higgs, J., Titchen, A. and Neville, V. (2001) 'Professional practice and knowledge', in J. Higgs and A. Titchen (eds) *Practice Knowledge and Expertise in the Health Professions*. Oxford: Butterworth-Heinemann. pp. 3–9.

Hill, H. and Kenyan, R. (2007) *Promoting Equality and Diversity: A Practitioner's Guide*. Oxford: Oxford University Press.

HM Government (2006) *Working Together to Safeguard Children: A Guide to Inter-Agency Working to Safeguard and Promote the Welfare of Children*. London: TSO.

HM Government (2007a) *Care Matters: Time for Change*. London: TSO (Cm 7137).

HM Government (2007b) *Putting People First: A Shared Vision and Commitment to the Transformation of Adult Social Care*. London: TSO.

HM Government (2009a) *Shaping the Future of Care Together*. London: TSO (Cm 7673).

HM Government (2009b) *Multi-Agency Practice Guidelines: Handling Cases of Forced Marriage*. London: TSO

HM Government (2010) *Working Together to Safeguard and Promote the Welfare of Children*. London: TSO.

Hoggett, P. (2000) *Emotional Life and the Politics of Welfare*. Basingstoke: Macmillan.

Honey, P. and Mumford, A. (2000) *The Learning Styles Helper's Guide*. Maidenhead: Peter Honey Publications.

Horwath, J. (ed.) (2001) *The Child's World: Assessing Children in Need*. London: Jessica Kingsley.

Howe, D. (1992) *An Introduction to Social Work Theory*. Aldershot: Ashgate.

Howe, D. (1993) *On Being a Client: Understanding the Process of Counselling and Psychotherapy*. London: Macmillan.

Howe, D. (1995) *Attachment Theory for Social Work Practice*. London: Macmillan.

Howe, D. (1996) 'Surface and depth in social work practice', in N. Parton (ed.) *Social Theory, Social Change and Social Work*. London: Routledge. pp. 77–97.

Howe, D. (2008) *The Emotionally Intelligent Social Worker*. Basingstoke: Palgrave-Macmillan.

Howe, D. (2009) *A Brief Introduction to Social Work Theory*. Basingstoke: Palgrave-Macmillan.

Hugman, R. (1998) *Social Welfare and Social Value*. Basingstoke: Macmillan.

Humphrey, C. (2006) 'Tomorrow's social workers in the UK', *European Journal of Social Work*, 9 (3): 357–73.

Humphrey, C. (2007a) 'Safeguarding children: exploring the interfaces between policy, pedagogy, psychology and practice', *Journal of Social Work*, 7 (2): 197–216.

Humphrey, C. (2007b) 'Observing students' practice (through the looking glass and beyond)', *Social Work Education*, 26 (6): 723–36.

Humphrey, C. (2009a) 'By the light of the Tao', *European Journal of Social Work*, 12 (3): 377–90.

Humphrey, C. (2009b) 'The faith closet', *Journal of Practice Teaching and Learning*, 8 (3): 7–27.

Humphrey, J. C. (2002) *Towards a Politics of the Rainbow: Self-Organisation in the Trade Union Movement*. Aldershot: Ashgate.

Humphrey, J. C. (2003) 'New Labour and the regulatory reform of social care', *Critical Social Policy*, 23 (1): 5–24.

Humphries, B. (2009) 'Critical social work research', in R. Adams, L. Dominelli and M. Payne (eds) *Practising Social Work in a Complex World*. Basingstoke: Palgrave-Macmillan. pp. 308–20.

Hunt, R. and Valentine, G. (2008) *Love Thy Neighbour: What People of Faith Really Think about Homosexuality*. London: Stonewall.

Hussein, S., Moriarty, J., Manthorpe, J. and Huxley, P. (2006) *Diversity and Progression in Social Work Education in England: A Report on Progression Rates among DipSW Students*. London: GSCC.

Hussein, S., Moriarty, J. and Manthorpe, J. (2009) *Variations in the Progression of Social Work Students in England*, London: King's College and Social Care Workforce Research Unit.

International Federation of Social Workers (2000) 'Definition of Social Work'. Available at www.ifsw.org/en/p38000208.html (accessed 1 January 2009).

Jamrozik, A. and Nocella, L. (1998) *The Sociology of Social Problems: Theoretical Perspectives and Methods of Intervention*. Melbourne: Cambridge University Press.

Jay Committee (1979) *Report of the Committee of Inquiry into Mental Handicap Nursing and Care*. London: HMSO.

Jeffers, S. (2007) *Feel the Fear and Do it Anyway: How to Turn Your Fear and Indecision into Confidence and Action,* 20th anniversary edn. London: Vermillion.

Johns, C. (2000) *Becoming a Reflective Practitioner*. Oxford: Blackwell Science.

Jordan, B. (2004) 'Emancipatory social work: opportunity or oxymoron?', *British Journal of Social Work*, 34 (1): 5–19.

Karpman, S. (1968) 'Fairy tales and script drama analysis', *Transactional Analysis Bulletin*, 26 (7): 39–43.

Kendrick, A. (ed.) (2008) *Residential Child Care: Prospects and Challenges*. London: Jessica Kingsley.

Kennedy, M. (2002) 'Disability and child abuse', in K. Wilson and A. James (eds) *The Child Protection Handbook*, 2nd edn. London: Ballière-Tindall. pp. 147–71.

Killen, M. and Smetana, J. (eds) (2006) *Handbook of Moral Development*. Mahwah, NJ: Lawrence Erlbaum.

King, E., Mackay, R. and Lishman, J. (2002) 'Practice learning in the voluntary sector', in S. M. Shardlow and M. Doel (eds) *Learning to Practise Social Work: International Approaches*. London: Jessica Kingsley. pp. 179–99.

Kirton, D. (2009) *Child Social Work: Policy and Practice*. London: Sage.

Knowles, M. S. (1990) *The Adult Learner: A Neglected Species*. Houston, TX: Gulf.

Kohli, R. K. S. (2006) 'The sound of silence: listening to what unaccompanied asylum-seeking children say and do not say', *British Journal of Social Work*, 36 (5): 707–21.

Kolb, D. A. (1984) *Experiential Learning: Experience as the Source of Learning and Development*. Englewood Cliffs, NJ: Prentice-Hall.

Lafrance, J., Gray, E. and Herbert, M. (2004) 'Gate-keeping for professional social work practice', *Social Work Education*, 23 (3): 325–40.

Laird, S. (2008) *Anti-Oppressive Social Work: A Guide to Developing Cultural Competence*. London: Sage.

Laming, Lord (2009) *The Protection of Children in England: A Progress Report*. London: TSO.

Langan, M. and Lee, P. (eds) (1989) *Radical Social Work Today*. London: Unwin Hyman.

Lawrence, S., Lyons, K., Simpson, G. and Huegler, N. (eds) (2009) *Introducing International Social Work*. Exeter: Learning Matters.

Lee Badgett, M.V. and Frank, J. (2007) *Sexual Orientation Discrimination: An International Perspective*. Abingdon: Routledge.

Lefevre, M. (1998) 'Recognizing and addressing imbalances of power in the practice teacher/student dialectic: an anti-discriminatory approach', in H. Lawson (ed.) *Practice Teaching: Changing Social Work*. London: Jessica Kingsley. pp. 15–31.

Leslie, A. (2001) *Report of the Part 8 Review for Brighton and Hove Area Child Protection Committee into the Care and Protection of JAS*. Brighton: ACPC. (NB: Access to this report is restricted.)

Levey, J. (2000) *The Fine Art of Relaxation: Self-Guided CD*. Seattle, WA: Earth View.

Levin, E. (2004) *Involving Service Users and Carers in Social Work Education*. London: Social Care Institute for Excellence.

Lewis, G. (ed.) (1998) *Forming Nation, Framing Welfare*. London: Routledge.

Lewis, J. and Thornbory, G. (2006) *Employment Law and Occupational Health: A Practical Handbook*. Oxford: Blackwell.

Lishman, J. (ed.) (2007) *Handbook for Practice Learning in Social Work and Social Care: Knowledge and Theory*. London: Jessica Kingsley.

Llewellyn, A., Agu, L. and Mercer, D. (2008) *Sociology for Social Workers*. Cambridge: Polity Press.

Lynn, E. (1999) 'Value bases in social work education', *British Journal of Social Work*, 29 (6): 939–53.

Lyons, K. and Manion, H. K. (2004) 'Goodbye DipSW: trends in student satisfaction and employment outcomes. Some implications for the new social work award', *Social Work Education*, 23 (2): 133–48.

MacDonald, A. (2006) *Understanding Community Care: A Guide for Social Workers*, 2nd edn. Basingstoke: Palgrave-Macmillan.

Manthorpe, J. and Stanley, N. (1999) 'Dilemmas in professional education: responding effectively to students with mental health needs', *Journal of Interprofessional Care*, 13 (4): 355–65.

Manthorpe, J. and Stanley, N. (eds) (2004) *The Age of the Inquiry: Learning and Blaming in Health and Social Care*. London: Routledge.

Marsh, P. and Doel, M. (2006) *The Task-Centred Book*. London: Routledge.

Marsh, P. and Triseliotis, J. (1996) *Ready to Practise? Social Workers and Probation Officers: Their Training and First Year in Work*. Aldershot: Avebury.

Maslow, A. H. (1943) 'A theory of human motivation', *Psychological Review*, 50: 370–96.

Maslow, A. H. (1964) *Religion, Values and Peak Experiences*. New York: Viking.

Mayo, M. (2009) 'Community work', in R. Adams, L. Dominelli and M. Payne (eds) *Critical Practice in Social Work*, 2nd edn. Basingstoke: Palgrave-Macmillan. pp. 125–36.

McBeath, G. and Webb, S. A. (2002) 'Virtue ethics and social work: being lucky, realistic and not doing one's duty', *British Journal of Social Work*, 32 (8): 1015–36.

McCann, L. I. and Pearlman, L. A. (1990) 'Vicarious traumatisation: a framework for understanding the psychological effects of working with victims', *Journal of Traumatic Stress*, 3 (2): 131–49.

McLaughlin, H. (2006) *Understanding Social Work Research*. London: Sage.

McLaughlin, H. (2009) 'What's in a name: "client", "patient", "customer", "consumer", "expert by experience", "service user" – what's next?', *British Journal of Social Work*, 39 (6): 1101–17.

McLaughlin, K. (2007) 'Regulation and risk in social work: the General Social Care Council and the social care register in context', *British Journal of Social Work*, 37 (7): 1263–77.

McNamara, D. and Harris, R. (1997) *Overseas Students in Higher Education: Issues in Teaching and Learning*. London: Routledge.

Means, R., Richards, S. and Smith, R. (2008) *Community Care: Policy and Practice*. Basingstoke: Palgrave-Macmillan.

Menzies, I. (1970) *The Functioning of Social Systems as a Defence against Anxiety*. London: The Tavistock Institute.

Metson, D. (1998) 'The practice teacher and student dyad: using concepts from transactional analysis to enable effective learning and teaching', in H. Lawson (ed.) *Practice Teaching: Changing Social Work*. London: Jessica Kingsley. pp. 111–27.

Millar, M. (2008) ' "Anti-oppressiveness": critical comments on a discourse and its context', *British Journal of Social Work*, 38 (2): 362–75.

Miller, A. (1987) *For Your Own Good: Hidden Cruelty in Child-Rearing and the Roots of Violence*. London: Virago.

Miller, A. (1994) *The Drama of Being a Child: The Search for the True Self*. London: Virago.

Miller, A. (2005) *The Body Never Lies: The Lingering Effects of Cruel Parenting*. New York: W. W. Norton & Co.

Miller, W. R. (ed.) (1999) *Integrating Spirituality into Treatment: Resources for Practitioners*. Washington, DC: American Psychological Association.

Miller, W. R. and Rollnick, S. (2002) *Motivational Interviewing: Preparing People for Change*. New York: Guilford Press.

Mooney, G. (1998) 'Remoralising the poor? Gender, class and philanthropy in Victorian Britain', in G. Lewis (ed.) *Forming Nation, Framing Welfare*. London: Routledge. pp. 49–92.

Morris, K. (ed.) (2008) *Social Work and Multi-Agency Working: Making a Difference*. Bristol: Policy Press.

Morris, L. (1994) *Dangerous Classes: The Underclass and Social Citizenship*. London: Routledge.

Morrison, T. (1993) *Staff Supervision in Social Care: An Action Learning Approach*. London: Longman.

Morrison, T. (2007) 'Emotional intelligence, emotion and social work: context, characteristics, complications and contribution', *British Journal of Social Work*, 37 (2): 245–63.

Moss, B. (2005) *Religion and Spirituality*. Lyme Regis: Russell House.

Munro, E. (2008) *Effective Child Protection,* 2nd edn. London: Sage.

Neenan, M. and Dryden, W. (2002) *Cognitive Behaviour Therapy.* London: Whurr.

Newton, S. (2006) *Adult Placement: An Introduction to the Principles and Practice of Adult Placement.* Birmingham: Venture Press.

Ng, S. M. and Chan, C. L. W. (2009) 'Alternative intervention: a Chinese body–mind–spirit perspective', in R. Adams, L. Dominelli and M. Payne (eds) *Social Work: Themes, Issues and Critical Debates,* 3rd edn. Basingstoke: Palgrave-Macmillan. pp. 271–80.

Nicolson, P., Bayne, R. and Owen, J. (2006) *Applied Psychology for Social Workers.* Basingstoke: Palgrave-Macmillan.

Northern Ireland Social Care Council (NISCC) (2002) *NISCC Code of Practice for Social Care Workers.* Belfast: NISCC.

Northern Ireland Social Care Council (NISCC) (2003a) *The National Occupational Standards for Social Work.* Belfast: NISCC.

Northern Ireland Social Care Council (NISCC) (2003b) *Practice Learning Requirements for the Degree in Social Work.* Belfast: NISCC.

Northern Ireland Social Care Council (NISCC) (2009) *Report on the 5 Yearly Periodic Review of the Degree in Social Work.* Belfast: NISCC.

Oaklander, V. (1998) *Windows to Our Children: A Gestalt Therapy Approach.* St Moab, UT: Real People Press.

O'Hagan, K. (2001) *Cultural Competence in the Caring Professions.* London: Jessica Kingsley.

O'Hagan, K. (2007) *Competence in Social Work Practice: A Practical Guide for Students and Professionals.* London: Jessica Kingsley.

Oliver, M. and Sapey, B. (2006) *Social Work with Disabled People,* 3rd edn. London: Jessica Kingsley.

Oser, D. (2000) *Violence against Social Care Staff: A Report on Qualitative Research among Social Care Professionals.* London: DH.

Osmond, J. and O'Connor, I. (2004) 'Formalising the unformalised: practitioners' communication of knowledge in practice', *British Journal of Social Work,* 34 (5): 677–92.

O'Sullivan, T. (2009) 'Managing risk and decision-making', in R. Adams, L. Dominelli and M. Payne (eds) *Practising Social Work in a Complex World.* Basingstoke: Palgrave-Macmillan. pp. 196–203.

Palmer, G., MacInnes, T. and Kenway, P. (2008) *Monitoring Poverty and Social Exclusion.* York: Joseph Rowntree Foundation.

Parker, J. and Bradley, G. (2003) *Social Work Practice: Assessment, Planning, Intervention and Review.* Exeter: Learning Matters.

Parker, J. and Merrylees, S. (2002) 'Why become a professional? Experiences of care-giving and the decision to enter social work or nursing education', *Learning in Health and Social Care,* 1 (2): 105–14.

Parrott, L. (2009) 'Constructive marginality: conflicts and dilemmas in cultural competence and anti-oppressive practice', *Social Work Education,* 28 (6): 617–30.

Parsloe, P. (1999) *Risk Assessment in Social Care and Social Work.* London: Jessica Kingsley.

Parton, N. (1991) *Governing the Family: Child Care, Child Protection and the State.* London: Macmillan.

Parton, N. and O'Byrne, P. (2000) *Constructive Social Work: Towards a New Practice.* Basingstoke: Macmillan.

Payne, M. (1993) 'Standards of written and spoken English in social work education', *Issues in Social Work Education*, 13 (2): 37–51.

Payne, M. (1995) *Social Work and Community Care*. Basingstoke: Palgrave-Macmillan.

Payne, M. (2005a) *The Origins of Social Work: Continuity and Change*. Basingstoke: Palgrave-Macmillan.

Payne, M. (2005b) *Modern Social Work Theory*, 3rd edn. Basingstoke: Palgrave-Macmillan.

Payne, M. (2009a) 'Critical reflection and social work theories', in R. Adams, L. Dominelli and M. Payne (eds) *Critical Practice in Social Work*. Basingstoke: Palgrave-Macmillan. pp. 91–104.

Payne, M. (2009b) 'Doing literature searches and reviews', in R. Adams, L. Dominelli and M. Payne (eds) *Practising Social Work in a Complex World*. Basingstoke: Palgrave-Macmillan. pp. 271–83.

Peterson, T. and McBride, A. (eds) (2002) *Working with Substance Misusers: A Guide to Theory and Practice*. London: Routledge.

Phillips, T., Schostack, J. and Tyler, J. (2000) *Practice and Assessment in Nursing and Midwifery: Doing it for Real*. London: The English National Board for Nursing, Midwifery and Health Visiting.

Pierson, J. (2002) *Tackling Social Exclusion*. London: Routledge.

Pithouse, A. and Scourfield, J. (2002) 'Ready for practice? The DipSW in Wales: views from the workplace on social work training', *Journal of Social Work*, 2 (1): 7–27.

Popple, K. (1995) *Analysing Community Work: Its Theory and Practice*. Buckingham: Open University Press.

Powell, F. (2001) *The Politics of Social Work*. London: Sage.

Preston-Shoot, M. (2007) *Effective Groupwork*, 2nd edn. Basingstoke: Palgrave-Macmillan.

Pritchard, C. (2006) *Mental Health Social Work: Evidence-Based Practice*. Abingdon: Routledge.

Pritchard, J. (ed.) (2008) *Good Practice in Safeguarding Adults: Working Effectively in Adult Protection*. London: Jessica Kingsley.

Quality Assurance Agency (QAA) for Higher Education (2008) *Social Work*. London: QAA. Available at www.qaa.ac.uk/academicinfrastructure/benchmark/honours/ (accessed 25 August 2009).

Quinton, D. (2004) *Supporting Parents: Messages from Research*. London: Jessica Kingsley.

Razack, N. (2001) 'Diversity and difference in the field education encounter: racial minority students in the practicum', *Social Work Education*, 20 (2): 219–32.

Reder, P., Duncan, S. and Grey, M. (1993) *Beyond Blame: Child Abuse Tragedies Revisited*. London: Routledge.

Rees, D. (2001) *Death and Bereavement: The Psychological, Religious and Cultural Interfaces*. London: Whurr.

Reid, W. J. and Epstein, L. (1972) *Task-centered Practice*. New York: Columbia University Press.

Reupert, A. (2009) 'Students' use of self: teaching implications', *Social Work Education*, 28 (7): 765–77.

Riddell, S., Tinklin, T. and Wilson, A. (2005) *Disabled Students in Higher Education: Perspectives on Widening Access and Changing Policy*. Abingdon: Routledge.

Roberts, A. R. (ed.) (2000) *Crisis Intervention Handbook*. New York: Oxford University Press.

Robson, C. (1993) *Real-World Research: A Resource for Social Scientists and Practitioner Researchers*. Oxford: Blackwell.

Roger, S. (1991) *Gramsci's Political Thought: An Introduction*. London: Lawrence and Wishart.

Rogers, A. (2002) *Teaching Adults*. Maidenhead: McGraw-Hill Education.

Rogers, A. and Pilgrim, D. (1991) ' "Pulling down churches": accounting for the British mental health users' movement', *Sociology of Health and Illness*, 13 (2): 129–48.

Rogers, C. R. (1951) *Client-centered Counseling*. Boston, MA: Houghton-Mifflin.

Rogers, C. R. (1961) *On Becoming a Person: A Therapist's View of Psychotherapy*. London: Constable & Co.

Rose, M. (2003) 'Good deal, bad deal? Job satisfaction in occupations', *Work Employment and Society*, 17 (3): 503–30.

Rose, S. D. (1998) *Group Therapy with Troubled Youth: A Cognitive–Behavioral Interactive Approach*. Thousand Oaks, CA: Sage.

Ruch, G. (2000) 'Self and social work: towards an integrated model of learning', *Journal of Social Work Practice*, 14 (2): 99–112.

Ryan, T. and Walker, R. (2003) *Life Story Books*. London: British Agencies of Adoption and Fostering.

Ryan, V. (2002) 'Non-directive play therapy with children and adolescents', in K. Wilson and A. James (eds) *The Child Protection Handbook*, 2nd edn. London: Ballière-Tindall. pp. 423–41.

Sangharakshita (1996) *A Guide to the Buddhist Path*, 2nd edn. Birmingham: Windhorse Publications.

Satyamurti, C. (1981) *Occupational Survival: The Case of the Local Authority Social Worker*. Oxford: Blackwell.

Sayer, T. (2008) *Critical Practice in Working with Children*. Basingstoke: Palgrave-Macmillan.

Schön, D. A. (1987) *Educating the Reflective Practitioner: Towards a New Design for Teaching and Learning in the Professions*. San Francisco: Jossey Bass.

Scottish Executive (2006) *Changing Lives: Report of the 21st Century Social Work Review*. Available at www.scotland.gov.uk/Resource/Doc/91931/0021949.pdf (accessed 21 October 2009).

Scottish Social Services Council (SSSC) (2003) *The Framework for Social Work Education in Scotland*. Dundee: SSSC.

Scottish Social Services Council (SSSC) (2005) *Codes of Practice for Social Services Workers and Employers*. Dundee: SSSC.

Scottish Social Services Council (SSSC) (2008) *The Framework for Continuous Learning in Social Services*. Dundee: SSSC.

Secker, J. (1993) *From Theory to Practice in Social Work: The Development of Social Work Students' Practice*. Aldershot: Avebury.

Shapiro, J. and Clawson, T. (1988) 'Burnout', in L. McDerment (ed.) *Stress Care*. London: Social Care Association. pp. 111–36.

Shardlow, S. M. and Doel, M. (1996) *Practice Learning and Teaching*. Basingstoke: Macmillan.

Shaw, I. F. and Gould, N. (eds) (2001) *Qualitative Research in Social Work*. London: Sage.

Shulman, L. (2005) *The Skills of Helping Individuals, Families, Groups and Communities*, 5th edn. Florence, KY: Wadsworth.

Smith, A. M. (1994) *New Right Discourses on Race and Sexuality: Britain 1968–1990*. New York: Cambridge University Press.

Smith, D. (ed.) (2004) *Social Work and Evidence-Based Practice*. London: Jessica Kingsley.

Social Work Task Force (SWTF) (2009) *Building a Safe, Confident Future: The Final Report of the Social Work Task Force*. Available at http://publications.dcsf.gov.uk (accessed 3 December 2009).

Stanley, N., Manthorpe, G. and Penhale, B. (eds) (1999) *Institutional Abuse: Perspectives across the Life Course*. London: Routledge.

Stephenson, M., Giller, H. and Brown, S. (2007) *Effective Practice in Youth Justice*. Collompton, Devon: Willan Publishing.

Stepney, P. and Popple, K. (2008) *Social Work and the Community: A Critical Context for Practice*. Basingstoke: Palgrave-Macmillan.

Stryker, S. and Whittle, S. (eds) (2007) *The Transgender Studies Reader*. New York: Routledge.

Sutton, C. (2000) 'Cognitive–behavioural theory: relevance for social work', *Cognitive Behavioural Social Work Review*, 21 (1): 22–46.

Swain, J., Finkelstein, V., French, S. and Oliver, M. (eds) (1993) *Disabling Barriers – Enabling Environments*. London: Sage.

Symonds, A. and Kelly, A. (eds) (1998) *The Social Construction of Community Care*. Basingstoke: Macmillan.

Tew, J. (ed.) (2005) *Social Perspectives in Mental Health: Developing Social Models to Understand and Work with Mental Distress*. London: Jessica Kingsley.

Thoburn, J., Chand, A. and Proctor, J. (2005) *Child Welfare Services for Minority Ethnic Families*. London: Jessica Kingsley.

Thompson, N. (1998) *Promoting Equality: Challenging Discrimination and Oppression in the Human Services*. Basingstoke: Macmillan.

Thompson, N. (2006) *Anti-Discriminatory Practice*. Basingstoke: Palgrave-Macmillan.

Thompson, N. and Thompson, S. (2008) *The Social Work Companion*. Basingstoke: Palgrave-Macmillan.

Timonen, V. (2008) *Ageing Societies: A Comparative Introduction*. Maidenhead: Open University Press.

Tovey, W. (ed.) (2007) *The Post-Qualifying Handbook for Social Workers*. London: Jessica Kingsley.

Training Organisation for the Personal Social Services (TOPSS) (2002) *The National Occupational Standards for Social Work*. Leeds: TOPSS.

Trevillion, S. (2008) 'Research, theory and practice: eternal triangle or uneasy bedfellows?' *Social Work Education*, 27 (4): 440–50.

Trevithick, P. (2005) *Social Work Skills: A Practice Handbook*. Maidenhead: Open University Press.

Trevithick, P. (2008) 'Revisiting the knowledge-base of social work: a framework for practice', *British Journal of Social Work*, 38 (6): 1212–37.

Trotter, C. (1999) *Working with Involuntary Clients: A Guide to Practice*. St Leonards, NSW: Allen and Unwin.

Trotter, J. and Leech, N. (2003) 'Linking research, theory and practice in personal and professional development: gender and sexuality issues in social work education', *Social Work Education*, 22 (2): 203–14.

Tummey, R. and Tummey, F. (2008) 'Iatrogenic abuse', in R. Tummey and T. Turner (eds) *Critical Issues in Mental Health*. Basingstoke: Palgrave-Macmillan. pp. 126–41.

Wakeford, R. (1999) 'Principles of assessment', in H. Fry, S. Ketteridge and S. Marshall (eds) *A Handbook for Teaching and Learning in Higher Education*, London: Kogan Page. pp. 58–69.

Ward, A. (2006) *Working in Group Care: Social Work and Social Care in Residential and Day Care Settings*. Bristol: Policy Press.

Ward, D. (2009) 'Groupwork', in R. Adams, L. Dominelli and M. Payne (eds) *Critical Practice in Social Work*. Basingstoke: Palgrave-Macmillan. pp. 115–24.

Webb, S. A. (2006) *Social Work in a Risk Society: Social and Political Perspectives*. Basingstoke: Palgrave-Macmillan.

Webster, C., Macdonald, R. and Simpson, M. (2006) 'Predicting criminality? Risk factors, neighbourhood influence and desistance', *Youth Justice*, 6 (1): 7–22.

Weinstein, J. (2007) *Working with Loss, Death and Bereavement: A Guide for Social Workers*. London: Sage.

Weinstein, J., Whittington, C. and Leiba, T. (eds) (2003) *Collaboration in Social Work Practice*. London: Jessica Kingsley.

Welsh Assembly Government (2007) *A Strategy for Social Services in Wales over the Next Decade: Fulfilled Lives, Supported Communities*. Cardiff: Welsh Assembly Government.

Wheal, A. (2006) *The Foster Carer's Handbook*. London: Russell House.

Whittaker, A. (2009) *Research Skills for Social Work*. Exeter: Learning Matters.

Whyte, B. (2004) 'Effectiveness, research and youth justice', *Youth Justice*, 4 (1): 3–21.

Wilson, A. and Beresford, P. (2000) 'Anti-oppressive practice: emancipation or appropriation?', *British Journal of Social Work*, 30 (5): 553–73.

Wilson, D. and Game, C. (2006) *Local Government in the United Kingdom*, 4th edn. Basingstoke: Palgrave-Macmillan.

Wilson, G. (ed.) (1995) *Community Care: Asking the Users*. London: Chapman and Hall.

Wilson, K., Ruch, G., Lymbery, M. and Cooper, A. (2008) *Social Work: An Introduction to Contemporary Practice*. Harlow: Pearson Education.

Woodroofe, K. (1961) *From Charity to Social Work in England and the United States*. London: Routledge and Kegan Paul.

Yalom, I. with Leszcz, M. (2005) *The Theory and Practice of Group Psychotherapy*, 5th edn. New York: Basic Books.

Index

Page numbers in *italics* represent figures and tables.